"Czerny and Brandoff have developed an incredible resource for clinicians serving clients who have experienced relationship abuse in any of its varying and diverse forms. They deftly integrated the latest research on the phenomenon and its treatment. Culturally diverse case vignettes, weaved throughout, help the reader understand the concepts and therapeutic applications offered through the lens of the client experience. Twelve holistic experiential art interventions offer a path to sovereignty for clients by bringing all the sectors of the Empowerment Wheel to life. This is a must-have resource for any therapist helping clients to overcome relationship abuse."
—Reina Lombardi, ATR-BC, ATCS, LMHC-QS, Owner of Florida Art Therapy Services, LLC and Host of *The Creative Psychotherapist Podcast*

"The Empowerment Wheel model offers a helpful framework for understanding and treating victims of relationship abuse. This book adds suggested art therapy interventions for each sector of the model, thereby enhancing its potential to heal."
—Judith A. Rubin, PhD, ATR-BC, Licensed Psychologist and Former President of the American Art Therapy Association

"The Empowerment Wheel is a must-have resource for any counselor working with survivors of domestic violence. The authors combine research and information with relevant case examples to clearly illustrate concepts. The creative exercises to explore healing are amazing!"
—Jennifer Geddes Hall, PhD, Licensed Clinical Mental Health Counselor, Registered Play Therapist, and Associate Clinical Professor at Clemson University

"Essential for clinicians working with survivors of relationship abuse, Czerny and Brandoff's comprehensive guide seamlessly weaves theory and practical application. Their integration of art therapy amplifies therapeutic effica⁻ crucial for trauma healing. This bo(in training, and a must-include for
—Sarah Ness Luke, P and Foun(

by the same author

Quick and Creative Art Projects for Creative Therapists with (Very) Limited Budgets
Rachel Brandoff and Angel Thompson
ISBN 978 1 78592 794 2
eISBN 978 1 78450 787 9

of related interest

Written on the Body
Letters from Trans and Non-Binary Survivors of Sexual Assault and Domestic Violence
Edited by Lexie Bean
Foreword and additional pieces by Dean Spade, Nyala Moon, Alex Valdes, Sawyer DeVuyst, and Ieshai Bailey
ISBN 978 1 78592 797 3
eISBN 978 1 78450 803 6

Working with Domestic Violence and Abuse Across the Lifecourse
Understanding Good Practice
Edited by Ravi K. Thiara and Lorraine Radford
ISBN 978 1 78592 404 0
eISBN 978 1 78450 758 9

Intimate Partner Sexual Violence
A Multidisciplinary Guide to Improving Services and Support for Survivors of Rape and Abuse
Edited by Louise McOrmond-Plummer, Patricia Easteal AM, and Jennifer Y. Levy-Peck
ISBN 978 1 84905 912 1
eISBN 978 0 85700 655 4

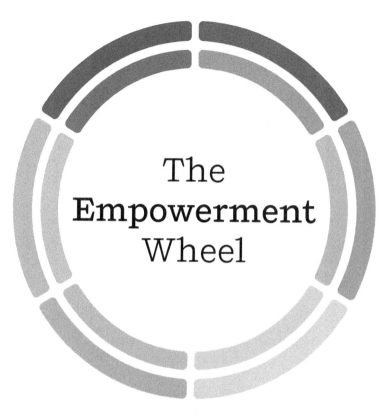

The Empowerment Wheel

Helping Clients Heal
from Relationship Abuse

Astra B. Czerny and Rachel Brandoff

Jessica Kingsley Publishers
London and Philadelphia

First published in Great Britain in 2024 by Jessica Kingsley Publishers
An imprint of John Murray Press

1

Copyright © Astra B. Czerny and Rachel Brandoff 2024

The right of Astra B. Czerny and Rachel Brandoff to be identified as Authors of the Work has been asserted by them in accordance with the Copyright, Designs and Patents Act 1988.

All rights reserved. No part of this publication may be reproduced, stored in a retrieval system, or transmitted, in any form or by any means without the prior written permission of the publisher, nor be otherwise circulated in any form of binding or cover other than that in which it is published and without a similar condition being imposed on the subsequent purchaser.

All case studies in this book are fictional and are not directly reflective of any one living individual.

A CIP catalogue record for this title is available from the British Library and the Library of Congress

ISBN 978 1 83997 766 4
eISBN 978 1 83997 767 1

Printed and bound by CPI Group (UK) Ltd, Croydon, CR0 4YY

Jessica Kingsley Publishers' policy is to use papers that are natural, renewable and recyclable products and made from wood grown in sustainable forests. The logging and manufacturing processes are expected to conform to the environmental regulations of the country of origin.

Jessica Kingsley Publishers
Carmelite House
50 Victoria Embankment
London EC4Y 0DZ

www.jkp.com

John Murray Press
Part of Hodder & Stoughton Ltd
An Hachette Company

Contents

About the Authors 7
Introduction 8

Part One: Current Paradigm

1. Understanding Relationship Abuse 15
2. Understanding Treatment Protocols. 44
3. Understanding Empowerment 67
4. Understanding Art Therapy 78

Part Two: A New Direction

5. The Empowerment Wheel. 93
6. Red Flags 108
7. Boundaries 120
8. Locus of Control 133
9. Relationship Authenticity 150
10. Self-Talk 168
11. Integrated Self 182

Part Three: Additional Considerations

12. Implications for Clinical Use 203
    Appendix: Definitions 212
    Index 218

Figures

Figure 1: *The Empowerment Wheel*, by E.J. Herczyk (2020) 92

Figure 2: *Broken Frame Flag*, by an anonymous artist (2022) 118

Figure 3: *He Barks & I Bite My Tongue*, by Lauren Strailey (2023) . . . 118

Figure 4: *Holes in My Boundaries*, by Savannah (2023) 131

Figure 5: *Bound*, by Jacey Ludlam (2023) 131

Figure 6: *Where We're Headed*, by an anonymous artist (2023) 146

Figure 7: *The Unloved*, by Rachel Woerner (2023). 147

Figure 8: *Hidden*, by Melissa Paolercio (2023) 165

Figure 9: *Pull and Flow*, by Betsy Weiss (2023). 165

Figure 10: *Authentically Me*, by an anonymous artist (2018). 166

Figure 11: *Untitled*, by Makeiah Milbourne (2023) 179

Figure 12: *Finding Your Voice*, by Rachel Woerner (2023). 180

Figure 13: *Solving Me*, by an anonymous artist (2018) 197

All figures on pages marked with ⬇ can be downloaded and most can be viewed in color at https://library.jkp.com/redeem using the voucher code: LFCAMRQ

About the Authors

Dr. Astra B. Czerny is a licensed counselor (LCMHC-NC, LPC-PA) and a National Certified Counselor (NCC). She maintains a small private practice for clients and a supervision and consultation practice with clinicians. Dr. Czerny is an Associate Professor at Lenoir-Rhyne University in Hickory, NC, where she is the Clinical Coordinator and the developer of the Trauma Certificate program. Dr. Czerny is an active presenter at both state and national conferences. Her areas of interest include healing from trauma and empowerment.

Dr. Rachel Brandoff is a Registered, Board-Certified Art Therapist (ATR-BC) and credentialed supervisor (ATCS). She is an Associate Professor and Coordinator of the Art Therapy Concentration in the Community and Trauma Counseling program at Thomas Jefferson University. Dr. Brandoff maintains a clinical practice specializing with individuals who are coming out of crises and coping with trauma. She provides supervision and consultation to art therapists and professional counselors. Dr. Brandoff has served on the boards of various professional organizations and is a regular presenter at regional and national conferences. Her first book, *Quick and Creative Art Projects for Creative Therapists with (Very) Limited Budgets*, was published in 2019.

Introduction

The Me Too Movement (2017) put a spotlight on relationship violence and the prevalence of sexual harassment and abuse in both private and public spaces. Mental health clinicians work with individuals who have experienced inter-personal abuse that can range from financial or emotional boundary violations to sexual assault and other physical traumas. Clinicians must be equipped with tools that can be readily implemented and which provide an avenue for trauma-responsive healing for their clients. Interventions that can be delivered in a variety of settings, that are preventive in nature, and that aid in the transition from disempowerment to empowerment are needed. While survivors should never be blamed for experiencing relationship violence, they are tasked with coping with the repercussions and legacy of their abuse. Ideally, their legacy should include healing.

THE EMPOWERMENT WHEEL

One way to incorporate the goal of empowerment into treatment for domestic violence or other types of relationship abuse is by using the Empowerment Wheel model (Czerny and Lassiter 2016) combined with art therapy. The Empowerment Wheel includes six sectors, which are: *red flags, boundaries, locus of control, relationship authenticity, self-talk,* and *integrated self.* The Empowerment Wheel model provides a simple, effective, and powerful tool that can aid survivors in healing and in recognizing the signs of future abuse. It also provides a therapeutic structure for intra- and inter-personal reflection, which encourages survivors to examine their self-in-relationship experience through the lens of the six Empowerment Wheel sectors. It offers an holistic process that addresses the social, cognitive, and emotional experiences of relationship, as well as the non-linear and recursive nature of the healing process.

Since the 2016 introduction and publication of the Empowerment Wheel (Czerny and Lassiter 2016), we have added art therapy interventions into each of the six sectors to enhance the client's active engagement and understanding of their personal healing journey from relationship abuse and disempowerment. Art therapy has been known to help heal the wounds of domestic violence by helping individuals process traumatic events and trauma responses, enhance communication, and build self-esteem (Buschel and Hurvitz Madsen 2004; Cohen, Barnes, and Rankin 1995; Miller 2008). More specifically, art therapy may help to reduce symptoms resulting from trauma and which relate to arousal, avoidance, and the intrusive, fragmented nature of traumatic memory due to its non-verbal and experiential nature (Schouten *et al.* 2018). Each of the six sectors is presented and discussed in its own chapter, and specific corresponding art therapy-based interventions are identified to increase self-awareness, aid growth for victims, and support the empowerment process.

CLINICAL AND RESEARCH APPLICATIONS

The Empowerment Wheel model provides a structure for both clinical treatment and research applications. The sectors are specifically designed to answer a common question that survivors frequently ask, "What can I do to make sure this doesn't happen to me again?" The six sectors provide a roadmap for clinicians working with survivors of relationship abuse. The topics broached in therapy through exploration of the sectors will resonate with clients across cultural, racial, and ethnic backgrounds.

Clients and clinicians alike need research on therapeutic interventions or treatment protocols for use with victims of domestic and intimate partner violence. The Empowerment Wheel model provides a researchable tool for clinical use with this population.

Studies could reveal the relative short- and long-term success of survivors who use the Empowerment Wheel and art therapy to guide their healing, emotional and psychological change, and behavior and biomarker measurements. Researchers could examine and contrast the experience of clients who engage in therapy with the Empowerment Wheel and art therapy versus clients who may engage in traditional talk psychotherapy, for example.

INTENDED AUDIENCE

In writing this book, we have chosen to speak to a clinical audience. However, although the Empowerment Wheel model is conceptualized as a treatment intervention best applied by licensed therapists working with survivors of relationship abuse, we have also kept in mind that books such as this may attract someone working from a self-healing perspective. It is also possible that clinicians using this book may also be survivors of relationship abuse themselves, and thus find personal meaning in the Empowerment Wheel, while also finding it to be a useful intervention for their clients. As such, we speak to licensed therapists intending to use the Empowerment Wheel model professionally as well as to a larger audience interested in doing their own healing work. For the unlicensed individual reading this book, we strongly recommend working with a licensed therapist who can hold space for your healing journey and the painful past you are working to heal from. We believe that being in therapy, especially after experiencing trauma, is essential.

WHO WE ARE

We live and work in the United States, where there continues to be an increase in mass murders, school shootings, and workplace violence. The increase in instances of relationship violence is both devastating and heart-wrenching. In some cases, those are our clients. We both have professional experience working with survivors of relationship abuse and intimate partner violence. The creation of the Empowerment Wheel model, the inclusion of art therapy into this model, and the writing of this book were not only born out of a clinical understanding of this issue; we both tend the wounds associated with relationship abuse from personal experiences in our own lives. This issue has affected us professionally and personally. We are both passionate about wanting to help survivors of abuse find their way to empowerment, which ultimately was the motivation for writing this book.

WHY WE WROTE THIS BOOK

Relationship abuse continues to be a significant and devastating problem in our society. The COVID-19 pandemic and subsequent lockdowns exacerbated an existing issue by making it even harder to access services and support in a society that is struggling with a burgeoning mental healthcare crisis. Our world continues to be violent and dangerous, and this includes the increase in domestic and intimate partner violence. The media often minimizes and neuters these stories by reporting on these events using language such as "domestic dispute," "domestic altercation," or "domestic conflict." To those of us who work in the field, we know and see the tragic truth behind these stories. These aren't disputes or altercations; they are violent attacks from one partner or another in an attempt to gain or maintain power and control.

If you are a clinician working with victims of relationship abuse, it is our sincere hope that you will find this book useful. If you are a victim or survivor yourself, we hope this book helps you to find a new, stronger place for yourself in our world, a place that brings healing and hope. The six sectors of the Empowerment Wheel will grow with you as you embrace your own healing journey. They are flexible and adaptable, and will hopefully help you turn inward to soothe the wounded spaces in yourself. In addition to the six sectors of the Empowerment Wheel, we have added breakout boxes and reflection notes throughout this book that will offer opportunities for consideration and development. These are designed to deepen inquiry and understanding on a personal level that will buttress the growth that results from working through the six empowerment sectors. We hope, ultimately, that this book inspires you to nurture and strengthen your own inner wisdom, which is the most powerful tool any of us have.

REFERENCES

Buschel, B.S. and Hurvitz Madsen, L. (2004) "Strengthening connections between mothers and children: Art therapy in a domestic violence shelter." *Journal of Aggression, Maltreatment & Trauma 13*, 1, 87-108. https://doi.org/10.1300/J146v13n01_05

Cohen, B., Barnes, M., and Rankin, A. (1995) *Managing Traumatic Stress Through Art.* Lutherville, MD: The Sidran Press.

Czerny, A.B. and Lassiter, P.S. (2016) "Healing from intimate partner violence: An empowerment wheel to guide the recovery journey." *Journal of Creativity in Mental Health 11*, 3-4, 311-324. https://doi.org/10.1080/15401383.2016.1222321

Me Too Movement (2017) United States [Web archive]. Library of Congress, www.loc.gov/item/lcwaN0025442

Miller, G. (2008) "Bruce Perry's impact: Considerations for art therapy and children from violent homes." SlideShare. www.slideshare.net/gretchenmilleratrbc/PerryAATAPanelGretchen2

Schouten, K.A., van Hooren, S., Knipscheer, J.W., Kleber, R.J., and Hutschemaekers, G.J.M. (2018) "Trauma-focused art therapy in the treatment of posttraumatic stress disorder: A pilot study." *Journal of Trauma & Dissociation 20*, 1, 114-130. https://doi.org/10.1080/15299732.2018.1502712

Part One

CURRENT PARADIGM

Chapter 1

UNDERSTANDING RELATIONSHIP ABUSE

Relationship abuse, often also called domestic violence or intimate partner violence, is a pervasive and insidious crime that occurs in all levels of society regardless of economic status, race, education, or ethnicity. It occurs in relationships spanning the gender and sexual spectrum, including heterosexual, same sex, and transgender; research suggests, however, that most often it is women and transgender persons who are victimized (Flores *et al.* 2021). Relationship abuse typically begins with some form of verbal or emotional abuse and escalates to physical, sexual, or psychological assaults.

DEFINING TERMS
There is inconsistency in the definition and use of the terms "domestic violence," "intimate partner violence," and "relationship abuse." Domestic violence is typically defined as physical, mental, sexual, or emotional abuse caused by a loved one, but can also be used more broadly to define abuse by a member of someone's household (including parents, children, or even roommates). In the United Kingdom, the term "domestic abuse" refers to a broader definition of abuse by any member of a household. In the United States, the term "domestic violence" is utilized in legal cases where a victim and aggressor are either in a current or previous intimate relationship, and specific definitions vary according to state law.

Violence between people in a relationship is not exclusive to couples: the term "intimate partner violence" can now also be applied to cohabiting and unmarried couples.

Throughout this book, we use the term *relationship abuse* to describe the general experience of coercive or abusive behavior taking place within a current or former intimate partnership. At times, we may use the terms *intimate partner violence*, *domestic violence*, or *domestic abuse* interchangeably depending on the term used in resources that we cite. We consider "relationship abuse" to be an umbrella term that encompasses all such abusive behavior, including intimate partner violence, domestic violence, and domestic abuse.

We also use pronouns interchangeably, including she/her, he/him, and they/them, to indicate that anyone can be a victim or perpetrator of relationship abuse. In some cases, we use the pronouns that are used in an original source.

There are many ways to describe someone who commits abuse against another individual, such as "abuser," "abusive individual," "perpetrator," and "violent partner." These terms have varying meanings and values in the clinical world, as well as in the legal realm and society in general. In clinical work, we typically espouse the value of using person-first language. That is, a person exists independent of their diagnosis, thoughts, feelings, and behaviors. This can feel especially challenging in light of behaviors that are severely harmful to another person. That said, we make an attempt throughout this book to refer to people as people first, knowing that the circumstances that shape their behaviors are complicated, traumatic, and nuanced.

Similarly, we refer to the individual who is impacted by the abuse as "victim" or "survivor," depending on where that person is in their healing journey. We may also use terms to identify individuals that are reflective of the resources that we cite. We understand that not every person who has experienced relationship abuse will identify with the term *victim* or the term *survivor*, but we find these to be the most universal in describing the trajectory of healing that is an integral part of the recovery process from relationship abuse.

ELEMENTS OF RELATIONSHIP ABUSE
Relationship abuse can occur between any type of partner. Heterosexual, homosexual, and gender-fluid or non-binary relationships are all subject to the trappings of abusive, controlling relationships (Ard and Makadon 2011; Finneran and Stephenson 2013; Laskey, Bates, and Taylor 2019). While it is still true that physical and sexual violence is more often perpetrated onto female, non-binary, or female-identifying persons (Black *et al.* 2011), a person of any demographic could be a victim or perpetrator of relationship violence. Research shows that there is a significant record of underreporting from victims (Gracia 2004; Tjaden and Thoennes 2000).

Relationship abuse and intimate partner violence may include emotional, financial, spiritual, religious, and occupational or vocational manipulation. One common manner of abuse is when an individual attempts to isolate a partner by cutting off their family, social circle, contacts, and support systems. Abusive partners often maintain control through dictation of financial earning and spending (Johnson *et al.* 2021). A combination of other abusive controlling behaviors may be employed, leaving the victim with a seriously diminished self-esteem and a lack of confidence in their own ability to assert themselves and achieve self-sufficiency.

TYPES OF RELATIONSHIP ABUSE
Pence and Paymar developed the Power and Control Wheel (Domestic Abuse Intervention Programs n.d.) as part of their batterer intervention model, the Duluth Model (Pence and Paymar 1993; see Chapter 2 for a discussion of treatment for perpetrators), which has become a standard in explaining and defining types of abuse that typically occur in controlling or violent relationships. The Power and Control Wheel is divided into sections highlighting abusive behaviors, including emotional abuse; isolation; minimizing, denying, or blaming activities; using children as a means to exert control; male privilege; economic abuse; coercion and threats; and intimidation.

Emotional abuse
Emotional abuse includes any behavior that minimizes or attacks a person's self-esteem or confuses them enough to cause them to doubt themselves more than the perpetrator. Name-calling, mind games, humiliation, bullying, and gaslighting are variations of emotional abuse with the end goal of making the victim easier to control.

Isolation
Isolation occurs when an individual has limited access to support networks, including family and friends, as well as any outside of the home involvement. Controlling who a victim has contact with, what a victim reads, watches, or has exposure to, results in a form of destructive dependency that makes accessing support for leaving a relationship almost impossible.

Minimizing, denying, or blaming
In the 1990s, Freyd (2023) coined the acronym DARVO, meaning "Deny, Attack, and Reverse Victim and Offender." Perpetrators who minimize, deny, or blame the victim refuse to take responsibility for their actions and often reverse-blame the victim, telling them they are overreacting or that the abuse simply didn't happen. An abuser can make a victim believe that they are the cause of the abuse. These types of behavior weaken a victim's sense of self and self-worth, leaving that person confused and unable to seek help.

Using children as a means to exert control
Many victims stay in abusive relationships due to perpetrator threats to take their children away or deny visitation should the victim attempt to leave. The typical objective is to make the victim feel guilty and afraid, as a means to control the victim and keep them trapped in the relationship. Some victims may stay to protect their children, feeling that their children are more at risk from the abuser if they leave. This category can include pets as well.

Male privilege
Some forms of intimate partner violence tend to be more common in households with traditional gendered partner roles. This occurs in situations where the male partner is the "head of the house" and makes all the decisions, including those related to responsibilities and activities that family members are expected or allowed to have and experience.

Economic abuse
Economic abuse includes having limited or no access to finances, restrictions on being allowed to work or participate in work affairs, or demanding that the victim forfeit earned income (or sequestering such income) if they are allowed to work. It can also include making the victim ask for money or keeping the victim on an allowance, or denying financial access for necessary items.

Coercion and threats
Coercion and threats includes making or carrying out threats to harm or hurt the victim in some way. It also may include threats to abandon the victim or attempt suicide. Abusers may threaten to report the victim to the authorities (welfare, child services, etc.), even when aggressive acts are committed by victims in their own defense. Abusers may exert their control by making the victim do things that the victim does not want to do, including taking or using drugs or alcohol or other illegal activities.

Intimidation
In intimate relationships, so much can be communicated without saying a single word. Facial expressions, intense eye contact, non-violent physical actions, or gestures can convey intentions, expectations, and messages of grave consequences. These motions can covertly or overtly threaten and intimidate, and may include aggressive behaviors such as destruction of property, throwing or smashing household items, or displaying weapons.

OTHER FORMS OF ABUSE OR PROTECTIVE BEHAVIORS

The following terms are gaining popularity to describe behaviors that abusive partners use to take advantage of the victims with whom they are in a relationship:

- *Gaslighting:* psychological abuse that is specifically meant to make the victim feel as if they are losing their mind or slowly going mad, by creating doubt as to what they know is factual or true.

- *Love-bombing:* being showered with gifts, attention, affection, and compliments that often result in the relationship moving forward extremely rapidly.

- *Benching:* the victim feeling that their partner is playing them and holding out for someone better by staying active on an online dating app, or that their partner isn't committing to them in case someone better comes along.

- *Breadcrumbing:* leaving a low-commitment, low-investment trail of contact that keeps the victim guessing.

- *Haunting or orbiting:* orbiters or haunters essentially ghost their partners, but continue to passively interact via social media by "liking" messages, viewing all posts, and engaging in behaviors that can feel like social media stalking but without direct contact.

The following term describes behaviors that victims use to create some protection for themselves from their abusive partners:

- *Grey rocking:* being as unresponsive and neutral as possible when engaging with an abusive or toxic person; not responding, showing emotion, or making minimal eye contact as a way to reinforce boundaries and stop the negative behavior.

Other terms that have gained in popularity describe behaviors that could be used by an abusive partner or a victim. For example:

- *Ghosting:* the act of ceasing all contact without an explanation, including blocking avenues that might open contact (phone, social media, etc.) and possibly even relocating to a different location.

Finally, we have seen an increase in gestures and words that are meant to signal a safety issue and need for help to bystanders or responders. These are gestures or phrases that work only if the abusive partner is unaware of them or out of hearing or sight range:

- *Distress hand signal, indicating violence at home:* tucking your thumb into the palm and closing all four fingers over the thumb is a universal distress signal that indicates there is violence at home.

- *Ordering an Angel Shot:* if you are out and need help, ordering an Angel Shot drink signals to the bartender or waiter that you need help. If you order an Angel Shot neat, the bartender or waiter will escort you to your car; if you order an Angel Shot *with ice*, the bartender or waiter will call for a ride such as Uber or Lyft; and if you order an Angel Shot *with lime*, the bartender or waiter will call the police.[1]

The rise of online dating apps and social media posters continues to create new vocabulary to describe controlling acts and behaviors related to abuse and protection from abuse.

> Maggie was a young and very successful real estate agent who had just ended her relationship with Newell, whom she had met on an online dating forum. Maggie explained how her relationship with Newell went from a single date to moving in together in less than three months. From the minute they met, Maggie had the sense that everything about Newell was a perfect fit for her. He complemented her in so many ways—not only was he also employed in real estate (he was a rental manager), but his background and interests also matched

---

[1] In the UK, "Ask for Angela" (i.e., asking venue staff for "Angela") works in a similar way to ordering an Angel Shot in the USA.

hers almost perfectly. Newell was charming and handsome, and he showered Maggie with gifts and flowers. Maggie was quickly pulled into the seductive and romantic swirl that Newell orchestrated around her. He surprised her with tickets to concerts and sporting events, and she willingly rearranged her schedule to accommodate these thoughtful gestures. Over time, however, Newell's behaviors began to feel somewhat smothering. When Newell told her he had purchased tickets to Tahiti for the two of them as a surprise, without checking with her first or making sure the trip would fit around her work schedule, she said she couldn't go. He was furious. Maggie found herself suddenly dealing with a version of Newell she didn't recognize. Newell became vindictive and angry, and Maggie began to fear for her safety. It took her over six months to extricate herself from the relationship. In the end Maggie had to stay at a domestic violence shelter for several weeks before she could secure new housing for herself that was far enough away from where Newell worked and lived. Maggie was constantly exhausted and worried, as she told her story in counseling and tried to figure out her life. It would take another two years of therapy before Maggie would feel "herself" again.

BARRIERS TO LEAVING AND FEMICIDE

Not all victims leave and pursue a life beyond their abusers due to the significant barriers to departure that exist and which prevent or hinder victims from leaving (NCADV n.d.-a). One such barrier is the fear that the violence will escalate or become lethal. Indeed, the most dangerous time for a victim is during the termination of the relationship (Tjaden and Thoennes 2000), as this is when 77 percent of domestic violence-related homicides occur. When a victim decides to leave their abuser, there is a 75 percent increase in violence for at least two years (BWSS 2020). An abuser who feels they are losing power in the relationship will typically escalate control tactics.

Other barriers, such as lacking knowledge on how to access resources for safety and support, fear of isolation from friends and family, uncertainty about being able to gain employment and financial stability, or fear of separation from or loss of custody of children or pets, can make leaving an abusive relationship difficult or even impossible.

Femicide, the homicide of women, is increasing in the USA and globally. According to the NCADV (National Coalition Against Domestic Violence), the presence of a gun in a domestic violence situation increases the risk of homicide for the victim by 500 percent (Campbell *et al.* 2003). The United Nations (UN) reports that 81,100 women were intentionally killed in 2021, 45,000 of whom were killed by their intimate partners or family members (UN Women 2022). According to the same report, there was a 9 percent increase in femicide in North America in 2020, pointing to the impact of the COVID-19 pandemic lockdown protocols that kept people at home.

Sites that track data and analysis relating to femicide

- In the USA, Dawn Wilcox, RN, BSN, tracks data on femicide by collecting information on murdered women and publishes it on her website, Women Count USA,[2] of which she is the founder and executive director.

- The Murdered & Missing Indigenous Women website tracks murdered and American Indian and Alaska Native missing women, girls, and two-spirit persons.[3,4]

- MMIW (Murdered and Missing Indigenous Women) USA works to bring missing Indigenous women home

---

[2] https://womencountusa.org
[3] www.nativewomenswilderness.org/mmiw
[4] A third gender found in some Indigenous Native American cultures, often involving birth-assigned men or women taking on the identities and roles of the opposite sex. A sacred and historical identity, two-spirit can include, but is by no means limited to, LGBTQ identities.

and support the families of murdered Indigenous women through the grief process.[5]

PREVALENCE OF THE PROBLEM

It is suggested that one in four women and one in nine men have experienced severe intimate partner physical or sexual violence or stalking (Truman and Morgan 2014), which result in serious injury, pervasive fearfulness, or other physical or mental health sequelae. Also, one in three women and one in four men have experienced some form of physical or coercive violence by an intimate partner (Black *et al.* 2010). This includes a wide range of behaviors, from those that might not necessarily result in physical injury (such as slapping or shoving) to more severe forms of physical violence and injuries requiring medical intervention. A complicating factor to these statistics is not just the fact that underreporting occurs (Tjaden and Thoennes 2000), but also that abusive behaviors are often miscategorized or misidentified by those who are experiencing it. Charlot and Joel (2023, p.2) conducted a study in which they recruited participants both with and without professional expertise in relationship abuse. They then asked participants to categorize a series of behaviors (e.g., "Justin[e]'s partner did not let him[her] make decisions") as either abusive or non-abusive. The professionals consistently rated more behaviors as abusive than the participants with less understanding of what comprises abusive behavior. This demonstrates that not only is underreporting a problem, but that a lack of awareness of what constitutes abuse also contributes to the problem.

The Centers for Disease Control and Prevention (CDC) define *intimate partner violence* as "abuse or aggression that occurs in a romantic relationship" (2022, para. 1), where relationship refers to both current and former spouses and/or dating partners. Intimate partner violence is defined as a wide array of behaviors, including: acts of physical violence, sexual violence, stalking, or psychological

---

[5] https://mmiwusa.org

aggression (CDC 2022). Intimate partner violence can start as early as an intimate partnership starts and can continue across the lifespan.

Victims, groups, and trends
Adolescent dating violence
In a recent study that examined adolescent dating violence in 9th and 10th graders in Canada, researchers found that over one in three Canadian dating teens had experienced or perpetrated adolescent dating violence in the past 12 months (Exner-Cortens 2021). Similarly, the CDC reports that, based on the Youth Risk Survey completed in 2019 (Basile *et al.* 2020), one in twelve high school students in the USA experienced either physical and/or sexual dating violence. They also found that female high school students and students who reported being lesbian, gay, bisexual, transgender, or queer (LGBTQ), or those who were questioning their sexual identity, experienced higher rates of physical and sexual violence than their heterosexual counterparts. When looking at a broader age range (12- to 19-year-olds), the following statistic indicates the depth of the problem: 10 percent of adolescents report being the victim of physical violence by a dating partner (Office of Family Violence and Prevention Services 2023; youth. gov 2023). Adolescent dating violence can occur in various ways, including in-person and through the use of technology. It can result in physical, sexual, or psychological aggression, as well as stalking. It can have profound consequences on the health and wellbeing of those impacted, including depression, anxiety, illicit drug use, alcohol or tobacco use, antisocial behaviors such as bullying, theft, or aggression, and even suicide (Exner-Cortens, Baker, and Craig 2021). The fact that in the USA we now have a Teen Dating Violence Awareness Month (February) is an indication that adolescent dating violence is an increasing problem that demands our attention (youth.gov 2023).

COVID-19 pandemic
Initial reports in the aftermath of the COVID-19 lockdown, which started in March 2020, suggest that domestic violence

reports increased internationally at alarming rates. France saw a 30 percent increase in domestic violence reports, Argentina a 25 percent increase, and Singapore experienced a 33 percent increase in domestic violence helpline calls (Boserup, McKenney, and Elkbuli 2020). In the USA, the National Commission on COVID-19 and Criminal Justice noted an 8 percent increase in the reporting of domestic violence after governments imposed the lockdown in 2020 (Piquero *et al.* 2021). The increase is attributed to a variety of factors including isolation resulting from the lockdown, social distancing measures when in public, increased unemployment, decreased financial security, increased childcare demands within the home including home-schooling, and the inability to access support services for those who needed them.

Elder abuse and domestic violence

For the elderly, relationships are often complicated by health issues, physical limitations, and dependency on caregivers, which can contribute to the prevalence of relationship abuse (Bows *et al.* 2022; Yunus, Abdullah, and Firdaus 2021). The NCADV estimates that approximately 4 million older Americans are victims of physical, psychological, or other forms of abuse and neglect each year (NCADV 2018). It also reports that over 76 percent of elder physical abuse is perpetrated by a family member, and that the majority of elder sexual abuse cases involve a female victim and a male perpetrator. The World Health Organization (WHO) reported that the global prevalence of domestic violence for women aged 65–69 was 22 percent (2013), although this is likely an underestimate. They also reported not having data for women over the age of 70—Knight and Hester (2016, p.465) reported that "most of the data does not include information for women over the age of 49." This confirms a large gap in what we know.

In a British study, researchers found that the miscategorization of violence against the elderly contributed to how social support services were or were not delivered (Bows *et al.* 2022). The researchers found cases where there was a "tendency to see the abuse as *abuse in a domestic context, rather than domestic abuse*" (Bows *et al.* 2022, p.3; original emphasis). Elements of domestic abuse were completely overlooked in 35 out of the 119 Section 42 case files reviewed.[6] This study, which also considered risk factors and causes, suggests that there are challenges in properly identifying abuse and then describing it in a way that will alert the appropriate services. Since elder abuse can be physical, emotional, sexual, psychological, or financial, constructing social services policies written with an eye towards gaps identified in research could ensure that appropriate services are rendered to those who need it. Experiencing abuse later in life has profound consequences, including shorter lifespans, loss of independence, loss of life savings, and loss of dignity.

Sporting events and violence

Research supports a positive correlation between certain major sporting events and an increase in calls to the police and/or domestic violence hotlines. While sporting events and team fandom can build connections and community in positive ways, it can also fuel aggression. One study in Texas found a significant increase in police service calls reporting crimes against persons that correlated with most major professional sports, and by certain teams. The findings were significant enough for the authors to recommend increased policing on game days (Bagwell *et al.* 2023). Another study that looked at FIFA World Cup tournaments in the UK between 2002 and 2010 found an increase of 26 percent in the risk of domestic violence when the national team won, and a 38 percent increase when the national team lost (Kirby, Francis, and O'Flaherty 2014). In Calgary, Alberta researchers found an increase of 40 percent in domestic violence reports during Grey Cup football games in which Calgary played (Boutilier *et al.* 2017). In a study that examined the role of alcohol and emotions in connection to domestic abuse after major football (called "soccer" in the USA) games in Manchester, England, researchers found that there was a 5 percent decrease in domestic abuse incidents in the first 2 hours of a game, indicating a "substitution effect" between football and domestic abuse. However, they also found that domestic abuse

---

6   Section 42 cases are reports that are referred to local authorities involving abuse or neglect of elderly citizens.

incidents rose significantly (8.5%) and peaked 10 hours after the game. The increase was driven by two factors: perpetrators who imbibed alcohol, and when games were started prior to 7pm (Ivandić, Kirchmaier, and Torres-Blas 2021).

Sex trafficking

The United States Department of Justice (USDOJ) defines sex trafficking as "the recruitment, harboring, transportation, provision, obtaining, patronizing, or soliciting of a person for the purpose of a commercial sex act in which a commercial sex act is induced by force, fraud, or coercion, or in which the person induced to perform such an act has not attained 18 years of age" (USDOJ n.d.). Although it may not be apparent at first, there is an overlap between the experience of relationship abuse and the experience of being sex trafficked. Sex trafficking often occurs within the context of a relationship; traffickers often prey on young or vulnerable individuals by using coercion and control tactics that are similar to the dynamics of intimate partner violence (Verhoeven *et al.* 2015; Walsh 2016). Sex traffickers can present as intimate partners and convince their victims that they are in love. These relationships can be violent and volatile, and the dynamics of attachment and affection are used to keep the victim trapped and isolated. Other forms of abuse frequently present in sex trafficking are also present in domestic and intimate partner violence, including financial abuse, emotional abuse, and intimidation. In spite of the parallels between the experience of sex trafficking and domestic or intimate partner violence, research that examines the two experiences and makes recommendations for treatment is scant. However, there is consensus in the research that does exist that using interventions from the domestic violence or intimate partner violence literature can be useful when working with victims of sex trafficking (Macy and Graham 2012; Verhoeven *et al.* 2015; Walsh 2016).

Male victims

It is commonly acknowledged that the stigma associated with being a male victim often results in this being an underreported phenomenon (Walker *et al.* 2019). Because of this, we may not have an accurate understanding of the problem. Some research supports that the current terminology (for example, "domestic violence" and "intimate partner violence") is gendered to the degree that men do not relate to the language that is commonly used in research. A 2019 study that used the term "boundary crossing" in lieu of the term "domestic violence" or "intimate partner violence" resulted in more men (50% of the 258 participants) being willing to disclose their experiences of abuse (Walker *et al.* 2019). The same study found that male victims experienced physical, sexual, verbal, and controlling behaviors from their female partners, and that help-seeking often resulted in secondary abusive experiences, including "ridicule, doubt, indifference, and victim arrest" (Walker *et al.* 2019, p.1). Morgan and Wells (2016) concluded that female perpetrators used social norms to their advantage, as previous research had indicated about male abusers. This may indicate a similarity between male and female victim experiences. Finally, Dziewa and Glowacz (2022) noted in their qualitative study of both men and women leaving abusive relationships that the trajectories and stages of leaving (they propose an eight-stage process of leaving) are similar for both genders, with nuanced differences based on individual and environmental factors only. It is clear that more research is needed that can support services that are inclusive of men and women's experiences of abuse, including language that invites disclosure.

SHORT- AND LONG-TERM CONSEQUENCES

The consequences of intimate partner violence may include physical or mental injury, such as: damage to cardiac, digestive, reproductive, and nervous systems; depression and posttraumatic stress symptoms; and even disability or death. In addition, there is a social and economic impact that includes, among others, an impact to employers for injuries and time off; strain on the medical system and child welfare systems; and demands on the criminal justice systems.

Individuals who have been victims of relationship abuse can face a myriad of health issues. These can appear as physical, spiritual, or psychological disorders. Common long-lasting mental health concerns include depression, anxiety, posttraumatic stress disorder (PTSD), suicidality, and social phobias (Karakurt, Smith, and Whiting 2014; Lagdon, Armour, and Stringer 2014; Resick and Schnicke 1992). Serious, long-term physical health issues can include reproductive concerns, as well as autoimmune issues such as fibromyalgia and asthma, and other autoimmune disorders. Sexual health issues that frequently stem from the impact of relationship violence include infertility, sexually transmitted diseases and subsequent infections, AIDS, rectal or uterine prolapse, and substance abuse.

Two studies linked relationship abuse with increased risk of experiencing health issues later in life, including symptoms complicating menopause in women. Gibson and colleagues (2019) found that emotional abuse and PTSD correlated with an increase in sleep problems, and vasomotor (hot flashes and night sweats) and vaginal symptoms (dryness, itching, irritation, odor, discharge, pain during intercourse, pain during urination, bleeding, and prolapsed organs); physical abuse was correlated with night sweats; and sexual abuse was associated with vaginal symptoms. Similarly, Stubbs and Szoeke (2022) found that women who had experienced relationship abuse were more likely to experience an increase in distressing menopausal symptoms as well as an increased risk for diabetes, sexually transmitted infections, drug and alcohol abuse, and chronic diseases and pain. Furthermore, accessing, managing, and paying for what are often long-term healthcare issues as a result of experiencing an abusive relationship almost always falls to the victim.

Countless statistics demonstrate the very serious nature and impact of relationship abuse for victims, both in the immediate aftermath of violence and also across the lifespan. And yet the statistics do not tell the whole story, as it is widely known that relationship abuse is underreported. The National Violence Against Women Survey (Tjaden and Thoennes 2000) estimated that a mere one-quarter of all physical assaults, one-fifth of rapes, and one-half of stalkings are reported. Underreporting of rapes, stalking, and relationship abuse is attributed to a number of factors, including:

- fear of retribution from the abuser;
- fear of not being believed;
- being ostracized by the community;
- fear of prosecuting and losing a court judgment;
- concern for future social consequences (e.g., "Who will ever love me if they know that this has happened?");
- fear of losing opportunities (e.g., jobs, scholarships, earned merits);
- lack of understanding of what constitutes rape, stalking, or relationship abuse—consequently not believing that what they experienced was a crime;
- negative past experiences with medical professionals, law enforcement, abusive intimate partners, counselors, and/or family members;
- physiological and psychological effects of trauma, leaving the person voiceless, isolated, and disempowered;
- exhibiting psychological defense mechanisms such as repression and denial;
- a lack of reliance on memory storage and recall triggered by trauma imprinting, which compromises a person's ability to sequentially narrate their experience;
- lack of trust in oneself and one's own motivation;
- expectation of social maltreatment based on living in a culture that promotes male domination;
- power differentials caused by gender, ethnicity, race, occupation, socioeconomic status, or social standing.

More recently, the WHO's *Violence Against Women Prevalence Estimates, 2018* (2021) lists numerous issues that contribute to challenges and gaps in accurately assessing reliable data. These include variations in definitions of intimate partner violence, disaggregation of the various forms of abuse (physical, sexual, psychological), lack of data on intimate partner violence in same-sex relationships, victims living with intersecting forms of discrimination (such as refugees, transgender women, and women living with disabilities), a lack of standardized assessment measures, and a lack of measures that capture a wide range of age groups. Still, the WHO reported staggering statistics we have known for years, namely that more than 30 percent of women have been victims of physical or sexual violence from a current or former male partner at least once in their lifetime (WHO 2021). The challenges in accurately capturing the true numbers and prevalence of intimate partner violence highlight the complexity of such abuse, and the myriad ways that long-established power dominates and controls social institutions and structures.

Did you know?
Public policy
In the USA, the Violence Against Women Act (VAWA) was enacted as federal law under President Clinton in 1994 with bipartisan support until 2012, when conservative House politicians mounted opposition against it. At the time of VAWA's inception, the USA was moving on a worldwide trend to take action on addressing an antiquated legal system that prioritized men in society and consequently limited opportunities for women (Cepeda, Lacalle-Calderon, and Torralba 2022; World Bank 2020).

VAWA was eventually reauthorized in 2013, and then expired in 2018 during a government shutdown. A short-term spending bill kept the law going from January 2019 through February 2019, after which the House voted to reauthorize the law in April 2019. Increased opposition stalled the law from reenactment until President Biden reauthorized it on March 15, 2022. These fluctuations have real consequences in financial support and service delivery and show how critical issues are manipulated at the whim of politicians. VAWA creates comprehensive and cost-effective responses to sexual assault, domestic violence and intimate partner violence, dating violence, and stalking. However, VAWA has not fully addressed or standardized victim care, legal proceedings, or support systems, and the responsibility for creating laws about domestic violence and intimate partner violence has fallen to each state. This explains the significant difference of philosophical approach, legal protections, punitive damages, and funding that exist across the USA. Attempts to grow much-needed victim services ebb and flow, corresponding to the relative priority placed on this issue by political parties and representatives.

THE ROOT OF THE PROBLEM

How is it that people perpetuate violence and abuse in their relationships? In general, most people do not intentionally decide to be abusive to their partners. And certainly no one wakes up one day and thinks, "Today, I'm going to be really horrible to my partner." So what happens to someone that turns them into someone who can be labeled as abusive? The old adage "hurt people hurt people" is true. Our adult relationships are mirrors of the relational patterns we experience in childhood. If we were lucky enough to experience sufficient love and support and validation in our childhood, then we, in turn, can more likely give love and support and validation as adults. Alternatively, if we experienced love that was conditional, or if we experienced harsh punishment for small crimes, or worse, physical or sexual abuse, then our adult relationships, especially our intimate partnerships, are going to be based on a different kind of "relational map," one that is based on and mirrors our experience. In other words, what we experience relationally in childhood will show up in our adult relationships, most specifically in our intimate partnerships. Regardless of how loving and supportive parents may be, often we still learn that love has conditions. Well-intentioned parents, like well-intentioned partners, do not always excel at gaining insight, knowing their own triggers, or emotional regulation. Well-intentioned parents, after all, come to parenting with their own relationship histories. When we experience maladaptive relationship patterns in childhood, such as attachment wounding or ruptures, or outright abuse, those experiences may have a negative impact on our adult relationships, if patterns persist.

> Jan was finally able to leave an abusive relationship after 14 years of marriage. Her understanding of why her husband behaved the way he did was a focus of many therapy sessions. Finally, she was able to make the connection between his childhood and the way he showed up as her husband. Tommy had grown up in a household where addiction had a firm grasp on both of his parents. As a child, and the youngest of three, he often relied on his older siblings for his basic needs. He was also exposed to the drunken rages of his father, and struggled in school and with mood regulation. Tommy quickly learned how to be charming and witty as a way to disarm his parents, and initially this was something that Jan found attractive in Tommy. Their relationship progressed quickly, and within six months they were married and Jan was pregnant. During her pregnancy, Tommy's behavior started to change and Jan began to see a very different side of Tommy. He would rage at Jan about money and household expenses. Jan was completely caught off guard. The episodes got worse, and one night Tommy punched a hole in the kitchen wall. The next morning Jan found a bouquet of flowers with a note from Tommy apologizing for his behavior, swearing he would never do it again, and declaring his love for her. Apologizing after violent episodes became a pattern, and Tommy himself seemed confused by his own outbursts.

The reasons why a person might engage in abuse towards a loved one are complicated. The dynamics of relationships can challenge people immensely. Those who have been mistreated should never be assumed to be abusive themselves based on their history. Increased social understanding about relationship abuse can help individuals to avoid or escape this. Awareness around relationship abuse has increased recently, in part due to the #MeToo movement as well as high profile cases, such as the Harvey Weinstein, Bill Cosby, Larry Nassar, Jeffrey Epstein, and Jerry Sandusky sexual abuse cases. These underscore that predatory violence, grooming, sexual assault, and coercion can exist at all levels of power and privilege and across demographics.

MISCONCEPTION OF ANGER AS THE SOURCE

A common misconception about relationship abuse is that it is related to problems around anger management, or that anger management is an effective treatment. While perpetrators of relationship abuse can certainly demonstrate anger issues (Giordano *et al.* 2016), the fact is that anger problems are characterized by emotional outbursts that may cause an individual to lose control and respond in misaligned or maladaptive ways to a situation that often feels threatening, stressful, or fearful. In contrast, relationship abuse is a pervasive pattern of behavior that seeks to exert power and control over another in an attempt to maintain dominance over that individual. Perpetrators of relationship abuse might experience anger at home and in other settings, such as work, but the need to dominate and control others occurs within an intimate, interpersonal relationship and not, for example, against a co-worker, supervisor, or manager.

CHARACTERISTICS OF THE PERPETRATOR

Relationship abuse is a learned or socialized behavior and is the result of multiple factors or life experiences, including the way in which men and women are socialized and gendered. It tends to be more common in households or cultures that cling to more traditional gender roles (Kury, Obergfell-Fuchs, and Woessner 2004), or in communities where the male partner is seen as the "head of household" and the female partner's role is to be submissive, although this dynamic can also play out in same-sex relationships (Frankland and Brown 2014).

The use of abuse, power, and control against women continues to be normalized, on a societal scale and in a multitude of ways that range from hidden, subtle messages to messages that are more overt and direct. A good example of this is the popular *Fifty Shades* book trilogy (James 2011, 2012a, 2012b). The first book, *Fifty Shades of Grey*, depicts a relationship between the characters Christian Grey and Anastasia Steele. When examined, researchers found that emotional abuse or sexual violence, including stalking, intimidation, isolation, the use of alcohol to compromise consent, disempowerment, and entrapment, is present in some form in almost every interaction between the two main characters (Bonomi, Altenburger, and Walton 2013). However, following publication, *Fifty Shades of Grey* was banned from public libraries in several US states based on the semi-pornographic content of the novel and not on the patterns of abuse that occur between the two main characters.

There is no typical profile or personality that indicates someone might have an abusive personality. However, there is research indicating that perpetrators of intimate partner violence tend to have histories of increased alcohol or drug use, mental health issues ranging from depression or PTSD to more serious personality disorders, or were abused as children including assault, sexual assault, or witnessing intimate partner violence themselves (Oriel and Fleming 1998; Singh *et al.* 2014; Tilley and Brackley 2005). Perpetrators can often display charming behavior and focus on their personal image. They are often able to garner and recruit support from others, including law enforcement or judicial officials, in a way that makes them appear believable (Rakovec-Felser 2014). While they can be law-abiding citizens without any criminal history, inside the home, they can be jealous, possessive, unpredictable, and controlling (NCADV n.d.-b).

Breakout box: Books and movies that look at relationship abuse

Several books and movies explore the phenomenon of relationship abuse in various ways. Engage these stories as a tool for reflection and discussion. Consider the movies (some are also books) *Fifty Shades of Grey* (Foley and Taylor-Johnson 2015), *Gaslight* (Cukor 1944), *Mommie Dearest* (Frank 1981), and *Big Little Lies* (Vallée and Arnold 2017). Invite your client to consider one of these stories or another one with which they are familiar. Invite them to reflect on and consider their reactions to the story, including the action or inaction of the protagonist.

TYPOLOGY OF CONTROL AND VIOLENCE IN RELATIONSHIPS

According to Johnson (2008), not all intimate partner violence is the same. Johnson delineated the different types of intimate partner violence to promote understanding of the mechanisms and characteristics that contribute to violent behaviors. His typology of relationship violence describes common patterns. The four distinct types are: intimate terrorism; violent resistance; mutual violent control; and situational couple violence.

Intimate terrorism is coercive, violent, and produces terror and fear in the victim, and makes help-seeking a challenge. It does not necessarily indicate the level of violence (although these relationships can be extremely violent) but rather the pattern of tactics used to gain control over the partner across time. Johnson estimates that somewhere between 2 and 4 percent of couples experience coercive control by one partner over the other. Coercive control has been a crime in the UK since 2015, but was recently amended to include intimate partners, former intimate partners, or family members as opposed to just persons who are cohabitating. Coercive control is punishable by up to five years in prison. Perpetrators of intimate terrorism tend to fall into two broad categories of personality type: emotionally dependent (the main source of murder-suicides) or antisocial (Holtzworth-Munroe and Stuart 1994).

Violent resistance can look like self-defense against a perpetrator of intimate terrorism, but can also be acts of retaliation against an abusive partner. It can result in acts of violence as serious as homicide, but more typically they are attempts at retaliation that are meant to mitigate or allow for escape from the violent relationship.

Mutual violent control occurs when both partners exert violence against each other in attempts to gain control over the relationship.

Situational couple violence is by far the most common, and estimated to affect one in eight couples. These are relationships in which arguments escalate to violence, and where either or both partners perpetrates the violence. Since men are typically bigger and often stronger than women, their violent acts can result in significantly more injury and fear to women victims. Situational couple violence can include a number of variables including chronic conflict, substance use and abuse, anger issues, and communication issues. Perpetrators of situational couple violence may have struggles in multiple areas of their lives including issues around poverty and substance abuse, especially alcohol (Johnson 2008).

RESPONSES TO ABUSE: FIGHT, FLIGHT, FREEZE, OR FAWN

The fear associated with relationship abuse and other related traumas has a profound impact on the nervous system. We move from a regulated state (calm) into a dysregulated state (agitated, anxious, nervous, panicked) generally by becoming activated when faced with cues that signal danger or lack of safety. Activation is generally characterized by "fight" or "flight;" we will fight to resolve the situation or we will try to escape it. If those options don't work, the next level of dysregulation is "freeze," where our body begins to move into immobilization, preparing for imminent attack. If these cycles happen frequently enough, we can get caught in either chronic activation (anxiety) or chronic immobilization (depression) or both (alternating between anxiety and depression) (Porges 2010). For some of us, however, a fourth option of survival exists. In this option we develop people-pleasing behaviors, known as a "fawn" response, which is meant to pre-empt conflict by establishing a sense of safety before anything bad can happen.

Clients who come to therapy are often struggling with dysregulation. This is especially true for victims of relationship abuse.

> Bryanna came to counseling while she was still living with her abusive partner, Camille. Bryanna was in her mid-40s and struggling with depression that, according to her, had plagued her for years. She stated that she did not love Camille, but that the thought of leaving her was simply impossible. Bryanna worried about how leaving Camille would impact her family, who thought Camille was wonderful. They did not see the belittling and hurtful behavior that Camille inflicted on Bryanna daily. Bryanna also worried that their two children would be negatively impacted by a divorce. Bryanna worried about everyone, in fact, except herself. She went out of her way to make sure that everyone else in her life was taken care of. She rarely considered her own needs or emotions, and her concern for others kept her trapped in a dysfunctional relationship. It took many years for Bryanna to learn that her own needs mattered. It took a few years more for her to be able to make her own needs a priority.

Many survivors of relationship abuse state that the bruises, broken bones, and wounds they sustained from their abusers, while terribly painful and often difficult to heal from, were nothing compared to the emotional and psychological damage they incurred. Relationship abuse is insidious in that way; the internal damage and long-term effects attack the very core of the victim's internal ego structure. It is not uncommon for survivors to state that after years of abuse they don't know themselves anymore, that somewhere along the way they lost who they really are. Survival tactics and coping behaviors take over and all else is often lost. The road to recovery is difficult, but not impossible. Healing can happen, and discovering (or rediscovering) the lost self is possible.

REFERENCES

Ard, K.L. and Makadon, H.J. (2011) "Addressing intimate partner violence in lesbian, gay, bisexual, and transgender patients." *Journal of General Internal Medicine 26*, 8, 930–933. https://doi.org/10.1007/s11606-011-1697-6

Bagwell, R., Block, K., Leal, W.E., and Piquero, A.R. (2023) "The association between professional sporting events and police calls for service in San Antonio, Texas." *Journal of Crime and Justice*. https://doi.org/10.1080/0735648X.2023.2201891

Basile, K.C., Clayton, H.B., DeGue, S., Gilford, J.W., et al. (2020) "Interpersonal violence victimization among high school students—Youth Risk Behavior Survey, United States, 2019." *Morbidity and Mortality Weekly Report Supplements 69*, Suppl-1, 28–37. http://dx.doi.org/10.15585/mmwr.su6901a4

Black, M.C., Basile, K.C., Breiding, M.J., Smith, S.G., et al. (2011) *National Intimate Partner and Sexual Violence Survey: 2010 Summary Report*. Atlanta, GA: National Center for Injury Prevention and Control, Centers for Disease Control and Prevention. www.cdc.gov/violenceprevention/pdf/nisvs_report2010-a.pdf

Bonomi, A., Altenburger, L.E., and Walton, N.L. (2013) "'Double crap!' Abuse and harmed identity in *Fifty Shades of Grey*." *Journal of Women's Health 22*, 9, 733–744. https://doi.org/10.1089/jwh.2013.4344

Boserup, B., McKenney, M., and Elkbuli, A. (2020) "Alarming trends in US domestic violence during the COVID-19 pandemic." *American Journal of Emergency Medicine 38*, 12, 2753–2755. doi: 10.1016/j.ajem.2020.04.077

Boutilier, S., Jadidzadeh, A., Esina, E., Wells, L., and Kneebone, R. (2017) "The connection between professional sporting events, holidays, and domestic violence in Calgary, Alberta." *The School of Public Policy Publications 10*, 12. https://ssrn.com/abstract=2997172

Bows, H., Penhale, B., Bromely, P., Pullerits, M., Quinn-Walker, N., and Sood, A. (2022) *Perpetrators of Domestic Abuse Against Older Adults: Characteristics, Risk Factors, and Professional Responses*. Durham: Durham University. www.dur.ac.uk/media/durham-university/research-/research-centres/research-into-violence-and-abuse-centre-for/pdf-files/Perpetrators-of-DA-report-v.5.pdf

BWSS (Battered Women's Support Services) (2020) "Eighteen months after leaving domestic violence is still the most dangerous time." June 11. www.bwss.org/eighteen-months-after-leaving-domestic-violence-is-still-the-most-dangerous-time

Campbell, J.C., Webster, D., Koziol-McLain, J., Block, C., et al. (2003) "Risk factors for femicide in abusive relationships: Results from a multisite case control study." *American Journal of Public Health 93*, 7, 1089–1097. https://doi.org/10.2105/ajph.93.7.1089

CDC (Centers for Disease Control and Prevention) (2022) "Fast Facts: Preventing Intimate Partner Violence." www.cdc.gov/violenceprevention/intimatepartnerviolence/fastfact.html

Cepeda, I., Lacalle-Calderon, M., and Torralba, M. (2022) "Measuring violence against women: A global index." *Journal of Interpersonal Violence 37*, 19–20, NP18614–NP18638. https://doi.org/10.1177/08862605211037424

Charlot, N. and Joel, S. (2023) "Differences in perceptions of intimate partner violence between professionals and nonprofessionals." PsyArXiv preprints, March 28. https://doi.org/10.31234/osf.io/5mjvx

Cukor, G. (Director) (1944) *Gaslight* [Film]. Metro-Goldwyn-Mayer Corp.

Domestic Abuse Intervention Programs (no date) "Wheel Information Center." www.theduluthmodel.org/wheels

Dziewa, A. and Glowacz, F. (2022) "Getting out from intimate partner violence: Dynamics and processes. A qualitative analysis of female and male victims narratives." *Journal of Family Violence 37*, 643–656. https://doi.org/10.1007/s10896-020-00245-2

Exner-Cortens, D., Baker, E., and Craig, W. (2021) "The national prevalence of adolescent dating violence in Canada." *Journal of Adolescent Health 69*, 3, 495–502. https://doi.org/10.1016/j.jadohealth.2021.01.032

Finneran, C. and Stephenson, R. (2013) "Intimate partner violence among men who have sex with men: A systematic review." *Trauma, Violence & Abuse 14*, 2, 168–185. https://doi.org/10.1177/1524838012470034

Flores, A.R., Meyer, I.H., Langton, L., and Herman, J.L. (2021) "Gender identity disparities in criminal victimization: National Crime Victimization Survey, 2017–2018." *American Journal of Public Health 111*, 4, 726–729. https://escholarship.org/uc/item/2gz31i23

Foley, J. and Taylor-Johnson, S. (Directors) (2015) *Fifty Shades of Grey* [Film]. Michael De Luca Productions; Trigger Street Productions; Perfect World Pictures.

Frank, P. (Director) (1981) *Mommie Dearest* [Film]. Paramount Pictures.

Frankland, A. and Brown, J. (2014) "Coercive control in same-sex intimate partner violence." *Journal of Family Violence 29*, 15–22. https://doi.org/10.1007/s10896-013-9558-1

Freyd, J.J. (2023) "What is DARVO?" http://pages.uoregon.edu/dynamic/jjf/defineDARVO.html

Gibson, C.J., Huang, A.J., McCaw, B., Subak, L.L., Thom, D.H., and Van Den Eeden, S.K. (2019) "Associations of intimate partner violence, sexual assault, and posttraumatic stress disorder with menopause symptoms among midlife and older women." *JAMA Internal Medicine 179*, 1, 80–87. doi: 10.1001/jamainternmed.2018.5233

Giordano, P.C., Copp, J.E., Longmore, M.A., and Manning, W.D. (2016) "Anger, control, and intimate partner violence in young adulthood." *Journal of Family Violence 31*, 1–13. https://doi.org/10.1007/s10896-015-9753-3

Gracia, E. (2004) "Unreported cases of domestic violence against women: Towards an epidemiology of social silence, tolerance, and inhibition." *Journal of Epidemiology & Community Health 58*, 7, 536–537. https://doi.org/10.1136/jech.2003.019604

Holtzworth-Munroe, A. and Stuart, G.L. (1994) "Typologies of male batterers: Three subtypes and the differences among them." *Psychological Bulletin 116*, 3, 476–497. https://doi.org/10.1037/0033-2909.116.3.476

Ivandić, R., Kirchmaier, T., and Torres-Blas, N. (2021) *Football, Alcohol and Domestic Abuse*. Centre for Economic Performance Discussion Papers, 1781. London: London School of Economics and Political Science. https://research.cbs.dk/en/publications/football-alcohol-and-domestic-abuse

James, E.L. (2011) *Fifty Shades of Grey*. New York: Vintage Books.

James, E.L. (2012a) *Fifty Shades Darker*. New York: Vintage Books.

James, E.L. (2012b) *Fifty Shades Freed*. New York: Vintage Books.

Johnson, L., Hoge, G.L., Nikolova, K., and Postmus, J.L. (2021) "Escala de abuso economico: Validating the scale of economic abuse-12 (SEA-12) in Spanish." *Journal of Family Violence 36*, 885–897. https://doi.org/10.1007/s10896-021-00251-y

Johnson, M.P. (2008) *A Typology of Domestic Violence: Intimate Terrorism, Violent Resistance, and Situational Couples Violence*. Lebanon, NH: Northeastern University Press.

Karakurt, G., Smith, D.B., and Whiting, J. (2014) "Impact of intimate partner violence on women's mental health." *Journal of Family Violence 29*, 7, 693–702. doi: 10.1007/s10896-014-9633-2

Kirby, S., Francis, B., and O'Flaherty, R. (2014) "Can the FIFA World Cup football (soccer) tournament be associated with an increase in domestic abuse?" *Journal of Research in Crime and Delinquency 51*, 3, 259–276. https://doi.org/10.1177/0022427813494843

Knight, L. and Hester, M. (2016) "Domestic violence and mental health in older adults." *International Review of Psychiatry 28*, 5, 464–474. https://doi.org/10.1080/09540261.2016.1215294

Kury, H., Obergfell-Fuchs, J., and Woessner, G. (2004) "The extent of family violence in Europe." *Violence Against Women 10*, 7, 749–769. https://doi.org/10.1177/1077801204265550

Lagdon, S., Armour, C., and Stringer, M. (2014) "Adult experience of mental health outcomes as a result of intimate partner violence victimization: A systematic review." *European Journal of Psychotraumatology 5*, 1, 1–12. https://doi.org/10.3402/ejpt.v5.24794

Laskey, P., Bates, E., and Taylor, J. (2019) "A systematic literature review of intimate partner violence victimization: An inclusive review across gender and sexuality." *Aggression and Violent Behavior 47*, 1–11. https://doi.org/10.1016/j.avb.2019.02.014

Macy, R.J. and Graham, L.M. (2012) "Identifying domestic and international sex-trafficking victims during human service provision." *Trauma, Violence, & Abuse 13*, 2, 59–76. https://doi.org/10.1177/1524838012440340

Morgan, W. and Wells, M. (2016) "'It's deemed unmanly': Men's experiences of intimate partner violence (IPV)." *The Journal of Forensic Psychiatry & Psychology 27*, 3, 404–418. https://doi.org/10.1080/14789949.2015.1127986

NCADV (National Coalition Against Domestic Violence) (2018) "What is abuse in later life?" Blog, June 12. https://ncadv.org/blog/posts/quick-guide-domestic-abuse-in-later-life

NCADV (no date-a) "Why do victims stay?" https://ncadv.org/why-do-victims-stay

NCADV (no date-b) "Signs of abuse." https://ncadv.org/signs-of-abuse

Office of Family Violence and Prevention Services (2023) "2023 Teen Dating Violence Awareness Month (TDVAM)." US Department of Health & Human Services. March 10. www.acf.hhs.gov/ofvps/teen-dating-violence-awareness-month-tdvam

Oriel, K.A. and Fleming, M.F. (1998) "Screening men for partner violence in a primary care setting: A new strategy for detecting domestic violence." *Journal of Family Practice 46*, 6, 493–498.

Pence, E. and Paymar, M. (1993) *Education Groups for Men Who Batter: The Duluth Model*. New York: Springer Publishing Company, Inc.

Piquero, A.R., Wesley, G.J., Jemison, E., Kaukinen, C., and Knaul, F.M. (2021) *Domestic Violence During COVID-19: Evidence from a Systematic Review and Meta-Analysis*. Washington, DC: Council on Criminal Justice.

Porges, S.W. (2010) *Polyvagal Theory: Neurophysiological Foundations of Emotions, Attachment, Communication, and Self-Regulation*. New York: W.W. Norton & Co.

Rakovec-Felser, Z. (2014) "Domestic violence and abuse in intimate relationship from public health perspective." *Health Psychology Research 2*, 3, 62–67. https://doi.org/10.4081/hpr.2014.1821

Resick, P.A. and Schnicke, M.K. (1992) "Cognitive processing therapy for sexual assault victims." *Journal of Consulting and Clinical Psychology 60*, 5, 748–756. doi: 10.1037//0022-006x.60.5.748

Singh, V., Tolman, R., Walton, M., Chermack, S., and Cunningham, R. (2014) "Characteristics of men who perpetrate intimate partner violence." *The Journal of the American Board of Family Medicine 27*, 5, 661–668. https://doi.org/10.3122/jabfm.2014.05.130247

Stubbs, A. and Szoeke, C. (2022) "The effect of intimate partner violence on the physical health and health related behaviors of women: A systematic review

of the literature." *Trauma, Violence, & Abuse 23*, 4, 1157–1172. https://doi.org/10.1177/15248380209855541
Tilley, D.S. and Brackley, M. (2005) "Men who batter intimate partners: A grounded theory study of the development of male violence in intimate partner relationships." *Issues in Mental Health Nursing 26*, 3, 281–297. https://doi.org/10.1080/01612840590915676
Tjaden, P. and Thoennes, N. (2000) *Extent, Nature, and Consequences of Intimate Partner Violence: Findings from the National Violence Against Women Survey.* Washington, DC: Department of Justice.
Truman, J.L. and Morgan, R.E. (2014) "Nonfatal domestic violence, 2003–2012." Special Report, April. US Department of Justice, Office of Justice Programs, Bureau of Justice Statistics, NCJ244697. https://bjs.ojp.gov/content/pub/pdf/ndvo312.pdf
UN (United Nations) Women (2022) "Five essential facts to know about femicide." News and Stories, November 25. www.unwomen.org/en/news-stories/feature-story/2022/11/five-essential-facts-to-know-about-femicide
USDOJ (United States Department of Justice) (no date) "Human trafficking." www.justice.gov/humantrafficking#:~:text=Sex%20trafficking%20is%20the%20recruitment,attained%2018%20years%20of%20age
Vallée, J.-M. and Arnold, A. (Directors) (2017) *Big Little Lies* [TV Series]. HBO Entertainment; Hello Sunshine; Blossom Films; David E. Kelley Productions.
VAWA (Violence Against Women Act) (2022) Reauthorization Act of 2022. www.congress.gov/bill/117th-congress/senate-bill/3623
Verhoeven, M., van Gestel, B., de Jong, D., and Kleemans, E. (2015) "Relationships between suspects and victims of sex trafficking: Exploitation of prostitutes and domestic violence parallels in Dutch trafficking cases." *European Journal on Criminal Policy and Research 21*, 1, 49–64. doi: 10.1007/s10610-013-9226-2
Walker, A., Lyall, K., Silva, D., Craigie, G., *et al.* (2019) "Male victims of female-perpetrated intimate partner violence, help-seeking, and reporting behaviors: A qualitative study." *Psychology of Men & Masculinities 21*, 2, 213–223. https://doi.org/10.1037/men0000222
Walsh, S.D. (2016) "Sex trafficking and the state: Applying domestic abuse interventions to serve victims of sex trafficking." *Human Rights Review 17*, 2, 221–245. doi: 10.1007/s12142-016-0404-8
WHO (World Health Organization) (2013) *Global and Regional Estimates of Violence Against Women: Prevalence and Health Effects of Intimate Partner Violence and Non-Partner Sexual Violence.* Geneva: World Health Organization Press.
WHO (2021) *Violence Against Women Prevalence Estimates, 2018.* March 9. Geneva: WHO. www.who.int/publications/i/item/9789240022256
World Bank Group (2020) *Women, Business and the Law 2020.* Washington, DC: International Bank for Reconstruction and Development and The World Bank. https://openknowledge.worldbank.org/server/api/core/bitstreams/6c2b5974-9a3b-5249-995b-2b22e5fd7909/content
youth.gov (2023) "Teen Dating Violence Awareness and Prevention Month." https://youth.gov/feature-article/teen-dating-violence-awareness-and-prevention-month
Yunus, R.M., Abdullah, N.N., and Firdaus, M.A.M. (2021) "Elder abuse and neglect in the midst of COVID-19." *Journal of Global Health 11.* doi: 10.7189/jogh.11.03122

Chapter 2

UNDERSTANDING TREATMENT PROTOCOLS

Relationship abuse is sadly a tale as old as time. The rise in the women's rights movements locally and globally helped to bring some power to women living in patriarchal societies, and some conviction that this problem warranted solutions. Around the world many women have taken action in their own communities, recruiting male allies to help, and inspiring other women in other communities.

Until the early 20th century, women were viewed as the property of their fathers, and then their husbands when they married. Subsequently, men were allowed by law to beat their wives in America, and in many other places (NOW 2023). What became known as the "battered women's movement" then started to gain traction through affiliation with the American temperance and suffrage movements, since relationship violence was thought to depend on alcohol use and intoxication (Hyer 2023; NOW 2023). In 1871, Massachusetts and Alabama were the first of the United States to criminalize assaults on wives by their husbands. North Carolina followed suit in 1874 (although sadly North Carolina didn't criminalize marital rape until 1993, the last of all 50 states to do so), and legal consequences against convicted offenders were added into the Maryland law. A movement started towards establishing and reforming laws across the states, but it did not happen quickly or without significant petitioning and lobbying efforts (Hyer 2023). We should note here, however, that enacting these laws did not necessarily translate to prosecution of offenders.

THE SHELTER MOVEMENT

Advocates against domestic violence have long been championing safe shelter for victims of relationship abuse who manage to escape their abuser; this often involved advocates taking the victim into their own homes. One of the earliest shelter residences, Haven House, was a shelter for battered women that was started in 1964 in Pasadena, California, sponsored by Al-Anon (NOW 2023). The shelter movement flourished in England with activist Erin Pizzey, who was a pioneer in creating a safe haven for battered women in a London suburb in 1971 (Haaken and Yragui 2003).

Similar initiatives were being taken around the world. In Canada, the Harbour Rescue Mission launched the Inasmuch House in Hamilton, Ontario in 1967 (Mission Services 2022). A group of local advocates in Hayward, California established the Emergency Shelter Program Inc. (now called Ruby's Place Inc.) in 1971 (Ruby's Place 2023). Women's Advocates, a non-profit collective, opened a shelter in St Paul, Minnesota in October 1974 (Kippert 2015). In Philadelphia, PA, local non-profit Women Against Abuse opened a part-time hotline center in 1976, and then a year later followed with the area's first women's shelter (Rivera 2021). In 1974, a group of advocates affiliated with the women's liberation group of Sydney, Australia, broke into two adjoining houses, changed the locks, and claimed residency through squatters' rights. They then opened the Elsie Refuge for Women and Children. In 1976, the Ministry of Family Affairs in Germany funded the creation of a shelter for battered women, which spurred the establishment of similar government-funded shelters started by the autonomous women's movement around the country (Schulz 2002). In the Netherlands, Stay-Off-My-Body Houses were started in the 1970s and operated in secret. Through grassroots advocacy efforts, a documented 700 shelters were serving 91,000 women in the USA by 1983 (NOW 2023).

The feminist shelter movement commenced shortly thereafter and differed somewhat from Pizzey's version in that the feminist-based shelters were usually in confidential locations and male visitors were strictly forbidden. The feminist shelter perspective expanded in Canada: Interval House in Toronto, Ontario opened in April 1973 (Interval House 2023), and the Ishtar Transition Housing Society[1] followed in June 1973, in Langley, British Columbia.

In the USA the shelter movement has generally progressed more or less in keeping with the feminist ideal of confidential and secretive locations that disallowed male visitors. Over the years organizations supporting the movement have transitioned from private homes and apartments to large facilities that are supported by state and federal funding. There has been a shift recently to move away from the strict confidentiality of shelter locations and limiting access strictly to residents and staff, both of which have been acknowledged to contribute to feelings of shame and guilt for survivors of relationship abuse (Goodman *et al*. 2020). In addition, there has been a shift toward a more multicultural view of healing from relationship abuse that makes space for a wide array of responses regarding safety as opposed to a one-size-fits-all approach. This broader, more inclusive approach acknowledges that empowerment can look different based on someone's cultural background, and is in keeping with current feminist principles of multicultural awareness and responsiveness.

The Global Network of Women's Shelters (GNWS) was established in 2015 in The Hague, the Netherlands. It is a volunteer organization that helps unite activists, hosts conferences, proposes legislation, unites communities, and educates the public about issues pertaining to relationship violence and individuals' need and right for safety (GNWS 2023).

TREATMENT SYSTEM: SHELTERS

Treatment for the lasting impact of intimate partner violence and other forms of relationship abuse almost always falls on the victim's

---

[1] Ishtar Women's Resource Society: https://ishtarsociety.org

shoulders. This includes everything from identifying the need for help, maintaining safety to the degree one is able, locating and procuring appropriate resources, and financing those resources. Much of the identified treatment for relationship abuse is focused on acute care, getting the victim to a stable, physically safe space separated from their abuser. Subsequent treatment for victims of abuse is frequently delivered in shelter settings (Allen and Wozniak 2010). Shelters can be a place of refuge and support for victims, providing much needed temporary housing, food, crisis support, and access to resources that can be helpful in the recovery process (such as navigating the legal system or securing protective orders); they can also be challenging in their own way.

Living in a shelter requires abiding by the regulations set by that facility. One study (Gregory, Nnawulezi, and Sullivan 2021) found that shelters could be notoriously inconsistent in how they delegated and administered rules. For example, the researchers found that shelter rules often impeded residents' ability to carry out day-to-day activities such as maintaining a job or transporting children. Difficulty maintaining life activities negatively affected the residents' mental wellbeing, and shelter rules are typically inflexible. When flexibility was displayed, it was inconsistent, revealing unequal treatment and favoritism. Another study examined literature on domestic and intimate partner violence between 2005 and 2022 (Kennedy *et al.* 2023). The researchers were seeking evidence on the trustworthiness of community-based intimate partner violence service providers in the USA, including domestic violence services, health and mental care, the legal system, and economic support services. They found a combination of factors that contributed to a lack of trustworthiness of services for survivors. These included a lack of shelter beds, services inaccessible due to language barriers, lack of affordable services, and harmful and discriminatory staff, especially for survivors who were sexual or gender minorities, impoverished, or brown-skinned. The study also found some providers who were incompetent due to insufficient training (Kennedy *et al.* 2023).

> When Maria worked her late shift at Walmart, and missed curfew returning to the shelter because the bus schedule was

erratic due to heavy storms in the area, she lost her place in the shelter. It was the third time that working late and being dependent on public transportation had caused her to be late returning to the shelter. When Maria reported that her bus was late, staff did not always believe her. Another resident reported to staff that they had seen Maria talking to a man on the corner while the bus drove by. Maria's motivations for treatment and judgment were questioned. All of Maria's life activities became scrutinized when she lived in the shelter setting. Despite actively engaging in other treatment protocols and working to save money to achieve independence, Maria and her child were removed from the shelter, and rendered homeless. Maria's story is not a unique one among shelter residents. Inflexibility in regulations contributed to Maria not being able to thrive in the shelter environment. Despite the good intentions by staff, Maria was no longer able to receive services there.

In terms of healing or recovery, the expectation is often that victims leave their partners. This may include the need to go into hiding and, depending on the level of threat that exists, the need to re-establish themselves in society, independent of their abuser, coupled with steps that are meant to ensure self-sufficiency rather quickly. Barriers to treatment may include the victim returning to or staying in the abusive relationship. In the USA and UK, shelter services are often limited by funding, and in the USA specifically there are almost always limits to the length of stay. Services tend to focus more on the social services components associated with case management (housing, employment, etc.) rather than reparative therapeutic work, although some shelters may also provide therapeutic services.

Shelter systems can benefit from national or even international affiliation that enhances service delivery. In the USA, individual shelters are unaffiliated with each other and operate as separate entities, with unique funding streams. In contrast, some countries operate an affiliated network of domestic violence shelters, which may lend toward sharing resources, tracking client treatment plans, and better understanding community service needs.

In contrast to the US shelter system, where victims are expected to leave their homes in order to stay safe, one program in Israel, Beit Noam, has flipped the expectation by allowing victims to stay in their homes and mandating perpetrators to treatment in shelter settings (Keynan et al. 2003). Residents of Beit Noam earn their right to reconnect with their family based on their progress with treatment goals. The victim, in contrast, is allowed to continue living in their home without their abuser, and without the disruption and upheaval that is more common in the USA and other countries.

In addition to temporary housing, which may have limitations on length of stay and rules, shelters have placed an emphasis on brief interventions that seek to establish stabilization and emotional wellbeing in a relatively short period of time. Such treatment options typically might include case management, brief interventions (e.g., medical, financial, safe placement, short-term therapy), support groups, and individual or group counseling. However, interventions should be tailored directly to the needs of the individual seeking treatment. The experience and response to relationship abuse is intensely personal, and the perceived level of threat and severity of abuse can impact treatment. Some counseling treatments emphasize working with the victim of relationship abuse, while others might emphasize working with the perpetrator.

> Myesha felt grateful to have secured a bed for herself and her two young children at the local domestic violence shelter, given that it was such short notice; she had finally escaped her abusive boyfriend after a particularly violent episode. Myesha was referred to the shelter from the local hospital by a social worker who recognized immediately that Myesha was in an abusive relationship. Myesha had received emergency surgery for a knife wound to her hand. After arriving at the shelter, Myesha was told that she would need to do the following: (1) change her children's enrollment to the local elementary school including transportation; (2) secure a new job, one where her boyfriend would not be able to find her; (3) save enough money to put

a down payment on new housing; (4) file a protective order against her boyfriend as soon as possible for safety reasons; (5) attend group twice weekly with the other shelter residents; (6) participate in a weekly chore rotation; and (7) meet with her assigned case manager on a weekly basis to track her progress on these goals. Myesha had every intention of doing her best to accomplish all of these goals, but she didn't count on her hand getting infected once she got to the shelter. Myesha ended up having to go back to the hospital for additional treatment. There was a flu-like bug going through the shelter and both of her children caught it, which meant Myesha was stuck in her room tending to her kids for several days. To make matters worse, Myesha was depressed, was prone to frequent crying spells, and missed her boyfriend. He had texted her and apologized multiple times and she could feel her resolve weakening. Myesha's boyfriend had been the sole wage earner while she stayed home with the children. Having not held employment in years, Myesha wasn't sure she could find a job or even keep one if she did find one. She missed the security of her boyfriend's income and their neat, clean apartment. The shelter was messy and her roommate left food everywhere in spite of the rules. After three weeks at the shelter, Myesha still hadn't found a job and the 30-day deadline was looming. She could ask for an extension, but that would only give her another 15 days. Myesha felt paralyzed and overwhelmed.

Myesha's situation, while typical, is concerning in that the expectations that were placed on her were unrealistic given the limited time and support available to her. A client-centric shelter system could better serve Myesha in a number of ways. For example, compassion given her hand injury and allowing extra time for healing before starting the length-of-stay "clock" would have been helpful. Myesha might have also benefited from a trained counselor who was willing to speak with her about the text messages from her boyfriend and the emotional pull that these had on her. A job readiness or interviewing skills program could have helped her feel more confident in her ability to secure employment. Childcare could have helped facilitate her ability to apply for jobs, interview, and obtain employment. Unless childcare can help facilitate school drop-off and/or pick-up, and aftercare, then the likelihood that a low-income parent with limited social support could maintain employment is slim. Securing housing may be more realistic for shelter residents who are provided with micro-loans to finance housing deposits, or lease co-signers in the case of those who are unemployed. Lastly, shelter residents could benefit from groups led by trained clinicians that implement the Empowerment Wheel model with art therapy. Most shelters do not provide these added services that would help ensure client program compliance and future life success. Many advocates have championed the idea that a fuller complement of services for abuse survivors should be delivered in a single location (Harbishettar and Math 2014). To achieve this, we likely need a system with greater communication and cooperation between education, health, legal, and judicial sectors (Kaur and Garg 2008).

> **Breakout box: Clinical considerations**
> If you're sitting with a client whose situation is like Myesha, you know that they have already been in the situation where they knew they had to get out of this relationship, and they left. Even if they are currently evaluating returning to the relationship, they have made the decision at least once to leave. Ask your client to think back to a *red flag* moment, to reflect on the moment that they knew something was off. They might discuss it verbally, or they might draw a picture, or they might just think about it in quiet moments. Their memory may be a time when they took action, or when they just gained insight into their abuser.

TREATMENT: COUPLES COUNSELING

There has been a historical hesitance to work with couples together, based on the assumption that the abusive patterns occurring in the home would show up in therapy, and that keeping a victim safe in a therapeutic setting would be difficult to guarantee. However, there has been a growing trend to work with couples over the last 20 years, and it is now commonly acknowledged that couples therapy is an effective treatment for a significant number of partners presenting together for relationship abuse issues (Hurless and Cottone 2018; Salis and O'Leary 2016). One domestic violence prevention program conducted art therapy couples groups for people who primarily wanted to end all relationship violence. In this program, "goals included both partners' commitment to changing their relationship through building on strengths and past successes, developing solutions, and cooperative conflict resolution" (Tucker and Treviño 2011, p.3).

Solution-focused domestic violence treatment is a model that emphasizes working with both members of a couple (Stith, McCollum, and Rosen 2007). In this structured group treatment model, couples that wish to eliminate violence and stay together participate in a series of psychoeducational, skill-building, and mindfulness exercises. Individuals are evaluated before the treatment and must demonstrate a shared understanding of the severity of violence in their relationship. Some practitioners assert that treating both partners in a couple together is more effective at teaching partners the tools of lasting healthy relationships, rather than separating the couple (Rosen *et al.* 2003). At least one study evaluated the impact of counseling multiple couples within a group in contrast to individual couples. Stith *et al.* (2004) found that couples participating in group therapy focused on intimate partner violence reported greater increases in marital satisfaction and decreases in violence as compared to couples that participated in individual couple therapy.

TREATMENT INTERVENTIONS
Perpetrators

While victims are often the ones who pursue treatment and healing from the impact of relationship abuse, it should be perpetrators who receive interventions that address their violent behaviors and to facilitate prevention. Batterer intervention programs (BIPs) are treatment interventions that seek to remediate violent behavior within intimate relationships. BIPs are frequently based on two main treatment approaches – psychoeducation and cognitive behavioral therapy (CBT) (Cramer *et al.* 2023; Ferraro 2017) – although a clear distinction between the approaches is sometimes difficult to determine. The Duluth Model (Pence and Paymar 1993), which has been operating since the early 1980s, is often categorized as psychoeducational and includes a coordinated community response that is meant to challenge patriarchal tendencies in society at large, and transfer blame or accountability for the violence from the victim to the perpetrator.

Regardless of their philosophical underpinnings, the research on the effectiveness of BIPs is mixed. In general, BIPs struggle with attrition rates, funding issues, recidivism, and low effect sizes of the interventions (Cheng *et al.* 2021; Ferraro 2017; Lila *et al.* 2014). Morrison and colleagues (2021) conducted a two-year ethnographic study that included 36 interviews with professionals working with BIPs that treat male perpetrators. They identified six themes that address the challenges of creating change in men who batter. These themes included social acceptance of relationship abuse, attitudes related to masculinity, emotional challenges, exposure to childhood violence, mental health issues, and denial, minimization, or blame.

Some researchers have suggested moving away from a one-size-fits-all model (i.e., the Duluth Model; see Pence and Paymar 1993) to more individualized treatment of relationship abuse perpetrators. Such interventions could incorporate trauma-informed care principles into treatment as a way to address the well-known issue of intergenerational patterns of abuse (Voith *et al.* 2018) or motivational strategies, specifically individualized motivational plans (Santirso, Lila, and Gracia 2020). Aaron and Beaulaurier (2017) argue the benefit of individualizing treatment based on the type of violence (see, for example, Johnson, 2008, and our discussion of his typology of domestic violence in Chapter 1) and creating profiles that consider the perpetrator's background and relationship dynamics.

Cramer and colleagues (2023) developed a 23-week BIP that included intervention groups plus additional one-to-one support for the male perpetrators and weekly one-to-one support for the female victims. The BIP intervention, named REPROVIDE, was based on a combination of the Duluth Model (Pence and Paymar 1993) as well as feminist, psychoeducation, and cognitive behavioral approaches. Results were positive, with 67 percent of the men and 80 percent of the women completing treatment. Both the male and female participants felt that the intervention was successful, and that perpetrator behavior had changed for the better.

Survivors

In a 2018 systematic review of the literature on interventions for victims of intimate partner violence, Trabold and colleagues (2018) identified a majority of interventions that met criteria for their study that were based on advocacy-related treatment. These interventions were often person-centered and strengths-based, and had at their core a foundation in empowerment theory, which focuses on autonomy, the claiming or reclaiming of control, decision-making, and the creation of opportunities for the victim that opened doors to an enhanced future without the threat of violence. Some of the more therapeutically aligned interventions tended to be either cognitive or behavioral-based (cognitive behavioral therapy, cognitive processing therapy, motivational interviewing, and dialectical behavior therapy). A few studies were cognitive but included "physiologic" approaches such as "narrative testimony or yoga breathing and poses" (Trabold *et al.* 2018, p.3). The remaining interventions utilized "empowerment principles, crisis models and feminist theories" (2018, p.4) as well as group interventions and psychoeducation. In general, the paucity of research coupled with the limited types of interventions and range of treatment settings has made making recommendations for treatment for relationship abuse difficult. However, this systematic literature review found that "interventions focused on problem-solving/solution seeking, enhanced choice making and the alteration in distorted self-thinking and perception are promising" (Trabold *et al.* 2018, p.1). In other words, interventions that help survivors move forward and away from abuse and violence, interventions that aid in the renegotiation of identity from victim to survivor, and perhaps even to thriver, are the interventions that seem to hold promise.

In recent years researchers have made progress in examining the healing journey from intimate partner violence (Trabold et al. 2018), and yet the literature pales in comparison to the magnitude of the problem. Existing interventions, such as dialectical behavior therapy (DBT) and narrative exposure therapy (NET), have been adapted for use with victims of relationship abuse. DBT is a very comprehensive therapeutic intervention that is used to treat emotion dysregulation among individuals with self-harming behaviors, borderline personality disorder, and interpersonal relationship problems. The modification of DBT for victims of relationship abuse is rather intuitive. Iverson, Shenk, and Fruzzetti (2009) adapted DBT with results of reduced depressive symptoms, hopelessness, and psychiatric distress in pre- and post-assessments. Modifications to the standard DBT intervention included incorporating all of the comprehensive DBT components into a time-limited 12-session group program for survivors of intimate partner violence, essentially eliminating the individual therapy that would normally be a part of the standard DBT intervention protocol. To compensate for this, the researchers encouraged phone calls to the therapists in the early weeks of the group intervention, especially if group members were contemplating treatment-interfering behaviors (such as skipping a group session due to anxiety or depression) as a means to help with *skill generalization* (one of the DBT skills taught early in the group). In addition, skills that were considered important for victims of intimate partner violence, such as self-validation, were included in the modification in addition to the core *mindfulness* skill that is central to DBT skills training.

Narrative exposure therapy was developed for survivors of multiple traumas such as war, cultural displacement, organized crime, and violence. NET was specifically designed to address PTSD symptoms, to be delivered in low-income countries, and in a relatively short-term manner. The treatment works well regardless of age, gender, or education, and can be delivered in a variety of settings. NET employs a structured, gradual approach to the traumatic material that is enhanced by the therapeutic relationship and the creation of a lifeline. The individual creates (with the therapist's help) a biographical overview of their life that includes their traumas (called "stones") as well as their moments of resilience and empathy (called "flowers"). The lifeline and each of the events on it are then processed and contextualized, pendulating between a "then" and "now" contrasting position (Neuner, Elbert, and Schauer 2020). Orang et al. (2018) used NET with a group of women with PTSD living under continuous intimate partner violence in Iran, and compared them to a treatment as usual (TAU—counseling) group. The NET group showed significant improvement in symptom reduction compared to the TAU group in PTSD, depression, and perceived stress at both the three- and six-month follow-ups.

Psychodynamic approaches have been used with some success with both victims and perpetrators of relationship abuse (Cogan and Porcerelli 2008; McKeown and Harvey 2018; Penone and Guarnaccia 2018). Some of the literature focuses on how psychodynamic approaches and psychodynamic concepts and terms, in particular, can help to conceptualize and treat violence (see, for example, Yakeley 2018). Ego state therapy approaches, such as internal family systems (Schwartz 1995) and the theory of structural dissociation of the personality (van der Hart, Nijenhuis, and Steele 2006), have been used for years to treat trauma and complex trauma, and have been combined with eye movement desensitization and reprocessing therapy (EMDR) as well.

EMDR, developed by Francine Shapiro in 1987 (Shapiro 2001), is an eight-phased process that focuses on the processing of traumatic memory, and helps to transform thought patterns or blocking beliefs that emerge from traumatic experiences. The adaptive information processing (AIP) model is the theoretical foundation for EMDR (Shapiro 2001). This argues that dysfunctionally stored memories are the root cause of maladaptive cognitions and behaviors that evolve out of traumatizing experience. Through the use of bilateral stimulation (eye movements, bilateral tapping, or bilateral auditory stimulation), EMDR therapists help facilitate the adaptive reprocessing of dysfunctionally stored memory, such that the distress that someone feels when thinking of or being reminded of the event begins to dissipate or disappear completely. Controlled studies with trauma victims where EMDR was employed as a treatment protocol demonstrated a decrease in distress and an increase in positive beliefs (Jiménez *et al.* 2020; Maxfield 2019; Talwar 2007). While EMDR is essentially a verbal therapy, it has more recently been combined with art therapy (Cohn 1993; Davis 2021; Davis *et al.* 2022; Fitzgerald 2021), and even inspired the creation of the art therapy trauma protocol (ATTP) designed for adult victims of trauma to integrate their experiences in productive and adaptive ways (Talwar 2007).

EMDR is an appropriate intervention for individuals of any age, race, gender, or cultural background. It has been approved by the American Psychiatric Association (APA) to treat PTSD, and is one of four recommended treatments for PTSD by the US Department of Veteran Affairs (the others are cognitive processing therapy, prolonged exposure therapy, and written exposure therapy). The research supporting EMDR as an intervention for PTSD and for complex PTSD (CPTSD, defined as experiencing PTSD and problems in affect regulation, negative self-concept, and disturbances in relationships) has grown steadily over the past 30 years (de Jongh *et al.* 2019). In spite of this, Lipscomb and Ashley (2021) provide a thoughtful and critical assessment of EMDR's "one-size-fits-all" treatment orientation, and suggest that adaptations for African American clients should be made, including considerations for "slower pacing, inquiries regarding identity, racialized experiences and oppression-based trauma, and clarification regarding the EMDR process" as well as considerations for the clinician including "the awareness of significant African American historical trauma by White therapists, acknowledgment of their own racial identity and social location, and willingness to explore power and privilege dynamics in therapeutic spaces" (2019, p.12). Lipscomb and Ashley's critique should also hold true for other cultures, and we should consider incorporating adjustments to make EMDR—and additional interventions as well—accessible to individuals across multiple populations and cultures.

Sáez *et al.* (2023) demonstrated benefits to victims of intimate partner violence through the use of adventure and wilderness therapy, approaches that centralize experimental activities that take place outdoors in nature and often in distant wild settings. Adventure and wilderness therapy has demonstrated the benefit for survivors of relationship abuse by promoting empowerment and addressing personal limitations and agency (Levine 1994; McBride and Korell 2005).

CULTURALLY APPROPRIATE INTERVENTIONS AND TREATMENT

Culturally appropriate treatment is designed to meet the unique needs of a specific population: "Mainstream interventions have often failed to reach certain racial or ethnic minority populations for various reasons from language barriers to isolation of these populations from mainstream American society because of cultural differences, prejudice, and racism" (Gillum 2008, p.921). Research supports that women from Anglo-Saxon or White populations are more likely to seek help than those from non-White populations (Cho *et al.* 2020; Flicker *et al.* 2011; Satyen *et al.* 2018). This has huge implications since engaging services can improve outcomes for survivors of relationship abuse (Meyer 2010). A qualitative thematic meta-analysis of studies representing 1286 survivors of intimate partner violence from 20 cultural groups evaluated the influence of culture on engagement of formal services, including those designed for family violence intervention, healthcare, or criminal justice. Researchers identified five themes that described the specific cultural norms that influence the engagement of formal services; they are: (a) gender roles and social expectations; (b) community recognition and acceptance of abuse; (c) honor-based society; (d) religion; and (e) cultural beliefs and attitudes about formal services (Green, Satyen, and Tombourou 2023). Consideration of these influential factors can help in the creation of effective and culturally relevant services in every community. Clinicians who treat relationship abuse should actively seek to meet the needs of their culturally diverse clients by increasing their self-awareness and cultural competence (Al'Uqdah, Maxwell, and Hill 2016), making every effort to validate and understand to the deepest degree possible the client's experience. Existing interventions may require adaptations to better serve a wide array of individuals from varying backgrounds.

While more scholars are considering the efficacy of treatment in various cultures (Vaddiparti and Varma 2009), there is still limited research that guides the adaptation of treatment programs across cultures. A small, but growing, body of literature seeks to better understand the impact of relationship abuse, intimate partner violence, and sexual abuse on specific cultures as a way of framing interventions that are relevant to the specific culture and the intervention setting. Some research looks at victim impact based on age or stage of life, educational or vocational setting, or religious affiliation. An individual's response to abusive behavior and to relationship violence can be influenced by their gender expectations, sexual orientation, culture, religion, and other deeply embedded societal roles (Azmat *et al.* 2003). Affiliation with a marginalized population or insular community, immigrant status, low socioeconomic status, and majority-spoken language barrier are also factors that can impact an individual reaching out for help, escaping an abusive relationship, or addressing their status as a relationship abuse victim (Abu-Ras 2003; Akinsulure-Smith *et al.* 2013; Alkhateeb, Ellis, and Fortune 2001; Oyewuwo-Gassikia 2020; Porter and Williams 2011).

In a study that used an imagery-based intervention with women in Pakistan (Ehsan and Rowland 2021), survivors of relationship abuse experienced a reduction in PTSD symptoms. Notable findings included that vivid imagery helped create a more "culturally friendly approach for treatment in non-Western populations" (2021, para. 9), since the women presented a low literacy level, and were not necessarily in the position, based on cultural expectations, to leave their abusive partners. As is often the case in therapeutic intervention, the goal here was to reduce PTSD symptoms, so treatment was successful.

A trauma-focused CBT-guided self-help intervention (Latif *et al.* 2021) was successfully developed and implemented for use with a group of female domestic violence victims in Pakistan by culturally adapting CBT tenets using themes and characters from local folklore and religion. The self-guided manual met several needs of the local domestic violence shelter, primarily by providing an intervention that had not previously been included in their services delivery model. This shelter typically helped with legal and financial advice, but not necessarily with symptom reduction. It also provided a much-needed and effective intervention that was relatively low in cost and easy to implement, and that could be easily delivered using available resources.

Gillum (2008) aggregates recommendations for culturally specific domestic violence treatment programs that target the African American community. She includes the incorporation of social support, which can be a motivating force for intervention participation for African American women, inclusion of the family—both immediate and extended—in the treatment process, and possible inclusion of religious leaders in the community who serve as a support to the client(s). Gillum presents a study reviewing the benefits of a culturally specific intimate partner violence intervention designed for African American survivors. After a series of authenticated interviews were analyzed, results confirmed that the services delivered were culturally specific due to the Afrocentric curriculum and environment, family-centered and spiritually based holistic approach, and representative staff and board. Treatment results revealed that benefit was derived from the family-centered focus of the agency (treatment was also provided for the children of the victims, which helped them to understand their parents' issues, and childcare was provided while the victims were receiving their own services), from the spirituality-based approach (women who were raised in the church environment could see their services as an extension of this spiritual space; for some women spirituality helped them to cope with and process their experiences of abuse; spirituality was allowed but not forced; and the agency was not tied to any one religious doctrine), and from the knowledge that the program was shaped and run by members of the African American community, and that the curriculum and agency environment were Afrocentric (promoted African values, and was located in a predominantly African American area of the city; see Gillum 2008).

Researchers who designed the myPlan web app[2] (Glass et al. 2017) safety planning intervention adapted it into a new tool called ourCircle, designed for Indigenous women victims of relationship abuse (Bagwell-Gray et al. 2021). Adaptations made in the ourCircle app include listing cultural and spiritual responsibility and "Connecting to Native Community" as an additional priority, something that women might consider when they are considering and possibly planning to leave an unsafe relationship. The ourCircle tool promotes a safety strategy called "Connecting to the Land/Homeland," which may involve an actual visit to the homeland, the woman learning her Indigenous language, or learning more about her people and homeland. It promotes an understanding of Indigenous knowledge, and encourages users to connect to this through cultural ceremony. The name of the app, *ourCircle*, reflects the value held by Indigenous persons who can metaphorically see themselves standing together in a circle promoting healing and empowerment, from which they can give and draw support. Another adaptation was the inclusion of *networks* in ourCircle, that acknowledge intergenerational violence and encourage users of the app to seek out wise tribal leaders or relatives who can speak out against relationship violence.

Researchers worked toward decolonizing their original myPlan (the precursor to ourCircle) intimate partner violence intervention by focusing on "strength, voice, and autonomy...while at the same time reject[ing] both externalized and internalized messages of oppression that have been instilled by a settler-colonial society" (Bagwell-Gray et al. 2021, p.174). There are limitations to this research that pertain to the use of and expectation that people have access to technology, the design of adapting a tool built for majority use, the assumption that Indigenous minority persons all have shared cultural values, and relying on therapeutic interventions that include no actual therapist. But this research does make strides in considering the cultural values that can be included in interventions that are targeted to a specific demographic.

Shortage of practitioners may impact successful trauma

---

2   www.myplanapp.org

treatment in much of the world, including the global south and countries where there are higher rates of poverty. One study looked at treatment for women who had experienced trauma in Tanzania, and found that the shortage of clinical psychologists prompted greater acceptance of art therapy treatment (Luzzatto et al. 2022). Additionally, there are some cultures in which creative arts practices are more socially embedded and accepted than western styles of mental health treatment; in these cultures, treatment approaches that utilize art, music, dance, drama, creative storytelling, and poetry may be easier to employ, and make more sense for individual clients to adopt.

REFERENCES

Aaron, S.M. and Beaulaurier, R.L. (2017) "The need for new emphasis on batterers intervention programs." *Trauma, Violence, & Abuse 18*, 4, 425–432. doi: 10.1177/1524838015622440.

Abu-Ras, W.M. (2003) "Barriers to services for Arab immigrant battered women in a Detroit suburb." *Journal of Social Work Research and Evaluation 4*, 1, 49–66.

Akinsulure-Smith, A.M., Chu, T., Keatley, E., and Rasmussen, A. (2013) "Intimate partner violence among West African immigrants." *Journal of Aggression, Maltreatment & Trauma 22*, 1, 109–126. doi: 10.1080/10926771.2013.719592.

Al'Uqdah, S.N., Maxwell, C., and Hill, N. (2016) "Intimate partner violence in the African American community: Risk, theory, and interventions." *Journal of Family Violence 31*, 877–884. https://doi.org/10.1007/s10896-016-9819-x

Alkhateeb, S., Ellis, S., and Fortune, M.M. (2001) "Domestic violence: The responses of Christian and Muslim communities." *Journal of Religion & Abuse 2*, 3–24. doi: 10.1300/J154V02N03_02.

Allen, K.N. and Wozniak, D.F. (2010) "The language of healing: Women's voices in healing and recovering from domestic violence." *Social Work in Mental Health 9*, 1, 37–55. https://doi.org/10.1080/15332985.2010.494540

Azmat, A., Khayr, Y., Mohajir, N., Reyna, M., and Spitz, G. (2023) "'They sit with the discomfort, they sit with the pain instead of coming forward': Muslim students' awareness, attitudes, and challenges mobilizing sexual violence education on campus." *Religions 14*, 1, 19. https://doi.org/10.3390/rel14010019

Bagwell-Gray, M.E., Loerzel, E., Sacco, G.D., Messing, J., et al. (2021) "From myPlan to ourCircle: Adapting a web-based safety planning intervention for Native American women exposed to intimate partner violence." *Journal of Ethnic & Cultural Diversity in Social Work 30*, 1–2, 163–180. https://doi.org/10.1080/15313204.2020.1770651

Cheng, S.-Y., Davis, M., Jonson-Reid, M., and Yaeger, L. (2021) "Compared to what? A meta-analysis of batterer intervention studies using nontreated controls or comparisons." *Trauma, Violence, & Abuse 22*, 3, 496–511. https://doi.org/10.1177/1524838019865927

Cho, H., Shamrova, D., Han, J.-B., and Levchenko, P. (2020) "Patterns of intimate partner violence victimization and survivors' help-seeking." *Journal of Interpersonal Violence 35*, 21–22, 4558–4582. https://doi.org/10.1177/0886260517715027

Cogan, R. and Porcerelli, J.H. (2008) "Psychoanalytic psychotherapy with people in abusive relationships." *Journal of Aggression, Maltreatment & Trauma 7*, 1–2, 29–46. https://doi.org/10.1300/J146v07n01_03

Cohn, L. (1993) "Art Psychotherapy and the New Eye Movement Desensitization (EMD/R) Method, an Integrated Approach." In E. Dishup (ed.) *California Art Therapy Trends* (pp.1–20). Chicago, IL: Magnolia Street Publishers.

Cramer, H., Gaunt, D.M., Shallcross, R., Bates, L., et al. (2023) "Randomised pilot and feasibility trial of a group intervention for men who perpetrate intimate partner violence against women." *Research Square.* https://doi.org/10.21203/rs.3.rs-2543341/v1

Davis, E. (2021) "EMDR and Expressive Arts Therapy: How Expressive Arts Therapy Can Extend the Reach of EMDR with Complex Clients." In A. Beckley-Forest and A. Monaco (eds) *EMDR with Children in the Play Therapy Room: An Integrated Approach* (Chapter 6). New York: Springer Publishing.

Davis, E., Fitzgerald, J., Jacobs, S., and Marchand, J. (2022) *EMDR and Creative Arts Therapies.* New York: Springer.

de Jongh, A., Bicanic, I., Matthijssen, S., Amann, B.L., et al. (2019) "The current status of EMDR therapy involving the treatment of complex posttraumatic stress disorder." *Journal of EMDR Practice and Research 13*, 4, 284–290. http://dx.doi.org/10.1891/1933-3196.13.4.284

Ehsan, M.K. and Rowland, D.L. (2021) "Possible role for imagery-based therapy in managing PTSD in Pakistani women experiencing domestic abuse: A pilot study using eidetic therapy." *International Journal of Environmental Research and Public Health 18*, 5, 2478. https://doi.org/10.3390/ijerph18052478

Ferraro, K.J. (2017) *Current Research on Batterer Intervention Programs and Implications for Policy.* Flagstaff, AZ: Family Violence Institute, Northern Arizona University. https://bwjp.org/wp-content/uploads/2022/08/batterer-intervention-paper-final-2018.pdf

Fitzgerald, J. (2021) "How artwork makes EMDR therapy more approachable." EMDRIA Focal Point blog, November 19. www.emdria.org/children/how-artwork-makes-emdr-therapy-more-approachable

Flicker, S.M., Cerulli, C., Zhao, X., Tang, W., et al. (2011) "Concomitant forms of abuse and help seeking behavior among white, African American, and Latina women who experience intimate partner violence." *Violence Against Women 17*, 8, 1067–1085. https://doi.org/10.1177/1077801211414846

Gillum, T.L. (2008) "The benefits of a culturally specific intimate partner violence intervention for African American survivors." *Violence Against Women 14*, 8, 917–943. https://doi.org/10.1177/1077801208321982

Glass, N.E., Perrin, N.A., Hanson, G.C., Bloom, T.L., et al. (2017) "The longitudinal impact of an internet safety decision aid for abused women." *The American Journal of Preventative Medicine 52*, 5, 606–615. https://doi.org/10.1016/j.amepre.2016.12.014

GNWS (Global Network of Women's Shelters) (2023) "Who we are." https://gnws.org/about-us/who-we-are

Goodman, H., Papastavrou Brooks, C., Price, O., and Barley, E.A. (2020) "Barriers and facilitators to the effective de-escalation of conflict behaviours in forensic high-secure settings: A qualitative study." *International Journal of Mental Health Systems 14*, 59. https://doi.org/10.1186/s13033-020-00392-5

Green, J., Satyen, L., and Tombourou, J.W. (2023) "Influence of cultural norms on formal service engagement among survivors of intimate partner violence: A qualitative meta-synthesis." *Trauma, Violence, & Abuse*, 1–14. https://doi.org/10.1177/15248380231162971

Gregory, K., Nnawulezi, N., and Sullivan, C.M. (2021) "Understanding how domestic violence shelter rules may influence survivor empowerment." *Journal of Interpersonal Violence 36*, 1–2. https://doi.org/10.1177/0886260517730561

Haaken, J. and Yragui, N. (2003) "Going underground: Conflicting perspectives on domestic violence shelter practices." *Feminism & Psychology 13*, 1, 49–71. https://doi.org/10.1177/0959353503013001008

Harbishettar, V. and Math, S.B. (2014) "Violence against women in India: Comprehensive care for survivors." *The Indian Journal of Medical Research 140*, 2, 157–159.

Hurless, N. and Cottone, R.R. (2018) "Considerations of conjoint couples therapy in cases of intimate partner violence." *The Family Journal 26*, 3, 324–329. https://doi.org/10.1177/1066480718795708

Hyer, S. (2023) "History of the battered women's movement." DCADV (Delaware Coalition Against Domestic Violence). https://dcadv.org/blog/history-of-the-battered-womens-movement.html

Interval House (2023) "Inside Interval House." https://intervalhouse.ca/inside-interval-house

Iverson, K.M., Shenk, C., and Fruzzetti, A. (2009) "Dialectical behavior therapy for women victims of domestic abuse: A pilot study." *Professional Psychology: Research & Practice 40*, 3, 242–248. doi: 10.1037/a0013476.

Jiménez, G., Becker, Y., Varela, C., García, P., *et al.* (2020) "Multicenter randomized controlled trial on the provision of the EMDR-PRECI to female minors victims of sexual and/or physical violence and related PTSD diagnosis." *American Journal of Applied Psychology 9*, 2, 42–51. https://doi.org/10.11648/j.ajap.20200902.12

Johnson, M.P. (2008) *A Typology of Domestic Violence: Intimate Terrorism, Violent Resistance, and Situational Couples Violence.* Lebanon, NH: Northeastern University Press.

Kaur, R. and Garg, S. (2008) "Addressing domestic violence against women: An unfinished agenda." *Indian Journal of Community Medicine: Official Publication of Indian Association of Preventive & Social Medicine 33*, 2, 73–76. doi: 10.4103/0970-0218.40871.

Kennedy, A.C., Prock, K.A., Adams, A.E., Littwin, A., *et al.* (2023) "Can this provider be trusted? A review of the role of trustworthiness in the provision of community-based services for intimate partner violence survivors." *Trauma, Violence, & Abuse*, 1–18. https://doi.org/10.1177/15248380231168641

Keynan, O., Rosenberg, H., Beili, B., Nir, M., *et al.* (2003) "Beit Noam." *Journal of Aggression, Maltreatment & Trauma 7*, 1–2, 207–236. https://doi.org/10.1300/J146v07n01_09

Kippert, A. (2015) "I helped open one of the first women's shelters." Domestic Shelters, December 9. www.domesticshelters.org/articles/heroes/i-helped-open-one-of-the-first-battered-women-s-shelters

Latif, M., Husain, M.I., Gul, M., Naz, S., *et al.* (2021) "Culturally adapted trauma-focused CBT-based guided self-help (CatCBT GSH) for female victims of domestic violence in Pakistan: Feasibility randomized controlled trial." *Behavioural and Cognitive Psychotherapy 49*, 1, 50–61. https://doi.org/10.1017/S1352465820000685

Levine, D. (1994) "Breaking through barriers: Wilderness therapy for sexual assault survivors." *Women & Therapy 15*, 3–4, 175–184. https://doi.org/10.1300/J015v15n03_14

Lila, M., Oliver, A., Catalá-Miñana, A., and Galiana, L. (2014) "The intimate partner violence responsibility attribution scale (IPVRAS)." *The European Journal of Psychology Applied to Legal Context 6*, 1, 29–36. https://doi.org/10.5093/ejpalc2014a4

Lipscomb, A. and Ashley, W. (2021) "A critical analysis of the utilization of eye movement desensitization and reprocessing (EMDR) psychotherapy with African American clients." *Journal of Human Services: Training, Research, and Practice 7*, 1. https://scholarworks.sfasu.edu/jhstrp/vol7/iss1/3

Luzzatto, P., Ndagabwene, A., Fugusa, E., Kimathy, G., Lema, I., and Likindikoki, S. (2022) "Trauma Treatment through Art Therapy (TT-AT): A 'women and trauma' group in Tanzania." *International Journal of Art Therapy 27*, 1, 36–43. https://doi.org/10.1080/17454832.2021.1957958

Maxfield, L. (2019) "A clinician's guide to the efficacy of EMDR therapy." *Journal of EMDR Practice and Research 13*, 4, 239–246. http://dx.doi.org/10.1891/1933-3196.13.4.239

McBride, D.L. and Korell, G. (2005) "Wilderness therapy for abused women." *Canadian Journal of Counselling 39*, 1, 3–14. https://files.eric.ed.gov/fulltext/EJ719916.pdf

McKeown, A. and Harvey, E. (2018) "Violent women: Treatment approaches and psychodynamic considerations." *Journal of Criminological Research, Policy and Practice 2*, 124–135. https://doi.org/10.1108/JCRPP-08-2017-0025

Meyer, S. (2010) "Responding to intimate partner violence victimisation: Effective options for help-seeking." *Trends & Issues in Crime and Criminal Justice 398*, 1–6. www.aic.gov.au/publications/tandi/tandi389

Mission Services (2022) "History." https://mission-services.com/about-mission-services/history

Morrison, P.K., Hawker, L., Cluss, P.A., Miller, E., et al. (2021) "The challenges of working with men who perpetrate partner violence: Perspectives and observations of experts who work with batterer intervention programs." *Journal of Interpersonal Violence 36*, 7–8, NP3524–NP3546. https://doi.org/10.1177/0886260518778258

Neuner, F., Elbert, T., and Schauer, M. (2020) "Narrative Exposure Therapy for PTSD." In L.F. Bufka, C.V. Wright, and R.W. Halfond (eds) *Casebook to the APA Clinical Practice Guideline for the Treatment of PTSD* (pp.187–205). Washington, DC: American Psychological Association. https://doi.org/10.1037/0000196-009

NOW (National Organization of Women) (2023) "The early years—Steps along the way." https://now.org/the-early-years-steps-along-the-way

Orang, T., Ayoughi, S., Moran, J.K., Ghaffari, H., et al. (2018) "The efficacy of narrative exposure therapy in a sample of Iranian women exposed to ongoing intimate partner violence—A randomized controlled trial." *Clinical Psychological Psychotherapy*, 1–15. doi: 10.1002/cpp.2318

Oyewuwo-Gassikia, O.B. (2020) "Black Muslim women's domestic violence help-seeking strategies: Types, motivations, and outcomes." *Journal of Aggression, Maltreatment & Trauma 29*, 856–875. doi: 10.1080/10926771.2019.1653411.

Pence, E. and Paymar, M. (1993) *Education Groups for Men Who Batter: The Duluth Model*. New York: Springer Publishing Company, Inc.

Penone, G. and Guarnaccia, C. (2018) "Intimate partner violence within same sex couples: A qualitative review of the literature from a psychodynamic perspective." *International Journal of Psychoanalysis and Education 10*, 1, 33–46.

Porter, J. and Williams, L.M. (2011) "Intimate violence among underrepresented groups on a college campus." *Journal of Interpersonal Violence 26*, 3210–3224. https://doi.org/10.1177/0886260510393011

Rivera, T. (2021) "How Philly's first domestic violence hotline maintained its mission amid COVID-19." *Al Día*, April 23. https://aldianews.com/en/leadership/advocacy/raising-awareness-women

Rosen, K.H., Matheson, J., Stith, S.M., and McCollum, E.E. (2003) "Negotiated time-out: A de-escalation tool for couples." *Journal of Marital and Family Therapy 29*, 3, 291–298.

Ruby's Place (2023) "It all started when..." www.rubysplace.org/our-story

Sáez, G., López-Núñez, C., Rojo-Ramos, J., Morenas-Martín, J., et al. (2023) "Evaluating the effectiveness of a psychological and adventure-based multicomponent therapeutic program for victims of intimate partner violence: A pilot study." *Journal of Interpersonal Violence*. https://doi.org/10.1177/08862605231169761

Salis, K.L. and O'Leary, K.D. (2016) "Treatment of Partner Aggression in Intimate Relationships." In K.T. Sullivan and E. Lawrence (eds) *The Oxford Handbook of Relationship Science and Couple Interventions* (pp.96–112). Oxford: Oxford University Press.

Santirso, F.A., Lila, M., and Gracia, E. (2020) "Motivational strategies, working alliance, and protherapeutic behaviors in batterer intervention programs: A randomized controlled trial." *The European Journal of Psychology Applied to Legal Context 12*, 2, 77–84. https://doi.org/10.5093/ejpalc2020a7

Satyen, L., Piedra, S., Ranganathan, A., and Golluccio, N. (2018) "Intimate partner violence and help-seeking behavior among migrant women in Australia." *Journal of Family Violence 33*, 7, 447–456. https://doi.org/10.1007/s10896-018-9980-5

Schulz, K. (2002) *Der lange Atem der Provokation [The Staying Power of Provocation]*. Frankfurt: Campus Verlag.

Schwartz, R.C. (1995) *Internal Family Systems Therapy*. New York: Guilford Press.

Shapiro, F. (2001) *Eye Movement Desensitization and Reprocessing: Basic Principles, Protocols, and Procedures* (2nd edn). New York: Guilford Press.

Stith, S.M., McCollum, E.E., and Rosen, K.H. (2007) *Couples Focused Domestic Violence Treatment: Treatment Manual for Couples Groups*. Blacksburg, VA: Virginia Tech University, Department of Human Development and Family Science.

Stith, S.M., Rosen, K.H., McCollum, E.E., and Thomsen, C.J. (2004) "Treating intimate partner violence within intact couple relationships: Outcomes of multi-couple versus individual couple therapy." *Journal of Marital and Family Therapy 30*, 3, 305–318. doi: 10.1111/j.1752-0606.2004.tb01242.x.

Talwar, S. (2007) "Accessing traumatic memory through art making: An art therapy trauma protocol (ATTP)." *The Arts in Psychotherapy 34*, 1, 22–35. https://doi.org/10.1016/j.aip.2006.09.001

Trabold, N., McMahon, J., Alsobrooks, S., Whitney, S., and Mittal, M. (2018) "A systematic review of intimate partner violence interventions: State of the field and implications for practitioners." *Trauma, Violence & Abuse 21*, 2, 311–325. doi: 10.1177/1524838018767934.

Tucker, N., & Treviño, A. L. (2011). An art therapy domestic violence prevention group in Mexico. *Journal of Clinical Art Therapy, 1*(1), 16-24. https://digitalcommons.lmu.edu/jcat/vol1/iss1/7

Vaddiparti, K. and Varma, D.S. (2009) "Intimate Partner Violence Interventions." In P.S. Chandra, H. Herrman, J. Fisher, M. Kastrup, et al. (eds) *Contemporary Topics in Women's Mental Health: Global Perspectives in a Changing Society* (pp.387–403). Chichester: John Wiley & Sons.

van der Hart, O., Nijenhuis, E., and Steele, K. (2006) *The Haunted Self: Structural Dissociation and the Treatment of Chronic Traumatization*. New York: W.W. Norton & Co.

Voith, L.A., Logan-Greene, P., Strodthoff, T., and Bender, A.E. (2018) "A paradigm shift in batterer intervention programming: A need to address unresolved trauma." *Trauma, Violence, & Abuse 21*, 4, 1–15. https://doi.org/10.1177/1524838018791268

Yakeley, J. (2018) "Psychodynamic approaches to violence." *British Journal of Psychiatric Advances 24*, 2, 83–92. https://doi.org/10.1192/bja.2017.23

Chapter 3

UNDERSTANDING EMPOWERMENT

> Fatimah sat on the blue couch in the therapy office, holding a round pillow in her lap. Tears flowed silently down her face, and she dabbed at them occasionally with a tissue. She was small in stature with a delicate frame and long, dark, curly hair. She had just finished sharing her story of abuse; her partner, Diego, had been emotionally, physically, and sexually abusive for years, and the pain of that relationship was still clearly visible on her face. She was filled with shame, was untrusting, and fearful of future relationships. She looked up and asked, "What do I do to make sure that this never happens to me again? What can I do to make sure I don't choose that kind of a man again?"

This is not an uncommon question among victims, and many are revictimized. Relationship abuse is sadly so common, and clinicians often wonder how they can help these victims heal in a way that helps prevent, or at least minimizes, the risk of future abuse.

Empowerment has been linked to many aspects of the experience of an abuse victim, including that of escaping an abuser, navigating the legal and court systems (Cattaneo and Goodman 2010), and the pursuit of and benefit from therapeutic intervention. Empowerment of victims of intimate partner violence and relationship abuse is now considered a standard goal in victim services (Cattaneo and Chapman 2010), although there may be some debate about how to implement and achieve this.

Empowerment is the process by which a person deprived of autonomy reasserts power and choice in their own life, including goal-setting, developing skills, accessing resources, and moving towards self-sufficiency. In most cases, professionals working with survivors of abuse are employing strategies of support and advocacy to help their clients become empowered. A large portion of the work of empowerment needs to be done by professionals who must understand systems of oppression and barriers experienced by survivors of intimate partner violence, including those specific to various cultures (Busch and Valentine 2000).

One of the most important tenets for those working with victims of abuse is an understanding that a victim's empowerment is shaped by context (Murphey-Graham 2010). That context includes the individual's cultural background, their racial identity and history of racial treatment, their socioeconomic status, their beliefs about themselves and their place in the world, their understanding of their role according to their identified gender, their religious affiliation, their familial context, and any other factors that add to the identity of that particular individual. Cattaneo and Goodman (2015, p.85) state that the term "empowerment" resonates in the anti-domestic violence movement because it "invokes ideals that resonate with feminist and social justice values; personal choice; finding voice; a focus on strength versus deficit; and transcending oppression."

The term "empowerment" is complex, however, in that it implies both concrete concepts, such as access to resources (a job, food, housing, etc.), and perhaps more aspirational concepts such as a "sense" of increased control or use of voice, which is harder to quantify. And yet, the felt sense that someone has more control over their life increases their perceived sense of empowerment, which is a measurable outcome included in research on intimate partner violence. This adds to the confusion surrounding the term, since it is unclear whether the word "empowerment" is more of a process or actually an outcome that results from a process, or both (Cattaneo and Goodman 2015).

We believe, and the research would generally support (Cattaneo and Chapman 2010; Falk-Rafael 2001), that empowerment is a process that begins in disempowerment, or powerlessness, and which is changed over time through critical awareness. Often, disempowered persons are aided by an advocate, who may be a mental health professional, but more importantly it is someone who can help the individual see their experience through a different set of eyes. In this journey towards empowerment, the individual begins to shift away from acceptance of the abuse or self-blame into an understanding of the abuse as not being their own fault. This personal, iterative process of shifting their view of their own experience, and moving away from internalized devaluation to feelings of worth, is an essential part of the empowerment journey.

POSTTRAUMATIC GROWTH

Some researchers report that focusing on empowerment as treatment for survivors of relationship abuse may result in individuals experiencing aspects of posttraumatic growth (Cobb *et al.* 2006; Ulloa *et al.* 2015). "Posttraumatic growth" has been defined as the "possibility of psychological growth in the aftermath of trauma" (Tedeschi and McNally 2011, p.19). The understanding that positive growth can occur in the aftermath of traumatic or distressing events is not new, and yet it was overlooked in the literature and research community until two researchers, psychologists Richard Tedeschi, PhD, and Lawrence Calhoun, PhD, coined the term in the mid-1990s.

Posttraumatic growth can occur in five different domains (Calhoun and Tedeschi 2013):

- *New possibilities:* discovering new life trajectories or activities that had not been previously considered, for example pursuing a career change because the individual's values or priorities have changed.

- *Relating to others:* finding new meaning in personal relationships, or relating to others with more compassion or in other new ways, for example an individual realizing that they are more open to self-disclosure or that they now value more honesty in relationships.

- *Personal strength:* realizing that you have strengths that you did not know about and might not ever have discovered had it not been for the event, for example a person discovering that they have greater capabilities than they realized or expected.

- *Spiritual change:* being more connected to the transcendent, or having a richer spiritual connection than previously, for example taking more pleasure in nature or in mindfulness or meditation practices.

- *Appreciation of life:* having a renewed gratitude for life in general or experiencing a shift in priorities, for example making more time for family and friends and spending less time working.

It is important to remember that posttraumatic growth does not mean that a person is grateful for a traumatic event; rather, that they can recognize growth that occurred in positive ways in spite of the traumatic event, which they wish had never happened. While experiencing posttraumatic growth does not happen for everyone, clinicians can listen for evidence of it and help their clients become more aware of it when it does occur (Calhoun and Tedeschi 2013).

CULTURAL CONTEXT

Empowerment is not something that can be bestowed on someone by another person. Rather, it is a journey of self-discovery or rediscovery that includes the reclaiming of voice, power, and autonomy, in a way that honors the background and culture of the individual. It is not necessarily the outcome of services, although some clients may come out of interventions feeling empowered. It is perhaps less likely to result from services prescribed in a one-size-fits-all manner (see Kasturirangan 2008, and more recently Gregory, Nnawulezi, and Sullivan 2021 for an excellent critique of the way in which the current shelter movement can sometimes do more harm than good), for example, by insisting that the best option for all victims of intimate partner violence is to leave their partners, or by assuming that empowerment that exclusively promotes individualism is always the best option. To understand this better, consider the story of Elena.

> Elena, a Chilean woman, was brought to the domestic violence shelter after child protective services had discovered that her husband was beating her. Elena was a member of a group of refugees from a very rural farming community, who spoke no English or Spanish, and could only communicate verbally in a rare Indigenous dialect. Child protective services had removed her four children from their home and put them in foster care, while simultaneously orchestrating for Elena to be brought to the domestic violence shelter for safe housing and support given the abuse she had suffered. Case workers tried in vain to communicate with her, and were unable to locate an appropriate translator. Elena was told in English that she needed to stay away from her husband, become financially independent and stable, and find housing on her own in order to have her children reunited with her. She had to, essentially, prove to child protective services that she was worthy of getting her children back and capable of supporting them according to standards set by western institutions and legal systems, and what they considered to be in the best interests for her and her children. None of this made sense to her, a woman who had lived within the boundaries of her small community her entire life. She was adjusting to life in a foreign country, and had suddenly lost everything, including the support of her community, because they now felt that *she* had turned her back on *them*. Her husband being charged with abuse resulted in her being ostracized from her own refugee community. She spent the first week of her stay in the shelter on the floor of the common room wailing in grief. Due to her dialect, it took over a week to get a translator before any of the shelter staff could speak with her. It was heart-breaking for shelter employees to witness; this particular shelter was promoted as an empowerment-informed domestic violence shelter. They advocated for empowerment in all of their literature and in all of their community outreach,

but that empowerment model did not translate to Elena. What happened to her was both disempowering and cruel.

What would have made this situation more empowering for Elena would have been to, first, promote reunification with her children, and second, to work with her community on helping to raise awareness of domestic violence and decreasing the stressors of being refugees suddenly transplanted from rural farm life into western, urban living. Empowerment for Elena might have addressed keeping the community safe and whole, and keeping each individual within that community safe as well. Empowerment for this community could only begin with trying to understand their way of life and placing importance on the things that they value. Effectively operating an empowerment-informed agenda with clients from different cultures includes understanding that the values promoted in one culture may not fit another. For example, separating husband and wife, as was done in Elena's case, is not a tenable solution in many cultures. Elena's case can serve as a reminder to clinicians that empowerment as a process can result in many different outcomes.

> **Breakout box: Clinical considerations**
> Consider the case of Elena, or another client you know whose needs may be at odds with the values promoted by local care systems. Make a list or draw a mind map (e.g., draw a circle around a central idea, and draw lines extending from the central idea, like rays from a sun; then write ideas on the extending lines, which may have subsequent branches for smaller supporting ideas), exploring potential avenues for action that could help Elena and her children. Consider exploring ideas for action on several levels: individual, familial, community, institutional, national. Remember that our clinical interventions and advocacy is sometimes marked by enormous movements and sometimes by very subtle ones. Also remember that inaction is a form of action.

In their article about perceived options for victims of physical abuse in a remote rural area of Northern India, Ragavan, Iyengar, and Wurtz (2015) lay out the complex and limited choices that victims face when dealing with violent husbands. Divorce, while legal in India, is the least desirable route. There are other options, such as enduring the abuse, reasoning with the abuser, having the victim return to her family of origin, or verbal intervention by an identified elder. These suggestions are culturally specific and necessitate a deeper understanding of the culture and norms that surround them, but the researchers acknowledge a lack of justice (as would be considered such in western culture) for the victim. Their study also highlighted the fact that victims educated about relationship dynamics were better able to make decisions that kept them safer and helped them feel more empowered as a result. These education efforts, however, needed to include both partners and not just the victim in order to be successful.

An individual who rejects a solution that may be empowering to someone else is not necessarily making a disempowering decision. In contrast, the very act of rejecting a solution that does not work well for an individual's unique cultural, historical, or familial situation is, in fact, making an empowered decision. This brings up another interesting aspect of empowerment: *inherent in the decision-making process is the privilege and freedom to learn from each decision so that a person can make a better or more informed decision in the future.* In other words, empowerment is a process that allows us to know ourselves better with each decision.

> Ta'lia had a soft, lyrical voice that belied the trauma of her marriage. She spoke about the abuse she had experienced and how she had managed to keep herself and her young son alive in spite of the relentless control of her husband, Tyrone. Ta'lia wasn't allowed to work or have money of her own; her husband believed that a mother should be at home caring for her child, and he said that she did not need money since he took care of all of the family expenses. Her comings and goings were strictly controlled and limited to only the most necessary outings; she lived under constant surveillance. She was permitted trips to

the market and could occasionally take her son to the playground, but was instructed not to talk to anyone. Most of the time, Ta'lia was exceptional at abiding by Tyrone's regulations, but if he thought that anything was amiss, he quickly escalated into fits of violent rage. In one episode, Ta'lia returned from the market 30 minutes after her husband expected she would be home. Ta'lia tried to explain that the market was crowded that day with shoppers preparing for the Thanksgiving holiday, but Tyrone was unmoved. Tyrone began to hit Ta'lia, and her verbal protests resulted in his escalating force. Ta'lia became silent. The incident resulted in a broken wrist and multiple bruises. After this incident, Ta'lia tried to be even more careful. She lived in constant fear of Tyrone's rages. Over time, Ta'lia's world became so small that even the most ordinary daily tasks felt exhausting and unbearable. She knew she had to get out, but she didn't know how to do it. With no money and no support, Ta'lia felt completely trapped.

Czerny, Lassiter, and Lim (2018) described the strategies that victims use to survive abuse that often result in a disconnection from self that occurs gradually over time—often so gradually that individuals do not see it until long after they have the courage to leave. This may be due in part to the fact that victims spend a tremendous amount of time and energy doing everything in their power to pre-empt their partner's bad moods. Additionally, it is simply impossible for someone to stay connected to the present moment and their current emotional state when that state is ruled by fear and hypervigilance.

In Ta'lia's case, a caring neighbor who had watched her and her husband for years intervened in a way that allowed Ta'lia to plan for escape. Judith, a kind elderly woman, lived across the street, and had always been friendly to Ta'lia; she had seen Ta'lia cradle multiple secret injuries over the years, and had heard Tyrone's yelling on many occasions. One day, when the yelling continued for quite some time, and Judith saw the couple's young boy sneak out the side door, she called the police.

A squad car was dispatched to the house, and Ta'lia and her son were transported to a local domestic violence shelter safe house.

As Ta'lia began her healing journey, she struggled to make any decisions for herself or her son. She continued to struggle with fear and hypervigilance, and she worried that her husband would use the legal system against her. The disconnection from self that is so common in victims of serious relationship abuse caused Ta'lia to question her decision-making abilities.

In the early days of her healing, Ta'lia still believed her husband was all-powerful and that she had no power at all. Over time, however, she began to break through that wall of fear, and to realize that Tyrone was not all-powerful. She began to listen to her inner wisdom, which, in the beginning, was nothing more than a whisper. But with encouragement from others and her therapist, she began to recognize when small glimmers of her old self appeared. For example, Ta'lia had always loved baking, but through years of abuse she had given up being creative and having fun in her kitchen. In her marriage she became perfunctory about cooking and baking, and had lost all enthusiasm for what she used to enjoy. It took time, but slowly she began to wonder about baking again. She started to collect recipes that she was interested in trying. She was invited by staff to utilize the shelter kitchen. One day, when she pulled a tray of hot muffins out of the oven, a small group of shelter residents circled around her in appreciation of the aroma. Eventually, she attended a community college baking class and started experimenting in her own apartment kitchen. After a while she realized that a significant amount of time had passed since she had woken up in fear. She began to make more plans for her future. Ta'lia was becoming her authentic self, and slowly, she was rediscovering the things that brought her joy and grounded her in her knowledge of self.

The journey was not smooth, and there were many bumps along the way. Because Ta'lia had not been connected to her emotions for so long, when she finally started to pay attention to what she was feeling, she frequently became overwhelmed.

She was angry at Tyrone for how he had treated her, and angry at herself for enduring his abuse for so long. When her anger started to emerge, she didn't always know what to do with it. Her healing journey was messy and non-linear. It was as if each critical experience in her post-abuse life taught her something new about herself, the knowledge of which was magical and wonderful, but also terrifying and overwhelming. In the beginning, Ta'lia frequently returned to old coping skills (such as shutting down, dissociating, and avoiding), but slowly, over time, the old coping skills became less effective and she found herself wanting to be more present and intentional in her life. She worked with an art therapist, and did a lot of creative interventions.

During this time Ta'lia's son was also seeing a counselor and doing play therapy to help him with his own healing journey. Ta'lia journaled, collaged, colored, and created sandtray scenes. While she loved being creative, it was also hard work expressing herself in ways that did not always allow full control. Living with Tyrone had taught her that nothing less than perfection was acceptable; in therapy she learned that perfection did not have to be her goal. They incorporated the six sectors from the Empowerment Wheel and created art that represented Ta'lia's growth in each area. Ta'lia took pictures of what she created and hung them on a bulletin board in her bedroom. They were a reminder for her of her growth journey. Art making, combined with the Empowerment Wheel sectors, bridged the disconnection *from* self that Ta'lia experienced and facilitated the return *to* self by helping her rediscover (or perhaps even discover for the first time) the parts of herself that had been lost as a way to cope and survive the distress and trauma of her abusive marriage.

REFERENCES

Busch, N.B. and Valentine, D. (2000) "Empowerment practice: A focus on battered women." *Affilia 15*, 82–95. https://doi.org/10.1177/08861090022093840

Calhoun, L.G. and Tedeschi, R.G. (2013) *Posttraumatic Growth in Clinical Practice.* Abingdon: Routledge.

Cattaneo, L.B. and Chapman, A.R. (2010) "The process of empowerment: A model for use in research and practice." *American Psychologist 65*, 7, 646–659. www.doi.org/10.1037/a0018854

Cattaneo, L.B. and Goodman, L.A. (2010) "Through the lens of therapeutic jurisprudence: The relationship between empowerment in the court system and well-being for intimate partner violence victims." *Journal of Interpersonal Violence 25*, 3, 481–502. www.doi.org/10.1177/0886260509334282

Cattaneo, L.B. and Goodman, L.A. (2015) "What is empowerment anyway? A model for domestic violence practice, research, and evaluation." *Psychology of Violence 5*, 1, 84–94. http://dx.doi.org/10.1037/a0035137

Cobb, A.R., Tedeschi, R.G., Calhoun, L.G., and Cann, A. (2006) "Correlates of posttraumatic growth in survivors of intimate partner violence." *Journal of Traumatic Stress 19*, 6, 895–903. https://doi.org/10.1002/jts.20171

Czerny, A.B., Lassiter, P.S., and Lim, J.H. (2018) "Post-abuse boundary renegotiation: Healing and reclaiming self after intimate partner violence." *Journal of Mental Health Counseling 40*, 3, 211–225. https://doi.org/10.17744/mehc.40.3.03

Falk-Rafael, A.R. (2001) "Empowerment as a process of evolving consciousness: A model of empowered caring." *Advances in Nursing Science 24*, 1, 1–16. doi: 10.1097/00012272-200109000-00004

Gregory, K., Nnawulezi, N., and Sullivan, C.M. (2021) "Understanding how domestic violence shelter rules may influence survivor empowerment." *Journal of Interpersonal Violence 36*, 1-2, 402–423. https://doi.org/10.1177/0886260517730561

Kasturirangan, A. (2008) "Empowerment and programs designed to address domestic violence." *Violence Against Women 14*, 12, 1465–1475. doi: 10.1177/1077801208325188

Murphey-Graham, E. (2010) "And when she comes home? Education and women's empowerment in intimate relationships." *International Journal of Educational Development 30*, 320–331. doi: 10.1016/j.ijedudev.2009.09.004

Ragavan, M., Iyengar, K., and Wurtz, R. (2015) "Perceptions of options available for victims of physical intimate partner violence in Northern India." *Violence Against Women 21*, 5, 652–675. www.doi.org/10.1177/1077801215573332

Tedeschi, R.G. and McNally, R.J. (2011) "Can we facilitate posttraumatic growth in combat veterans?" *American Psychologist 66*, 1, 19–24. doi: 10.1037/a0021896

Ulloa, E.C., Hammett, J.F., Guzman, M.L., and Hokoda, A. (2015) "Psychological growth in relation to intimate partner violence: A review." *Aggression and Violent Behavior 25*, A, 88–94. doi: 10.1016/J.avb.2015.07.007

Chapter 4

UNDERSTANDING ART THERAPY

Art making is a powerful process. Creating art as a tool for personal expression, emotional transformation, social communication, family documentation, and record keeping predates the emergence of the art therapy profession. Art therapy is both an innovative and an age-old therapeutic tool (Kaimal 2022; Magsamen and Ross 2023). As a professional discipline, it developed throughout the mid-20th century, with the establishment of professional associations and training programs and the publication of clinical literature (Junge 2016).

Art therapy sits at the nexus of art and healing. Healing can involve the physiological or somatic, psychological, psychic, or spiritual domains of development, and the art might include viewing, making, and reflecting on visual art and the creative process. Many different media (e.g., art materials) are used in art therapy, all with similar goals of facilitating creativity, encouraging expression, increasing self-awareness, improving communication with others, and the processing of past trauma experiences with the goal of alleviating distress caused by the trauma response (Brandoff and Thompson 2019).

Breakout box: Creative considerations
While some people identify as artists, others are quick to assert that they are not at all creative. In actuality, all people

have great capacity for creativity when encouraged and allowed. This creativity can be an essential tool in problem solving as well as personal expression. Create a list or draw a diagram of the ways in which you bring creativity to what you do—whether it is for work-related activities, for fun, or in service of others. How do you express yourself? Creativity may be artistic or inventive, but it can also be expressed in the mundane experiences of life. Do you cook well, knit, or doodle? Do you put together incredible outfits, or tableau installations in your home decor? Perhaps you are creative in the way you design space, or approach team leadership? Art is only one creative enterprise, but by thinking of what we do and how we do it, we can start to see the way that creativity manifests in our lives.

TALK VS. ART

While talk therapy can be beneficial for many clients coping with the impact of relationship abuse, it may also be contraindicated for some clients who may have difficulty verbalizing their experience and articulating feelings as a result of past trauma (Binkley 2013). In the wake of trauma, an individual's processing of cognitive and emotional experiences may change, and feelings and memories may not be easily accessed with language (van der Kolk 1996). Trauma experiences may be imprinted into traumatic memories stored in the brain's hippocampus and amygdala, and thus may be inaccessible via talk therapy (Shapiro 2001; Spring 2004; Talwar 2007; Tripp 2007). These areas of the brain guide emotional responses including acts of survival and self-preservation. Feelings of terror are often re-experienced when a person is emotionally processing their trauma; the limbic system can remain activated even when a person is no longer in a threat situation (Hass-Cohen 2008). The emotional components and non-verbal memories of trauma may be more important to explore in clinical treatment; moving beyond the verbal is often essential to the incorporation of the multisensory experience of trauma (Talwar 2007).

MEDIA

There are many different clinical art therapy applications used in treatment with clients who have experienced relationship violence. Sometimes the variations introduce new media, such as Photovoice (Ponic and Jategaonkar 2012; Vaddiparti and Varma 2009), animation (Austin 2009; Carlton 2014), green screen videography (Ehinger 2009), or virtual reality (VR; Kaimal *et al.* 2020). Other times, treatment may involve the use of media that is not traditionally associated with therapeutic treatment, such as tattooing (Alter-Muri 2020). Most often, art therapists employ conventional art materials such as pencils, paints, ink, yarn, and clay (Sholt and Gavron 2006; Thomson 2012; Wardi-Zonna 2020) in promoting the activities of drawing, painting, sculpture, printmaking, and textile arts (Bosgraaf *et al.* 2020; Collier 2011; Moon 2010). All of these can be valid, as the most important tool in any therapeutic discipline is the relationship between the clinician and client, which serves as a training ground for building healthy, dynamic, validating, and authentic relationships.

> **Breakout box: A creative exercise**
> Have you ever given yourself permission to create with non-traditional art materials? These are materials that can be used for creating art, but perhaps are not intended for use in that way. Non-traditional art materials are things that you can't buy in an art supply store but are likely to find around your house. Enterprising creators can make art with a variety of things, and there is a certain thrill to be had. Get a piece of paper and create an image with something non-traditional. This might mean painting with brewed coffee or tea; drawing with make-up; using your electric bill as a canvas; emptying a cardboard box and building a diorama; sculpting with aluminum foil and masking tape; collecting grass, acorns, and dandelions for a collage. Spices can be used as sand, or mixed with water to make crude paints. Cereal can be strung or glued on paper as a collage material. Non-traditional materials keep art quality

expectations low and inventive problem-solving skills high. See what you can make.

ART DIRECTIVES

Various creative directives may be employed in art therapy. They exist along a spectrum of approaches, ranging from highly directed art therapy practices to relatively unstructured or autonomously initiated (Bosgraaf *et al.* 2020). In some cases, tasks in art therapy treatment are specific and clearly identified (Rankin and Taucher 2003), while in others, the creative process may be more organic and exploratory.

> Aiyana was processing her relationship with her emotionally and sexually abusive spouse in a therapy session when she accidentally dropped her tea mug, which shattered as it hit the floor. As Aiyana and her therapist moved together to clean up the shards, she began to spontaneously view the resulting tea spill and ceramic pieces as a work of art, observing and ascribing meaning to each of the ceramic pieces beyond the initial site of impact. Using her phone, she began to photograph the fragments, seeing value in each individual chip, as well as in considering the gestalt of the mug of tea. This reframing of her own accident (dropping the mug) as an intention (making art from the photographs of broken shards) became a metaphor for her relationship; the resulting tea spill and broken shards held more specific metaphors for the way in which she connected with others.

Arts-based interventions engaged in art therapy may be planned or spontaneous, as seen in Aiyana's story. Aiyana's broken tea mug could have been discarded or used for collage; she decided to photograph it. Another approach would be to use the broken ceramic shards to reconstruct the object using the ancient Japanese art of Kintsugi, which uses liquid gold to mend and bond pieces together. This approach highlights the cracks even after the trauma of breakage, and promotes celebrating the broken parts as inclusive of the whole (Princer 2022; Wardi-Zonna 2020). Metaphor is a strong ingredient in art making and in art therapy (Moon 2007). In the case of the ceramic mug, seeing the beauty in an object even after it's damaged serves as a powerful metaphor for the process of recovering self-esteem in survivors of relationship abuse.

HOMEWORK

Some clients in therapy appreciate being given homework, or tasks to consider outside of session that can extend the work done within therapy. In art therapy, these often include journal prompts, art projects, doodles, worksheets, or even just things to think about. Homework is not requisite, however; for some clients the important trauma work of therapy and recovering from relationship abuse should be conducted exclusively in the presence of a therapist, where an educated and supportive professional can help to maintain safety for possible trauma responses and limit the possibilities of retraumatization.

> Lin was a young woman who had always been told what to do, first by her father, and then by her husband. She learned early that it was safer to comply. In therapy, while processing her relationship abuse, homework assignments served as an opportunity for her to continue her therapeutic work between sessions. Lin was a motivated client who wanted to get as much as she could out of treatment; she repeatedly requested homework activities from her therapist. One week, she returned to art therapy with the look of a guilty child, preparing to be scolded. She confessed that she had not had time to complete her homework that week and apologized profusely. The work of learning and change can take as long as it needs to take (considerations of payment, pre-set time frames, and the treatment trajectory set by institutions notwithstanding). The therapist explained to Lin that it was completely acceptable for her to opt out of homework. She was surprised that no one was angry with her and that she was not in trouble. She shared that she

had considered canceling the session since she was unprepared, and assumed that her lack of participation in homework was a sure sign of both laziness and non-compliance. Lin had long identified that she was a "people pleaser," but did not always understand the way that this manifested in her life. In addition to using art therapy and the Empowerment Wheel model, homework also became a tool that she could employ to both engage outside of sessions, and also to practice assessing her locus of control and personal authenticity.

Art therapy is employed as both a preventative (Tucker and Treviño 2011) and a responsive approach to working with individuals around issues of relationship violence. Preventative work is needed due to a legacy of socially sanctioned inequality in gender identities, differing understandings of gender, and relationship roles varying over time and by culture (Tucker and Treviño 2011).

RECLAMATION OF SELF AND VOICE

Art therapy provides a path to self-discovery, reclamation of self, and establishment of personal empowerment. Survivors of relationship abuse can benefit from the creative problem-solving opportunities presented in art therapy (Brooke 2008). The process of art making in therapy can allow for the externalization of negative feelings and memories, and a negative view of self that often accompanies survivors of relationship abuse. Art therapy offers a forum for individuals to reconnect with part of their identity beyond their survivor self, and to re-establish a healthy sense of who they are (Ikonomopoulos et al. 2017). This reconnection with self is attained through the use of the Empowerment Wheel model and art therapy, and promotes resilience in survivors of relationship abuse. Resilience is fostered through repeated experiences that provide moderate, predictable, and manageable stress (Winfrey and Perry 2021). Creating a piece of art is the process of identifying and solving a problem, which creates in the artist a certain amount of moderate stress that can serve as a practice platform for resilience building.

The use of voice is psychologically connected to power and empowerment, and this is especially true for survivors of relationship abuse since silencing voice is often a tactic used by abusers. One of the most common designs in art therapy treatment is to give survivors an opportunity and space to express themselves. As they move out of life experiences and relationships where their voices and other means of expression were limited, controlled, and often silenced, relationship abuse survivors may use the camaraderie built with a non-judgmental therapist and the creative process to give form to their own ideas; through this, survivors can find and re-establish their own voice. One group art therapy program for victims of relationship violence was "designed to provide survivors of intimate partner violence and sexual assault with an opportunity to express themselves and connect with others through arts-based interventions...and [give] voice to survivors" (Murray *et al.* 2017, p.192).

GROUP TREATMENT

Art therapy can be experienced individually, but many professionals espouse the benefits of working with survivors of relationship abuse within a group context (Bird 2018; Buschel and Madsen 2006; Riley 2001; Stronach-Buschel and Hurvitz-Madsen 2006). While group work in therapy originated as a cost-cutting measure and a response to a limited professional pool, research has demonstrated great benefit. The literature theorizing and supporting group therapy practice has grown and been shaped largely by the work of Yalom (1995).

Group work can help to combat the inherently isolating impact of relationship violence (Tutty, Babins-Wagner, and Rothery 2016). Skop *et al.* (2022) researched the impact of group art therapy on survivors of intimate partner violence in Canada, with the intention of better understanding the aspects of group process that may be beneficial to survivors in treatment. Thematic analysis of client interviews post treatment demonstrated that clients made meaning of their experience in group art therapy by creating connections, using visual metaphors in art making, reclaiming their own empowerment, and building resilience (Skop *et al.* 2022). Group art therapy treatment has demonstrated the benefit both with adult survivors of relationship abuse as well as for children who are processing exposure to relationship abuse or domestic violence (Malka 2021; Mills and Kellington 2011).

IMPACT OF RELATIONSHIP ABUSE ON CHILDREN

Children are deeply impacted in so many ways by the trauma of relationship violence (Winfrey and Perry 2021). Children of abusive relationships often bear witness to the violence perpetrated by and on their parents. There is ample evidence to suggest that children repeat what they learn, and in the case of relationship abuse, children are taught that violence is the way to address issues. Since children who grow up in families with relationship abuse are more likely to perpetuate cycles of abuse (Dube *et al.* 2005), we know that children, too, can benefit from the Empowerment Wheel model.

There is ample literature examining the impact on children, both in terms of direct abuse, and also as witnesses to the abuse of others. Research has demonstrated that the use of CBT with art therapy can be beneficial in helping to build resilience in children who are victims and witnesses to domestic violence (Basyiroh and Yuniarti 2020). Further, a body of research supports that children coping with the lasting impacts of trauma from abuse can benefit from art therapy, play therapy, and other creative action methods (Buschel and Madsen 2006; Callaghan, Fellin, and Alexander 2019; Camilleri 2007; Fellin *et al.* 2018; Haen and Boyd Webb 2018; Perry 2014; Pliske, Stauffer, and Werner-Lin 2021; Singh 2001; Weber and Haen 2005; White and Morgan 2006).

ART THERAPY WITH THE EMPOWERMENT WHEEL MODEL

Art therapy can help to lessen anxiety and the distress caused by symptoms of trauma, including relationship abuse (Rowe *et al.* 2017).

It can also help clients to facilitate expression, including subconscious ideas, and suppressed or preverbal memories (Rubin 2011). These outcomes and the strength-based approach that is inherent in art making suggest that art therapy is an optimal psychotherapeutic discipline to be combined with the Empowerment Wheel model. In Part Two of this book, we will introduce the Empowerment Wheel model in full, and explore the six sectors of the wheel. In the chapter that corresponds to each sector, we present more specific ways of incorporating art therapy into the treatment for individuals healing from relationship abuse.

REFERENCES

Alter-Muri, S. (2020) "The body as canvas: Motivations, meanings, and therapeutic implications of tattoos." *Art Therapy 37*, 3, 139–146. www.doi.org/10.1080/0742 1656.2019.1679545

Austin, B.D. (2009) "Renewing the debate: Digital technology in art therapy and the creative process." *Art Therapy: Journal of the American Art Therapy Association 26*, 2, 83–85. https://doi.org/10.1080/07421656.2009.10129745

Basyiroh, A.N. and Yuniarti, W.Y. (2020) "Applying art therapy in improving resilience in child victims of domestic violence." *Indigenous: Jurnal Ilmiah Psikologi 5*, 2, 119–130. https://doi.org/10.23917/indigenous.v5i2.9812

Binkley, E. (2013) "Creative strategies for treating victims of domestic violence." *Journal of Creativity in Mental Health 8*, 3, 305–313. https://doi.org/10.1080/154 01383.2013.821932

Bird, J. (2018) "Art therapy, arts-based research and transitional stories of domestic violence and abuse." *International Journal of Art Therapy 23*, 1, 14–24. https://doi.org/10.1080/17454832.2017.1317004

Bosgraaf, L., Spreen, M., Pattiselanno, K., and van Hooren, S. (2020) "Art therapy for psychosocial problems in children and adolescents: A systematic narrative review on art therapeutic means and forms of expression, therapist behavior, and supposed mechanisms of change." *Frontiers in Psychology 11*, 584685. https://doi.org/10.3389/fpsyg.2020.584685

Brandoff, R. and Thompson, A. (2019) *Quick & Creative Art Projects for (Very) Limited Budgets*. London and Philadelphia, PA: Jessica Kingsley Publishers.

Brooke, S.L. (2008) *The Use of the Creative Therapies with Survivors of Domestic Violence*. Springfield, IL: Charles C. Thomas.

Buschel, B.S. and Madsen, L.H. (2006) "Strengthening connections between mothers and children: Art therapy in a domestic violence shelter." *Journal of Aggression, Maltreatment & Trauma 13*, 1, 87–108. https://doi.org/10.1300/J146v13n01_05

Callaghan, J.E.M., Fellin, L.C., and Alexander, J.H. (2019) "Promoting resilience and agency in children and young people who have experienced domestic violence and abuse: The 'MPOWER' intervention." *Journal of Family Violence 34*, 521–537. https://doi.org/10.1007/s10896-018-0025-x

Camilleri, V. (2007) *Healing the Inner City Child: Creative Arts Therapies with At-Risk Youth*. London and Philadelphia, PA: Jessica Kingsley Publishers.

Carlton, N.R. (2014) "Digital culture and art therapy." *The Arts in Psychotherapy 41*, 1, 41-45. https://doi.org/10.1016/j.aip.2013.11.006

Collier, A. (2011) *Using Textile Arts and Handcrafts in Therapy with Women: Weaving Lives Back Together*. London and Philadelphia, PA: Jessica Kingsley Publishers.

Dube, S.R., Anda, R.F., Whitfield, C.L., Brown, D.W., et al. (2005) "Long-term consequences of childhood sexual abuse by gender of victim." *American Journal of Preventive Medicine 28*, 5, 430-438. https://doi.org/10.1016/j.amepre.2005.01.015

Ehinger, J. (2009) "Exploring dreamspace through video art with at-risk youth." Master's thesis. New York: Pratt Institute. https://eric.ed.gov/?id=ED536536

Fellin, L.C., Callaghan, J.E.M., Alexander, J.H., Mavrou, S., and Harrison-Breed, C. (2018) "Child's play? Children and young people's resistances to domestic violence and abuse." *Children & Society 33*, 2, 126-141. https://doi.org/10.1111/chso.12302

Haen, C. and Boyd Webb, N. (2018) *Creative Arts-Based Group Therapy with Adolescents: Theory and Practice*. Abingdon: Routledge.

Hass-Cohen, N. (2008) *Art Therapy and Clinical Neuroscience*. London and Philadelphia, PA: Jessica Kingsley Publishers.

Ikonomopoulos, J., Cavazos-Vela, J., Vela, P., Sanchez, M., Schmidt, C., and Catchings, C.V. (2017) "Evaluating the effects of creative journal arts therapy for survivors of domestic violence." *Journal of Creativity in Mental Health 12*, 4, 496-512. https://doi.org/10.1080/15401383.2017.1328290

Junge, M.B. (2016) "History of Art Therapy." In D.E. Gussak and M.L. Rosal (eds) *The Wiley Handbook of Art Therapy* (pp.7-16). New York: Wiley. https://doi.org/10.1002/9781118306543.ch1

Kaimal, G. (2022) *The Expressive Instinct: How Imagination and Creative Works Help Us Survive and Thrive*. Oxford: Oxford University Press.

Kaimal, G., Carroll-Haskins, K., Berberian, M., Dougherty, A., Carlton, N., and Ramakrishnan, A. (2020) "Virtual reality in art therapy: A pilot qualitative study of the novel medium and implications for practice." *Art Therapy 37*, 1, 16-24. www.doi.org/10.1080/07421656.2019.1659662

Magsamen, S. and Ross, I. (2023) *Your Brain on Art: How the Arts Transform Us*. New York: Random House.

Malka, M. (2021) "Using drawing following a story technique for processing the child's exposure to intimate partner violence in a group intervention framework." *Social Work with Groups 44*, 1, 60-77. https://doi.org/10.1080/01609513.2020.1738976

Mills, E. and Kellington, S. (2011) "Using group art therapy to address the shame and silencing surrounding children's experiences of witnessing domestic violence." *International Journal of Art Therapy 17*, 1, 3-12. https://doi.org/10.1080/17454832.2011.639788

Moon, B.L. (2007) *The Role of Metaphor in Art Therapy: Theory, Method, and Experience*. Springfield, IL: Charles C. Thomas.

Moon, C.H. (2010) *Materials and Media in Art Therapy: Critical Understandings of Diverse Artistic Vocabularies*. Abingdon: Routledge.

Murray, C.E., Spencer, K.M., Stickl, J., and Crowe, A. (2017) "See the Triumph Healing Arts Workshops for survivors of intimate partner violence and sexual assault." *Journal of Creativity in Mental Health 12*, 2, 192-202. https://doi.org/10.1080/15401383.2016.1238791

Perry, B.D. (2014) *Creative Interventions with Traumatized Children*. New York: Guilford Press.

Pliske, M.M., Stauffer, S.D., and Werner-Lin, A. (2021) "Healing from adverse childhood experiences through therapeutic powers of play: 'I can do it with my hands'." *International Journal of Play Therapy 30*, 4, 244-258. https://doi.org/10.1037/pla0000166

Ponic, P. and Jategaonkar, N. (2012) "Balancing safety and action: Ethical protocols for Photovoice research with women who have experienced violence." *Arts & Health* 4, 3, 189–202. https://doi.org/10.1080/17533015.2011.584884

Princer, M.K. (2022) "Putting the pieces back together: Using a Kintsugi-influenced directive to promote self-forgiveness and resiliency in young adults with shame and guilt." Art Therapy: Theses and Dissertations, 4. San Rafael, CA: Dominican University of California. https://doi.org/10.33015/dominican.edu/2022.AT.03

Rankin, A.B. and Taucher, L.C. (2003) "A task-oriented approach to art therapy in trauma treatment." *Art Therapy* 20, 3, 138–147. https://doi.org/10.1080/074216 56.2003.10129570

Riley, S. (2001) *Group Process Made Visible: Group Art Therapy*. New York: Brunner-Routledge.

Rowe, C., Watson-Ormond, R., English, L., Rubesin, H., et al. (2017) "Evaluating art therapy to heal the effects of trauma among refugee youth: The Burma art therapy program evaluation." *Health Promotion Practice 18*, 1, 26–33. https://doi.org/10.1177/1524839915626413

Rubin, J.A. (2011) *The Art of Art Therapy: What Every Art Therapist Needs to Know*. Abingdon: Routledge.

Shapiro, F. (2001) *Eye Movement Desensitization and Reprocessing: Basic Principles, Protocols, and Procedures* (2nd edn). New York: Guilford Press.

Sholt, M. and Gavron, T. (2006) "Therapeutic qualities of clay-work in art therapy and psychotherapy: A review." *Art Therapy* 23, 2, 66–72. https://doi.org/10.1080/07421656.2006.10129647

Singh, A. (2001) "Art therapy and children: A case study on domestic violence." MA research paper. Concordia University Libraries: Spectrum Research Repository. https://spectrum.library.concordia.ca/id/eprint/1350

Skop, M., Darewych, O.H., Root, J., and Mason, J. (2022) "Exploring intimate partner violence survivors' experiences with group art therapy." *International Journal of Art Therapy* 27, 4, 159–168. https://doi.org/10.1080/17454832.2022.2124298

Spring, D. (2004) "Thirty-year study links neuroscience, specific trauma, PTSD, image conversion, and language translation." *Art Therapy: Journal of the American Art Therapy Association 21*, 4, 200–209. https://doi.org/10.1080/07421656.2004.10 129690

Stronach-Buschel, B. and Hurvitz-Madsen, L. (2006) "Strengthening connections between mothers and children: Art therapy in a domestic violence shelter." *Journal of Aggression, Maltreatment & Trauma 13*, 1, 87–108. https://doi.org/10.1300/J146v13n01_05

Talwar, S. (2007) "Accessing traumatic memory through art making: An art therapy trauma protocol." *The Arts in Psychotherapy 34*, 1, 22–35. https://doi.org/10.1016/j.aip.2006.09.001

Thomson, S. (2012) "Out of the Fire: Women Survivors of Violence Use Clay as a Medium for Social Change." In H. Burt (ed.) *Art Therapy and Postmodernism: Creative Healing Through a Prism* (pp.118–134). London and Philadelphia, PA: Jessica Kingsley Publishers.

Tripp, T. (2007) "A short-term therapy approach to processing trauma: Art therapy and bilateral stimulation." *Art Therapy* 24, 4, 178–183. https://doi.org/10.1080/07421656.2007.10129476

Tucker, N. and Treviño, A.L. (2011) "An art therapy domestic violence prevention group in Mexico." *Journal of Clinical Art Therapy 1*, 1, 16–24. https://digitalcommons.lmu.edu/jcat/vol1/iss1/7

Tutty, L.M., Babins-Wagner, R., and Rothery, M.A. (2016) "You're not alone: Mental health outcomes in therapy groups for abused women." *Journal of Family Violence 31*, 4, 489–497. https://doi.org/10.1007/s10896-015-9779-6

Vaddiparti, K. and Varma, D.S. (2009) "Intimate Partner Violence Interventions." In P.S. Chandra, H. Herrman, J. Fisher, M. Kastrup, *et al.* (eds) *Contemporary Topics in Women's Mental Health: Global Perspectives in a Changing Society* (pp.387–403). New York: Wiley. https://doi.org/10.1002/9780470746738.ch18

van der Kolk, B.A. (1996) "The Body Keeps the Score: Approaches to the Psychobiology of Post-Traumatic Stress Disorder." In B.A. van der Kolk, A.C. McFarlane, and L. Weisaeth (eds) *Traumatic Stress: The Effects of Overwhelming Experience on Mind, Body and Society* (pp.214–241). New York: Guilford Press.

Wardi-Zonna, K. (2020) "Finding Buddha in the clay studio: Lessons for Art Therapy." *Art Therapy 37*, 1, 42–45. https://doi.org/10.1080/07421656.2019.1656459

Weber, A.M. and Haen, C. (2005) *Clinical Applications of Drama Therapy in Child and Adolescent Treatment*. Abingdon: Routledge.

White, M. and Morgan, A. (eds) (2006) *Narrative Therapy with Children and Their Families*. Adelaide: Dulwich Centre Publications.

Winfrey, O. and Perry, B.D. (2021) *What Happened to You? Conversations on Trauma, Resilience, and Healing*. New York: Flatiron Books, An Oprah Book.

Yalom, I. (1995) *Theory and Practice of Group Psychotherapy*. New York: Basic Books.

Part Two

A NEW DIRECTION

Figure 1: *The Empowerment Wheel*, by E.J. Herczyk (2020)

In this rendering of the Empowerment Wheel the six sectors are named in the inner circle, while six areas of exploration in art therapy are identified in the outer circle.

Chapter 5

THE EMPOWERMENT WHEEL

The Empowerment Wheel (Czerny and Lassiter 2016) draws on the strengths of humanism, feminism, and multiculturalism. All three of these frameworks share a deep commitment to a wellness perspective as well as a deep respect for the individual, including their diverse backgrounds, values, subjective experiences, and strengths (Brady-Amoon 2011). The humanistic framework is based on the principle of irreducibility (i.e., seeing the individual as an holistic, whole person, and not as an object, reduced to a byproduct of other phenomena), as well as existential and phenomenological perspectives (Hansen, Speciale, and Lemberger 2014). This blends well with feminist and multicultural approaches that argue that the sociopolitical and cultural contexts as well as the inherent power imbalances that inevitably occur must be attended to and challenged.

Building on this foundation, the Empowerment Wheel seeks to understand the individual as an holistic being, situated in the context of their environment and culture, and with respect to their dignity and uniqueness. While all clients will benefit from the Empowerment Wheel model, this is not a one-size-fits-all treatment, however. Exploration within any of the six sectors can look a variety of different ways and produce distinct outcomes, and there is no one right path. By encouraging survivors to reflect on the breadth of their relational experiences, the Empowerment Wheel aids in the healing process from relationship abuse by encouraging individuals to examine relational aspects of themselves over which they have direct control.

The examination of self-in-relationship (i.e., the examination of relational needs and tendencies) cannot occur without an understanding of the social, cultural, political, intergenerational, and contextual realities in which each of us live. As such, each of the six sectors of the Empowerment Wheel is designed to encourage examination of the survivor's internal ego structure, including those parts of self that might have been lost or forfeited in an attempt to cope with the abuse. The sectors are also designed with flexibility in mind, understanding that each individual may define for themselves how the construct best applies to their life. We are mindful of the fact that, as humans, we are all social and relational creatures. The goal here is not rugged individualism, but rather, the creation of a post-abuse life and healing process that values and promotes connection to self as well as to others.

ATTACHMENT

To better understand healing from intimate partner and relationship abuse, it is important to have a basic understanding of early childhood attachment theory and how attachment ruptures in relationships due to abuse, violence, or neglect at key developmental points across the lifespan can have devastating consequences. Individuals who present for mental health treatment with early childhood trauma, especially traumas related to attachment wounding, are in many ways some of the most difficult clients to treat. Severe, chronic ruptures in relationship attachment due to abuse, violence, or neglect, especially early in life, result in what we now generally call developmental trauma (van der Kolk 2005; van der Kolk and Courtois 2005) or complex PTSD (CPTSD). The impact of CPTSD touches every aspect of the individual's being, including their sense of self (authenticity) and their ability to connect to others (attachment), including loved ones, family, community, and social supports.

Burlae (2004) explains further how the experience of violence against women, specifically, occurs through the invasion of space and captivity. These invasions attack a woman's body (physical assault or captivity), her personal space (invasion of private and/or safe spaces), or her psychological wellbeing (cognitive or emotional abuse). Repeated invasions, sometimes seemingly undetectable, result in fragmented ways of relating that make paying attention to red flags or warning signs difficult. When red flags are ignored long enough, boundary violations will always occur. This underscores the sometimes-subtle way that ruptures in attachment can occur. We are relational beings and relationships play a primary, central role in all of our lives. Contrary to the individualism that seems to be a dominant value in many western countries, on a lived level, we long for and seek out connection from the moment of birth. Boundaries are most effective when formed with regard to social cues. Boundaries that are established with regard to a person's need for connection and that are simultaneously self-protective, in ways that are also respectful of cultural background, are essential. When applied properly, boundaries allow for connection and safety, which can, in turn, foster authenticity and feelings of worth. Conversely, when we ignore our own needs and open our boundaries in the hope that pleasing others will help us avoid conflict, we in fact demonstrate a lack of self-worth and sacrifice authenticity.

From the moment of birth, we need a reciprocal, attuned, and engaged relationship, which includes physical touch, with a primary caregiver in order for our brains to develop and for us to learn that we matter, that we exist, and that we are deserving of love. This produces a secure attachment. Attachment ruptures occur when a caregiver fails to provide consistent and predictable responses to an infant or child's needs. Occasional breaches in attachment with opportunities for repair are easily recovered from and relatively non-damaging. For example, a caregiver may be distracted by a job or financial crisis that lasts off and on for a week, but manages to return quickly to the same level of attention and care with their child as soon as the crisis subsides. In such cases the disruption is unlikely to result in long-term harm to the child because the disruption was brief, and both parent and child are quickly able to return to their previous level of interaction and engagement.

However, if we are born into a family or to a parent who is distracted by their own trauma, or who is doing everything they can to provide for their child but simply doesn't have the time to hold, cuddle, or soothe their child, or who believes in letting their child "cry it out," then the child doesn't necessarily get that all-important, foundational, primary caregiver relationship that is, in fact, a non-negotiable need for development. Or worse, if we are born into an abusive or violent home, or one where neglect is rampant, and there isn't the opportunity for recovery or relief, then at some point the child will either cry louder and try harder to get their needs met (anxious attachment), or they will shut the longing down (avoidant attachment). These early childhood attachment experiences actually build a neurological roadmap for all future relationships. A child's brain is a mirror of what they experience. The younger the child, the more sponge-like and impressionable the brain is, which is exactly the opposite of what many of us have been taught (Winfrey and Perry 2021).

> Vivienne had a really hard time remembering exactly when things had started to go wrong. She couldn't remember anything before that first incident of abuse when it had gotten really physical and Brendon had pushed her up against the kitchen wall. That fight was really bad, and she knew there were things leading up to it that she should have noticed; she just couldn't remember what they were. They were fighting about money; they were always fighting about money. Vivienne had bought a roast because she thought it would make him happy. She was cooking in the kitchen, cutting up green beans to sauté as a side dish. She had a small fruit pie in the oven and some potatoes simmering on the stove. She was feeling anxious, she remembered that much. Brendon had gotten a job promotion and there was a chance they might need to move. She didn't want to move. Her family was here and her friends; her whole life was in this city. But she was terrified of losing Brendon, in spite of the fighting and the arguing and the sleepless nights. She didn't think she could live without him. He was everything to her. When they got married, she

believed it was forever; ending a marriage was not an option. And besides, she loved him. She would do anything for him, and had made up her mind a long time ago that no matter what Brendon did to her, she needed him and was going to stay. The good outweighed the bad. He was a good man who had some bad days every now and then. She believed he needed her, too, and he had even said so after their last bad argument. That's what she needed to focus on, the good stuff.

In Vivienne's story we see evidence of her attachment to Brendon. Her need to stay in the relationship seems to outweigh her desire to protect herself or get her own needs met. In her attempts to placate Brendon, she misses warning signs (red flags) that perhaps she cannot or does not want to see. She spends a lot of time talking herself into staying with Brendon, which would indicate that she has an inner sense that the relationship is abusive, but she doesn't quite know how to listen to her own wisdom or what to do with that information.

Breakout box: Attachment myth busting
Myth buster #1: Attachment isn't always love
One of the most challenging things about the English language is that we have one word to describe *love*, regardless of whom we are talking about. We use the word *love* to describe a wide array of relationships: the love of a parent for a child, and conversely, the love of a child for their parent, the love that exists between siblings, the love we feel for our friends (both besties and more casual acquaintances), the love we might feel for a special co-worker, even the love we have for certain types of food, and finally, the love we feel for our romantic partners. None of these different ways of feeling *love* are exactly the same, and yet we use the same word for each. In Vivienne's story, we hear her talk about how much she *loves* Brendon, and yet some might question whether loving someone who is actively hurting you is really possible. While it is possible that Vivienne has

strong feelings of attachment to Brendon, the word *love* might need some further clarification for it to accurately depict what she feels for him.

Take a moment and reflect on the different ways that *love* shows up for you in your life. Are there words that better describe your relationships? Words such as affection, devotion, passion, admiration, fondness, infatuation, allegiance, ardor, fidelity, devotedness, or lust might help you better define your feelings of *love*.

Myth buster #2: First impressions

Often when we meet someone we make a relatively quick decision on who that person is. For example, we might go on a date with a person who treats us well, who compliments us and seems to align with our values, and because of this we might make a decision that this person is a *good person*; we may want this person to be a good person. Subsequent dates or conversations seem to confirm this belief, and we might even ignore some of the behaviors we see that indicate otherwise. Mental health practitioners call this *confirmation bias*; we continue to look for evidence to confirm our previous belief about something, and ignore evidence that indicates our belief needs to be adjusted. We see this in Vivienne's story. She states, "He is a good man who has some bad days every now and then." In fact, it is very possible that Brendon is not a "good man," but that Vivienne wants to see him as a good man. Brendon is a man with some very serious problems, who is able to rein in his bad behavior to make a good first impression.

Trusting yourself in your assessments of others is a process. Love that happens fast and fierce is romantic and passionate, but security also comes from investing in the process and not the outcome. Learning to stay open to incorporating new knowledge about someone's character after initial encounters is an aspect of empowerment. A supportive and compassionate partner should be able to demonstrate these qualities over time.

> Take a moment to reflect on your past relationships. Have there been times when you failed to reassess your belief about someone in spite of the evidence you were shown? What are some of the red flags that you saw but didn't pay attention to? As you think about this, take a moment to write down a few of your thoughts.

AUTHENTICITY

The counterpart to attachment is authenticity. In the same way that we need attachment to a primary caregiver for survival, we also need to develop an understanding and relationship with our inner *self* that is equally imperative, and which, according to Maté (2022), is the other non-negotiable need we are born with. Authenticity evolves in a similar way as attachment in that we grow to understand that our inner, emotional, felt experience (the *me* that is inside us) is real and matters when that inner experience is validated through interactions with those who love us. For example, when a child is frustrated because they can't get a toy to operate the way they want it to, and the parent of that child allows for that frustration and even names it for the child, the child learns that the emotion they are feeling is okay and that they are okay for feeling it too. What sometimes happens, however, in this example is that the caregiver might say something like "Oh no, we don't get frustrated when things don't work the way we want in this house," which puts the child in the dilemma of having to choose between the emotion they are feeling versus pleasing the caregiver they love. The child will choose the caregiver every time and push down the emotion they are feeling instead. If this happens enough times, authenticity is compromised. It's no surprise, then, that there is such a high correlation between early childhood trauma or abuse and experiencing domestic violence as an adult (Dube *et al.* 2005; Fleming *et al.* 1999). This underscores the need for interventions that emphasize empowerment, self-awareness, and growth, and which are simultaneously respectful of cultural differences and each person's unique and individual values.

It took Vivienne several years before she was able to leave Brendon and stay away permanently. Like many victims of relationship abuse, she was pulled back into the relationship for a variety of reasons. Each time she went back, though, she saw the relationship through different eyes. With the help of a therapist, Vivienne began to see how abusive Brendon was and how much the relationship was taking from her. She began to pay more and more attention to that small voice inside her, and with each step toward independence, that voice grew stronger and louder. Vivienne worked hard on identifying and articulating her own needs, including her emotional, spiritual, and physical needs. Paying attention to her own needs helped her connect to herself in a new way, and eventually, over time, Vivienne realized that she liked herself, a realization that was new and surprising, and that she deserved an intimate partnership that honored who she was. Vivienne felt empowered by this realization, and she no longer felt that she *needed* to be in a relationship, but rather that she *wanted* to be in one if the right person came along.

SOME RECOMMENDATIONS FOR USING THE EMPOWERMENT WHEEL MODEL WITH GROUPS

Art therapy is often delivered in group settings. Interventions that address domestic violence and relationship abuse, especially psychoeducation and awareness interventions that are delivered in shelter settings, are also frequently delivered in group settings. As such, we make a few recommendations here on how to use the Empowerment Wheel model with art therapy for groups.

Consider having a defined starting point

In general we suggest that there is no defined starting point and that the Empowerment Wheel is not a linear or sequential treatment model. However, for groups and for ease of implementation, we recommend a defined starting point, beginning with *red flags* and ending with *integrated self*. Having a defined starting point for groups will allow clinicians to plan appropriately in terms of materials for the art-making portion of each session. Additionally, a defined path through the Empowerment Wheel model will allow for group members to join together in their process.

Review the concept of empowerment
We recommend that facilitators review the concept of empowerment and provide a definition as well as examples from Chapter 3 on empowerment. We also suggest using Elena's story as an example of how empowerment can look very different for individuals from different cultures. What may be an empowered choice for one person may not fit the values or needs of another.

Use the "Breakout boxes" activities as group discussion tools
We recommend using the "Breakout box" activities from Chapters 1 to 4 as group discussion tools. These prompts, designed to increase awareness and invite reflection, can serve as opportunities to bring the group focus to a single concept related to relationship abuse. There are also some "Did you know?" boxes to provide further information.

Use structured questions to guide the inquiry of each section: think–pair–share
We recommend using the "Easing into reflection" prompts from Chapters 6 to 11 to guide the inquiry and conversation for each of the sectors. These prompts will work well for groups facilitated by a trained mental health therapist who invites members to write (think), turn to a neighbor to share (pair), and then, after the prompts have been answered, opens up the topic for larger group discussion (share). The prompts can be edited or revised as needed. The think–pair–share exercise is an educational strategy frequently used to facilitate conversation—sharing may be easier for some clients when done with an individual or smaller group (Gunter, Estes, and Schwab 1999; Lyman 1981). For ease of reference, we have repeated the reflection points from the relevant chapters here.

Red flags:

- Think back on your past relationships. What red flags can you identify now that you may or may not have seen or recognized at the time? Take a moment and write these down.

- How did you know it was a red flag? Where in your body did you experience that red flag? Was it a thought? Was it a feeling? Give as much detail as you can.

Boundaries:

- How have you intentionally set boundaries in your life? How have boundaries unintentionally emerged in your life? Take a moment to reflect on your experience with boundaries. Write down a few things that stand out to you.

- Consider your relationships (both past and present). Choose one relationship to focus on. Imagine a color that represents that person, and then imagine a color that represents you. Now imagine that the two of you are in a room and the two colors are filling up the space. How much of the room is your color and how much of the room is the other person's color? How much of the room is mixed?

Locus of control:

- How does the way others treat you affect you? Take a moment and reflect on your relationships with others. What is it like for you when others treat you well? What is it like for you when others treat you poorly? Write down a few thoughts.

- Now write down a few thoughts about how it feels when someone gives you feedback about you. How do you respond? Do you immediately agree? Are you defensive or do you shut down? Can you hear what they say and reflect on it?

Relationship authenticity:

- Reflect on the relationships in your life, both past and present. What kinds of things have you given up or compromised on in order to be in a relationship? Take a moment and write these things down.

- As you look at the list you made, are the items internal (parts of you) or external (activities, hobbies, friends)? Take a moment to categorize your list.

- Now look at your list and consider the following: are there things on your list that you would like to reclaim? Are there losses that you need to grieve?

Self-talk:

- Take a moment and think about a time when you felt anxious. Listen to the automatic thoughts that run through your mind as you reflect on that time. What are you telling yourself? Write the thoughts you had about yourself down.

- Now take a look at your list and ask yourself: whose voice do you hear when you read these thoughts? How does it feel to read these thoughts? Where in your body do you feel those feelings?

- Choose the most distressing thought and restate it in a positive way. How does it feel to read this new thought? Where in your body do you feel this feeling?

Integrated self:

- Imagine a past version of yourself. Take a moment to allow a full image of your younger self to form. What do you see? How old is this person? What is this person struggling with? What are this person's strengths? What could help this person? What do you think this person needs most? Take a moment to write down a few things that you notice.

- Now that you have written a few things down, how do you feel about this younger "you?" Do you identify with this person? What feelings show up in you? What else are you noticing? Whatever you feel is okay; just take note of it.

BRINGING ART THERAPY TO THE EMPOWERMENT WHEEL

Art provides a creative path for clients to share their feelings and ideas and to learn more about the ways that their experiences with relationship abuse have affected them. The content within the Empowerment Wheel model including the six sectors is both accessible, and also complex and layered. For this reason, art making and art exploration provide a useful way into exploring these topics.

While we encourage professionals to ensure that they have the proper training to engage in their practice activities, we also understand that art making is not only the domain of art therapists. We expect that without the proper education, supervised clinical work, and credentialing you are not holding yourself out as an art therapist. Art therapy is not just a series of activities or even organized techniques; it is a unique and specific professional discipline regulated by its own professional credentialing body. It is important to practice within the scope of your license, professional discipline, and training. Both the Art Therapy Credentials Board (ATCB 2021) and the American Art Therapy Association (AATA 2022) are useful places to learn more about the field of art therapy.

In this book we try to provide a useful overview of both art therapy, and the applications of it to the Empowerment Wheel model. In each of the next six chapters we explore a single sector of the Empowerment Wheel. After discussion about the sector and the principles that shape it, we give you a blueprint as to how you might incorporate the use of art into your use of the Empowerment Wheel model. Much like any recipe book, you may choose to follow it closely, or veer from our ideas, using them only as a jumping off point. This may depend on your own experience with clients with relationship abuse, art making in clinical treatment, and art making in your life, among other things. We have created a formula for each of these sections of the sectors. This is what it includes:

- **Art therapy project:** We'll introduce a main art project idea.

- **Purpose:** Here we'll give you some idea of what we are hoping to achieve in this project. We may also talk about the inspiration for the project, and related aspects of history, literature, or clinical tools.

- **Project goals:** Here we'll present a few goals that we have with clients when engaging the Empowerment Wheel model with art therapy interventions. Your goals may be the same, or they may be different.

- **Warm-ups:** Here are one or two suggested warm-up ideas that may be useful in working with your individual or group clients. A warm-up can serve as a check-in, and can also help introduce the topic or sector that is being explored. Warm-ups should not be underestimated, though; while they can be short activities that require little planning, they can often generate some important insights that are grist for the mill in therapeutic exploration.

- **Materials suggested:** Here we make some recommendations for the materials that you may need to execute a project. Art can be made with simple and ordinary materials, or, space and cost permitting, with more sophisticated materials. Use our lists as a guide, but consider what you or your client would like to work with. For more discussion of materials in art therapy, you may want to learn about the Expressive Therapies Continuum (Hinz 2019), a theory that can guide the use of material in the clinical space. Also, we encourage you to source a materials guide in the Customization Considerations list within the book *Quick & Creative Art Projects for (Very) Limited Budgets* (Appendix 2; see Brandoff and Thompson 2019).

- **Preparation:** In this section, we give you some recommendations when needed for how to prepare to engage your client with this art project. Preparation tips may have to do with art materials, reference materials, or emotional preparation for the art making.

- **Process:** The process will have suggestions on what to say to your client, and how to bring the topic up. This might include questions to pose to get your client thinking, feeling, or perhaps accessing memory.

- **Questions to spark reflection or discussion:** Just as it sounds, these are suggestions on how you might inspire some discussion about the creative process and/or the product. Experienced clinicians will likely use our ideas as a jumping off point. If you use the Empowerment Wheel model repeatedly, you may develop your own preferred questions that help you to encourage reflection and discussion.

- **Alternate art therapy project ideas:** Sometimes an idea does not appeal to a client. In this space we provide one or two alternatives on projects that you might do to engage the same topic in therapy. There is, of course, no limit to the projects that you could do. You might also come up with some of your own alternate projects.

- **Project examples:** Here we present some artwork that can give you some ideas of what a project might look like. There is no limit to the variety inherent in art, and for this publication we have limited the amount of artwork examples. But we hope this serves to give you some ideas.

These projects are intended to be a guide, and not to replace your own creativity or insight into what can be useful in the therapeutic journey of your own client. We look forward to hearing about how you found the project recommendations that have been paired with the Empowerment Wheel model.

REFERENCES

AATA (American Art Therapy Association) (2022) "About art therapy." https://arttherapy.org/about-art-therapy

ATCB (Art Therapy Credentials Board) (2021) "About the credentials." https://atcb.org/about-the-credentials

Brady-Amoon, P. (2011) "Humanism, feminism, and multiculturalism: Essential elements of social justice in counseling, education, and advocacy." *Journal of Humanistic Counseling 50*, 2, 135–148. https://doi.org/10.1002/j.2161-1939.2011.tb00113.x

Brandoff, R. and Thompson, A. (2019) *Quick & Creative Art Projects for (Very) Limited Budgets.* London and Philadelphia, PA: Jessica Kingsley Publishers.

Burlae, K.K. (2004) "The theory of mindful space: Identifying, understanding, and preventing violence." *Affilia 19*, 1, 85–98. https://doi.org/10.1177/0886109903260665

Czerny, A.B. and Lassiter, P.S. (2016) "Healing from intimate partner violence: An empowerment wheel to guide the recovery journey." *Journal of Creativity in Mental Health 11*, 3–4, 311–324. doi: 10.1080/15401383.2016.1222321

Dube, S.R., Anda, R.F., Whitfield, C.L., Brown, D.W., *et al.* (2005) "Long-term consequences of childhood sexual abuse by gender of victim." *American Journal of Preventive Medicine 28*, 5, 430–438. https://doi.org/10.1016/j.amepre.2005.01.015

Fleming, J., Mullen, P.E., Sibthorpe, B., and Bammer, G. (1999) "The long-term impact of childhood sexual abuse in Australian women." *Child Abuse & Neglect 23*, 2, 145–159. https://doi.org/10.1016/S0145-2134(98)00118-5

Gunter, M.A., Estes, T.H., & Schwab, J.H. (1999) *Instruction: A Models Approach* (3rd edn). Boston, MA: Allyn & Bacon.

Hansen, J.T., Speciale, M., and Lemberger, M.E. (2014) "Humanism: The foundation and future of professional counseling." *Journal of Humanistic Counseling 53*, 3, 170–190. https://doi.org/10.1002/j.2161-1939.2014.00055.x

Hinz, L.D. (2019) *Expressive Therapies Continuum* (2nd edn). Abingdon: Routledge.

Lyman, F. (1981) "The Responsive Classroom Discussion." In A.S. Anderson (ed.) *Mainstreaming Digest* (pp.109–114). College Park, MD: College of Education, University of Maryland. https://archive.org/details/mdu-univarch-027524/page/n9/mode/2up

Maté, G. (2022) "Authenticity can heal trauma." Mad in America: Science, Psychiatry, and Social Justice, December 11. www.madinamerica.com/2022/12/authenticity-can-heal-trauma-dr-gabor-mate-md

van der Kolk, B.A. (2005) "Developmental trauma disorder: Toward a rational diagnosis for children with complex trauma histories." *Psychiatric Annals 35*, 5, 401–408. https://doi.org/10.3928/00485713-20050501-06

van der Kolk, B.A. and Courtois, C.A. (eds) (2005) "Editorial comments: Complex developmental trauma." *Journal of Traumatic Stress 18*, 5, 385–388. https://doi.org/10.1002/jts.20046

Winfrey, O. and Perry, B.D. (2021) *What Happened to You? Conversations on Trauma, Resilience, and Healing.* New York: Flatiron Books, An Oprah Book.

Chapter 6

RED FLAGS

"I can't believe I didn't see this!" is what Faith would say repeatedly when in therapy, processing her abusive marriage. She frequently wondered how she could have been so blind, ignoring all of the warning signs that were trying to alert her to her husband's ulterior motives and hidden agenda. After five years of a marriage rife with sexual abuse, as well as alienation from her family and friends, she wanted out. She judged herself harshly for being so thoughtless, careless, and easily duped by someone who claimed to love her but who did not have her interests at heart. She was able to count dozens of signs along the way that she should have heeded but hadn't. Faith was identifying her red flags.

In simple terms, the experience of a red flag is the experience of a boundary violation. It is a physical reaction to a behavior that feels invasive, inappropriate, dismissive, invalidating, oppressive, or violent. It can be as subtle as an inner whisper that something feels "off," or as strong as a racing heartbeat. The ability to recognize a red flag or warning sign, however, is dependent on several key mechanisms that are rooted in the neurobiology of safety and danger. It is also connected to the way individuals are socialized to think about intimate partnerships and romance. Problematic behaviors that ultimately become abusive can feel rather flattering in the early stages of a relationship. For example, whirlwind romances and early signs of jealousy are easily dismissed when a relationship is new. In a 2011 study of college students, more than half (57%) of the participants reported that it was difficult to identify the warning signs of dating violence (Knowledge Networks 2011). Difficulty differentiating is likely complicated by the fact that things that eventually become warning signs of violence often start out as socially acceptable and even desirable overtures of affection. This was the situation in Sam's case.

> When Sam first met Drew, he loved that Drew was always ecstatic to see him. Drew would regularly drop by the library on his way to class, when Sam was on shift, restocking shelves. Sam loved the way Drew would surprise him, after he got off work. Every time Drew came to the library, he asked Sam who he was talking to—his boss Karen, his co-worker Renee, that blond pre-med student who was always studying in the third row. Drew seemed slightly jealous, but his attention was endearing, and Sam thought it was kind of cute.
>
> Sam was a friendly and supportive librarian, and just thought that Drew was curious and interested. It started to seem like Drew was always at the library, not only visiting, but also checking up on Sam. Drew's questions about various people never seemed to stop. Even when Drew knew perfectly well who Sam was talking to, he still asked. Sometimes he wondered about why Sam spent so much time talking to his co-workers. Sam just thought that this was the normal part of his job, and he felt like Drew was getting irrationally jealous. While Sam really loved Drew, he was starting to feel smothered by him.

The experience of relationship abuse and the ensuing trauma response can have a serious impact on an individual's ability to function in a number of domains. Psychological consequences can include a decline in mental health and emotional wellbeing, depression, low self-esteem, and isolation (Breiding *et al.* 2015). Repeated experiences of relationship abuse, aggression, or violence across the lifespan can result in a presentation of complex trauma in which individuals can become increasingly more emotionally detached from self and others as a means to self-protect from intrusive memories and other PTSD-like symptoms. While such coping skills are helpful in keeping an individual removed enough from the pain of their experience that they can function, they also impede their ability to connect and pay attention to internal signals and cues that are critically important when assessing their environment.

NEUROCEPTION, EXTEROCEPTION, AND INTEROCEPTION

Three neurological processes are connected to the ability to recognize and act on the experience of a red flag: neuroception, exteroception, and interoception. Neuroception represents the neural process that allows for recognition of environmental and/or visceral cues of safety, danger, or threat (Porges 2022), often outside of our conscious awareness. It is a neurological process that protects us by allowing us to cue into signs of danger or, conversely, signs of safety. Neuroception allows us to respond to environmental or visceral signals prior to the conscious ability to recognize what the signal is or where it is coming from. For example, we pull our hand away from a hot stove prior to our awareness of what is causing the pain. Or we experience deeper, more relaxed breathing and a slower heart rate because we have just entered a room where soft, rhythmic, and calming music is playing.

Two other neurological processes that are experienced consciously are exteroception and interoception. Exteroception is how we make sense of and assess our external environment through the use of our five senses (sight, taste, smell, touch, and hearing). Exteroception is useful in determining if a situation *feels* safe based on what we sense in our immediate surroundings.

Interoception, in contrast, is one of the additional three senses, which include proprioception (movement) and vestibular (balance) (Porges 2017). Interoception is sometimes experienced on a more conscious level; it is the recognition and interpretation of body signals that can indicate emotions and "gut" wisdom that are connected or experienced within the polyvagal system (Malchiodi 2020; Porges 2022). The vagus nerve is the tenth cranial nerve that is, in essence, a communication superhighway between the brain and key organs and systems within the body, such as the heart, lungs, and immune and digestive systems. The communication highway runs in both directions, from the brain to the organs and from the organs back to the brain. Interoception is our conscious perception of non-conscious body signals that are part of the vagus nerve network.

Research on interoception has exploded in the last 15 or so years and has heightened awareness of the mind–body connection. A growing body of research literature has demonstrated the importance of interoception related to cognitive and emotional processes such as decision making, awareness of social interactions, and, most importantly, body awareness and sense of self (Paciorek and Skora 2020). Interoceptive dysfunction has been connected to depression (Harshaw 2015), and can result in reduced sensitivity to body signals.

In the vignette above, we learned that Sam was feeling smothered by Drew's attention and jealousy, but he loved Drew and valued their relationship, so he dismissed his feelings about the behavior. Drew's focus on Sam's whereabouts and interactions with others continued to escalate. He continued to ask Sam a barrage of questions about who he was interacting with, and expressed envy when Sam talked to other people with any degree of interest.

The idea that paying attention to red flags or internal/external warning signs that might indicate safety or threat issues related to interpersonal violence has been examined in the literature, but generally more from a services perspective, that is, how to recognize warning signs in individuals seeking services (e.g., pregnancy care). There has been a reluctance to suggest that individuals in abusive relationships should recognize warning signs, as this would contribute to "victim blaming" that could hinder holding perpetrators responsible for their actions. However, part of the healing journey from relationship abuse includes a person's ability to appropriately assess red flags and act on them in a self-protective way. This is an essential part of the process, and is supported by the literature on interoception (Marx and Soler-Baillo 2005; Porges 2022).

Easing into reflection: Red flags

- Think back on your past relationships. What red flags can you identify now that you may or may not have seen or recognized at the time? Take a moment and write these down.

  ....
  ....
  ....
  ....

- How did you know it was a red flag? Where in your body did you experience that red flag? Was it a thought? Was it a feeling? Give as much detail as you can.

  ....
  ....
  ....
  ....

ART THERAPY PROJECT: RED FLAG
Purpose

Flags are deeply symbolic and are communication tools, which makes them ideal for exploration of therapeutic goals. "Flags are fabric signs, usually rectangular or triangular in shape, which have unique designs and meaningful colors on them" (Brandoff and Thompson 2019, p.34). Flags display our connection to place, our allegiance, self-concept, connection, and our pride. They are used as emblems of nationality, symbols of organizations, events, places, and even teams. For a variety of reasons people connect to self, one another, place, and cause through the marker of a flag. In this project, we invite clients to use the flag as a way to mark an event(s) or insight about a relationship, and communicate to themselves.

While there are still circumstances where flags in practice are useful communication tools, such as in designating a safe swim area at the beach, or indicating to racing cars what lap they have achieved, in many places flags are ornamental emblems of identity. In art therapy flags are sometimes conceived of as a symbol of the self (Buchalter 2009). For the purposes of this activity, it may be helpful to encourage clients to choose colors, designs, or symbols that represent themselves, or parts of their real or aspirational identity.

General history of flags

Utilitarian use: Flags have played an important part in many cultures throughout the ages. They have been used to indicate safety and security and to project power. They are used to initiate and to indicate peace. They have been used to mark both starts and completions. In prior eras that lacked the internet, cell phones, newspapers, radio, TV, and billboards, flags were sometimes used to communicate to many people quickly and with little resources.

Specialized use: Flags have been used as a tool to build community and connect people, and also to divide them. Every country has a flag, as do states, many cities, and regions. Flags connect people to causes and identities. They are also sometimes used to simply get our attention.

Artful use: Flags have been used frequently in art, in some cases as personal ornamentation on lawns, houses, and interiors. In the art world, one of the most famous depictions is the piece *Flag* (Johns 1954–55), an encaustic painting made by artist Jasper Johns shortly after his discharge from the army. It is a piece that ignited discussion in the artwork about the use of common symbols and icons, and raised questions about appropriation in artwork.

Symbolic ideas: In a literary and spoken sense, flags—and their action, which is to fly or wave—are used in a variety of idioms and expressions. A person could get flagged by an authority, a teacher, or a police officer for failing or falling short of expected norms and safety precautions. "To fly the flag" is an expression indicating a person's show of support. "To fly the coop" could indicate that someone has escaped, physically left, or mentally checked out. "To fly high" is an indication of success, while "to fly in the face of" is an open demonstration of beliefs contrary to the norm. "To fly off the handle" means to lose your temper, "to fly the nest" is a right of passage in leaving the parental home, and "to be on the fly" is an indication of being in motion. "To keep the flag flying" is both a champion of endurance and of maintaining the status quo.

Red flags specifically have been used to warn of danger or impending disaster. Colloquially we refer to them in speech as the point in a past experience where we knew or should have known that there was danger ahead. Synonyms for red flag are "caution" and "warning." In this project, red flags are used to create a literal warning, or a depiction of a warning.

Project goals

1. To consider the figurative *red flag(s)* in their lives, and render a literal flag. To identify qualities, values, or important aspects of self, and represent them with color, graphics, or symbols.

2. To encourage a greater awareness of personal qualities or traits, as well as qualities that an individual is aspiring to. To increase awareness of messages sent to the self.

3. To exemplify primary values and the potential clash of past experiences with these values.

Warm-up

Fabric check-in: This warm-up works particularly well if you are using fabric for the project. Invite your client to bring in a piece of fabric that is meaningful to them. People often bring in a fabric scrap, but sometimes they bring in a whole garment. We frequently attach meaning to fabric when we consider who it belonged to, where it came from, or what its use was. Frequent chosen pieces include baby blankets, favorite sweatshirts, t-shirts associated with a trip or memory, pot holders, tattered remnants, or something they wore during a pivotal experience. Invite your client to check in with you or the group by sharing their fabric piece and something about why it is important to them. It is always valuable to convey overtly that clients have the right to share as much or as little as they want, and that sometimes saying less is necessary.

Materials suggested

- Construction paper or fabric:
    - Flag forms can be pre-bought or pre-prepared, or cut by the client. You may want to consider the amount of creative time available, and the ability level of the client
    - Note that if you are cutting fabric, you will want to use fabric scissors. They are easier to maneuver and ensure a cleaner seam on the material
- Marker pens or gel pens:
    - If using fabric, you may want to use permanent marker pens or fabric markers
    - If using paper, you may want to put a table cover down beneath the flag material in case the marker pen bleeds through the paper or fabric

---

Materials note: Flags can be constructed of any size and many materials. You may want to consider what size, shape, and material will contribute to the most fulfilling art project here. This project has been executed in a number of ways with a number of groups, and found both benefits and frustrations based on materials. In one incarnation, participants used purchased red triangular flags, the type that you might see strung outside of a car dealership or a business announcing a grand opening. Although these were a great size to work on, their shape lent to associations with pennants, and the fabric only worked well with some marker pens while others bled on the fabric. In another setting, participants used tiny white paper flags attached to toothpick flagpoles, the kind that you might see adorning appetizers at a cocktail reception. These flags were affordable, as you could buy many in bulk, and they worked well with any traditional kind of 2D art media, but they were too small to give most people a fulfilling space to visually explore. In another session, construction paper was used that participants enjoyed, since they could have a flag in many different colors, and make it their desired size, but construction paper does not lend itself to "waving in the wind" in a flag-like manner—this made it feel like a static flag. You might want to consider your materials from this vantage point. Using fabric to construct a flag may feel more authentic to the nature of a flag, but then you may also want to secure fabric marker pens or paint for your project.

Preparation
Preparation for this project will be minimal and will depend in large part on what kind of surface you use and who your client is.

Process
Invite the client to consider a time in their life when there was a proverbial *red flag* or a signal that they may have felt that something was wrong or that danger lurked. It may have been a feeling in their gut or their heart, or a thought in the mind. Invite the client to create a flag (which may or may not be red) that represents the point at which they may have felt that something was dubious, uncertain, bad, or not to be trusted.

Questions to spark reflection or discussion

- What ideas inspired your flag?
- How did you make choices about color, shape, size, and design?

- Where would you consider hanging your flag?
- What does your flag communicate?
- While creating your flag, did you reflect on a particular incident or episode, or were you experiencing a collection of memories?
- Was your red flag experience obvious or subtle? How were you aware of the sign/signal that you were getting?
- Were you aware of your red flag at the time it occurred? If so, did it affect your actions or emotions?
- What do you think about intuition or inner voice? How do you know something? How does trust factor in to your learning?
- If working with a group, invite group members to consider how working among others influenced their design.

Alternate art therapy project ideas

Alternate art therapy project idea 1: Prayer flag

This project can be adapted to the inspiration of prayer flags, which are used in various cultures and traditions to identify a wish or a prayer, and to send it out into the world. This is done by creating a flag that represents a wish or prayer via written messages, artwork, symbols, and colors, and then hanging it so that it will be blown by the wind. In this way, the wind helps to disseminate the wish or prayer to the world.

Alternate art therapy project idea 2: Personal emblem

Invite the client to create a personal emblem to put on their flag. Picture symbols, words, colors, and patterns are often used to represent things. For example, for the US flag, the colors each hold meaning—the "red symbolizes hardiness and valor, white symbolizes purity and innocence, and blue represents vigilance, perseverance and justice" (PBS 2023).

PROJECT EXAMPLES

In *Broken Frame Flag* (Figure 2), the artist uses white construction paper to depict a piece of a memory when a violent partner shattered the glass of a meaningful framed piece of art. The artist attached a stick flagpole and hung the piece to appear as though it was waving. Red lines on the flag are intentionally hazy to convey the way that memories might fade over time.

Figure 2: *Broken Frame Flag*, by an anonymous artist (2022)

In *He Barks & I Bite My Tongue* (Figure 3), the artist uses red parachute fabric to build a flag that resembles a coat of arms. With careful sewing, embroidery, and stitching of ribbon, beads, and fringe, this artist created a representation of herself in relationships, and reflected on knowing her tendencies when in a relationship.

Figure 3: *He Barks & I Bite My Tongue*, by Lauren Strailey (2023)

REFERENCES

Anonymous artist (2022) *Broken Frame Flag* [Drawing]. Private collection.
Brandoff, R. and Thompson, A. (2019) *Quick & Creative Art Projects for (Very) Limited Budgets*. London and Philadelphia, PA: Jessica Kingsley Publishers.
Breiding, M.J., Basile, K.C., Smith, S.G., Black, M.C., and Mahendra, R. (2015) *Intimate Partner Violence Surveillance: Uniform Definitions and Recommended Data Elements. Version 2.0*. Atlanta, GA: National Center for Injury Prevention and Control, Centers for Disease Control and Prevention. https://stacks.cdc.gov/view/cdc/31292
Buchalter, S.I. (2009) *Art Therapy Techniques and Applications*. London and Philadelphia, PA: Jessica Kingsley Publishers.
Harshaw, C. (2015) "Interoceptive dysfunction: Toward an integrated framework for understanding somatic and affective disturbance in depression." *Psychological Bulletin 141*, 2, 311–363. doi: 10.1037/a0038101.
Johns, J. (1954–55) *Flag*. Museum of Modern Art (MoMA). www.moma.org/collection/works/78805
Knowledge Networks, Inc. (2011) *2011 College Dating Violence and Abuse Poll*. www.loveisrespect.org/pdf/College_Dating_And_Abuse_Final_Study.pdf
Malchiodi, C.A. (2020) *Trauma and Expressive Arts Therapy: Brain, Body, and Imagination in the Healing Process*. New York: Guilford Press.
Marx, B.P. and Soler-Baillo, J.M. (2005) "The relationships among risk recognition, autonomic and self-reported arousal, and posttraumatic stress symptomatology in acknowledged and unacknowledged victims of sexual assault." *Psychosomatic Medicine 67*, 4, 618–624. doi: 10.1097/01.psy.0000171809.12117.79.
Paciorek, A. and Skora, L. (2020) "Vagus nerve stimulation as a gateway to interoception." *Frontiers in Psychology 11*. https://doi.org/10.3389/fpsyg.2020.01659
PBS (2023) "The history of the American Flag." Frontline. www.pbs.org/a-capitol-fourth/history/old-glory
Porges, S.W. (2017) *The Pocket Guide to the Polyvagal Theory: The Transformative Power of Feeling Safe*. New York: W.W. Norton & Co.
Porges, S.W. (2022) "Polyvagal theory: A science of safety." *Frontiers in Integrative Neuroscience 16*, 871227. https://doi.org/10.3389/fnint.2022.871227
Strailey, L. (2023) *He Barks & I Bite My Tongue* [Tapestry]. Private collection.

Chapter 7

BOUNDARIES

> Jamie was excited to connect in love with another person who was intelligent and socially active, and who shared his interests in literature, politics, and education. Quickly into dating, the couple realized that shared interests in work created an overlap in their career activities and aspirations; they would often pull each other into their work activities to proofread an essay, review a PowerPoint, or solicit suggestions for a presentation. Within a year, they happily blended their libraries, their homes, their families, and their bank accounts, and started a business that they ran together. The business drew on both of their strengths, although not equally, and it didn't equally displace their other work. As things began to unravel it became clearer that neither partner had something or somewhere that was really exclusively theirs. As Jamie became more aggressive and territorial, his wife began to make herself smaller and smaller.

In simple terms, a boundary is a point of demarcation between self and others (Scott 1993). It is the knowing where one ends and where others begin, and an intentional awareness of the space (or lack of space) between. Boundaries can be physical or emotional, mental or spiritual. They can also be largely unconscious until they become uncomfortable and we are forced to pay attention to them. Boundaries define who we are and how we engage with others in the world. Boundaries can be established and manipulated with variables such as time, touch, physical space, and self-disclosure.

ATTACHMENT AND AUTHENTICITY

Boundaries are learned in early childhood through the examples set by our primary caregivers. Because of this, boundaries are often culturally bound. Cultures that value individualism and independence might put greater emphasis on more rigid or closed boundaries, whereas cultures that value interconnectedness and collectivist ideals might put greater emphasis on more open or permeable boundaries.

But there is more to boundaries than just our cultural background. Attachment style, formed in childhood through our primary caregiver relationship, also influences how our boundaries manifest across the lifespan. In fact, attachment is our very first, non-negotiable need. From the moment of birth, the relationship with a loving caregiver is essential for providing the basic needs of food, shelter, and connection. It is a primary need that shapes our growth and development. Susan Johnson, developer of Emotion Focused Therapy, defines attachment as "secure dependence," and states that attachment is "an innate and motivating force" (2004, p.25) that provides a safe haven from which we can grow and individuate into autonomous and self-confident adults.

When fear, uncertainty, or traumatic stress disrupt the attachment bond, it can result in one of two rather predictable responses: increased attachment anxiety or attachment avoidance. In other words, the individual either tries harder (cries louder, demands more) to get a response from the loved one, or they simply shut the longing down and retreat. An individual with a more anxious attachment style might look like they have very few or no boundaries at all, whereas an individual with an avoidant attachment style might come across as someone with rather rigid or closed boundaries.

There is, however, a second and equally important non-negotiable need that each of us is born with, namely authenticity. Authenticity is our ability to know, understand, and be deeply connected to ourselves and to our own inner experience. You might think of attachment as connection to other and authenticity as connection to self. Each is vitally important.

What happens for some of us, however, is that authenticity is sacrificed in service to attachment. Let's say, for example, that your parents were dealing with their own histories of trauma, and in response to that were unable to tolerate expressions of anger or rage. They might have given you clear messages that such emotions were to be tempered and any expression of anger or rage was met with swift reprimand. As a result, you learned very quickly to ignore or shut down your own anger whenever that emotion arose in order to make your parents happy. If this happens over and over, it can eventually lead to a lack of authentic understanding and connection to self. Authenticity is sacrificed while attachment is maintained. This, in turn, can influence how we view the space between us and others.

BOUNDARY FLEXIBILITY

It seems like a lot of boundary talk in the field of counseling is centered on the need for stronger or better boundaries in the lives of our clients. While this may, at times, be true, the fact is that what matters when considering boundaries is not the lack of strong or impermeable boundaries, but rather a person's ability to appropriately assess a situation based on environmental, inter- and intra-personal cues, and then respond appropriately based on an understanding of what the situation calls for. *Boundary flexibility*, a term coined by Scott (1988), emphasizes the need for the ability to move between closed and open or permeable and impermeable boundaries, depending on the situation. Someone with consistently closed boundaries will most likely stay relatively safe, but may lack the ability to access loving, supportive relationships. Conversely, someone with consistently open boundaries may be able to access loving, supportive relationships, but may also miss the cues that might signal the need for caution or stronger boundaries. Neither end of the spectrum is ideal as a permanent state. It is the ability to move, appropriately, between the two that defines flexibility and allows someone to access those relationships that provide the connections and relationships that enhance our development and growth while also staying aware that there may be times when more impermeable or closed boundaries are needed.

BOUNDARIES AND HEALING

The renegotiation of personal space boundaries is essential to the healing journey. However, boundaries can prove to be a challenge for survivors of relationship abuse or violence. The immediate and impulsive response for many survivors is to move into a period of hyper-strong boundaries that serve to keep the victim safe until they feel strong enough to venture back into community and relationships (for a more detailed description of this phenomenon, see Czerny, Lassiter, and Lim 2018). However, an individual's attachment style, their level of authenticity, and the presence of early childhood abuse can all complicate this response. Developing an increased awareness of boundaries and practicing boundary flexibility can aid the recovery journey. Practicing boundary flexibility can provide an opportunity to reassess where an individual's boundaries are most productive, and help to serve them in maintaining a sense of self as they engage in connection with another.

Easing into reflection: Boundaries

- How have you intentionally set boundaries in your life? How have boundaries unintentionally emerged in your life? Take a moment to reflect on your experience with boundaries. Write down a few things that stand out to you.

  ....
  ....
  ....
  ....

- Consider your relationships (both past and present). Choose one relationship to focus on. Imagine a color that represents that person, and then imagine a color that represents you. Now imagine that the two of you are in a room and the two colors are filling up the space. How much of the room is your color, and how much of the room is the other person's color? How much of the room is mixed?

....
....
....
....

BOUNDARIES ART THERAPY PROJECT: DRAWING LINES
Purpose
Using art to represent and convey concepts such as personal boundaries can be a useful way of giving form to things that are often unseen or unclear. It also serves as a practice field for individuals who are examining and establishing their personal boundaries. People who have suffered from relationship violence frequently need to reconsider and re-establish boundaries and then adjust them as needed while developing flexibility that serves them well.

The purpose of this art project is for the client to give reflection through creativity to their own boundary lines, where they have been neglected or established, and why. Special consideration may also be given to the permanence and permeability of boundary lines. It is typical that individuals may maintain multiple boundaries in life. Ultimately, "boundaries create an environment of safety and predictability" (Fenner and Gussak 2006, p.414), as well as avenues to connection, which help individuals to thrive in relationships.

Overview of boundary lines in art
One of the most common representations of boundary lines in art is that of maps, which conventionally draw boundaries between or around land areas. The Museum of Modern Art's (MoMA)

educational division has some project ideas that expound on the use of maps as both communicative tools, but also as artwork (MoMALearning n.d.). We also see boundaries tactfully employed in the art of mazes and some puzzles.

In classical and contemporary art, boundaries are often portrayed as divisions, establishing borders and differences. They may even heighten our awareness of differences. There is a rich history of artists exploring geo-political conflict via artwork (Wulkan 2017), such as in Fox's (1995) collected representations of the US–Mexico border. Some artists transcend boundaries by symbolically crossing borders set by a work's frame (The Frame Blog 2023). Boundaries as a philosophical divide help individuals to establish their authority and autonomy (Halpern 2012).

The art project suggested here borrows a material used in an entirely different professional domain, but which is designed to create a boundary: caution tape. Caution tape, or barricade or barrier tape, as it is also known, is often used by police detectives, fire marshals, hazmat investigators, or others concerned with promoting safety and conveying potential danger in the area. Caution tape comes in a variety of colors designed to convey something about the type of danger that exists (Safeopedia 2018). It is almost universally recognized as a warning to some sort of danger, although it may vary in color, text, or design across cultures.

Caution tape has made its way into the art world. In 2003, infamous and unidentified street artist Banksy snuck a painting into the Tate Museum in London and hung it on a wall. The painting depicted a classic landscape with a home marked with police crime scene tape (BBC News 2003); the artist was making a statement about personal and collective security. Puerto Rican artist Pepón Osorio used caution tape in a series of altar-like pieces examining culture from a voyeuristic perspective (Ramos Collado and Álvarez Lezama 2013). Artist Shelly Goldsmith (2015) staged an installation of her artwork incorporating custom-printed caution-style tape in crime scene layouts, to examine the phenomenon of bereavement. The portrayal of crime scenes in art has become a style of sorts, which may include the portrayal of symbols such as caution tape (Bray 2014).

In exploring the concept of boundaries, clients are invited through this project to use caution tape as a tool in their art making, along with a variety of other media. Caution tape easily lends itself to collage. Sometimes clients wrap objects or event spaces. Generally, it's a material that elicits some laughter initially (and there is room for humor in therapy), as it can be humorous to see caution tape used out of the context of keeping people within an identified safe zone. Caution tape can be purchased in large or small quantities at hardware and home renovation stores, or online. Additionally, artists can create their own caution tape.

Individuals need to establish boundaries in a variety of ways, including physical, emotional, psychological, financial, and spiritual. This art project can provide exploration into any of these specific domains, or more generally. In this project, a client can consider creating their boundaries as they appear currently, or perhaps aspirationally, as they wish they would be.

Project goals

1. To consider the literal and figurative boundaries that a person has set or may need to set for themselves within and between relationships.
2. To conceptualize relationship boundaries by externalizing and visualizing them through art.
3. To reflect on the permeability and flexibility of one's own boundaries.

Warm-ups

Idea 1, Fence check-in: Ask the client to create a fence on paper with any drawing material. They should consider the qualities that they want to include in the fence they make. They may want to reflect on fences that they've seen for inspiration. Anchor fences (also called chain link) allow you to see what is on the other side, while restricting access. Picket fences are typically lower, creating an attractive visual border, while retaining some relative access that, for example, children could typically climb over or squeeze under. Wood-paneled fences (often pressure-treated pine or cedar) are typically sturdy and offer more privacy by restricting sight. After drawing a fence, ask the client to fill in each side of the fence with something. In this way, they're considering the divide before adding in what it is that they are separating. Invite sharing about how this fence relates to their boundaries.

Idea 2, Build a boundary check-in: This is about bringing some silliness and whimsy to a very serious topic. Using their material of choice, ask the client to build a boundary around or between their space on the table. Their material should be something that is inherently soft or unstable, such as: gelatin cubes, mini marshmallows, dry sand, small stuffed animals, squeezable stress balls, hard pretzels, gummy worms, or crayons (whole or broken). They should try to build the safest, sturdiest boundary that they can, using these materials. Discussion or reflection can center round how they approached the act of building, what surprises came from the materials, what worked, what caused frustration, and what has been learned about establishing this boundary. Using unsturdy materials can lead to discussions about the holes or permeability of the boundary; these access points can be frustrating, but also valuable.

Materials suggested

- Caution tape (or alternately any sort of yellow "warning" or "do not cross" tape, as in those used by emergency personnel and police departments)
- Adhesives: glue, tape, stapler and staples
- Scissors
- Paper
- Magazine images for enhanced collage
- Marker pens

Preparation

When using collage with clients in art therapy or making artwork in counseling, we recommend including a bin of pre-cut images. This can make the collage process easier and quicker for clients who can simply select their images from the bin. Art therapists frequently recommend having several pre-cut image bins that divide images into categories by people, words, landscapes, and miscellaneous. These can help accelerate the art-making process, stimulate ideas and creativity in clients, and cut down on distractions. Whole magazines frequently have articles that clients can be distracted by, as well as associations with various publications, advertisers, or headlines. While in some cases these associations can be useful in therapy, in others, they constitute a distraction.

When using cut images for collage it can be beneficial to provide either a diverse array of images or a wide variety of magazines. This is especially important pertaining to magazines that show people of various races, genders, ages, ability levels, and with impairments. Western fashion and beauty magazines, for example, tend to only promote a certain cultural standard of beauty as well as certain gender expectations, body types, and ways of physically being in the world. This inevitably does not represent all clients. It is helpful for clients to see images of people who look like them, or share some of the real-world challenges that they face or see in their lives. Images that reflect physical disabilities, different ways of dressing, facial expressions, and ways that people come together can be both validating and inspiring. In this way, collage can help clients to embrace their own cultural identity, and to feel supported in doing so (Landgarten 1994; Tripp, Potash, and Brancheau 2019).

Process

You might suggest to the client that they make a piece of art exploring the idea of boundaries. For some, that will be enough to get them going. For those who need more specificity, suggest that they reflect on their boundaries within a specific relationship, perhaps the identified abusive relationship. Artwork may reflect any specific aspect of their boundaries, or may be a specific episode or event when boundaries were breached or boundary issues were highlighted.

Invite the client to consider first what they know and how they feel about their boundaries, or to dive right into the art material. Some art is made by artists who thoughtfully construct a plan in advance of working. In other cases, the art is the result of spontaneity, and the meaning evolves during the creative process. Both are useful and valid methods for approaching art making. And much like the concept of flexibility in boundaries, an individual does not have to work in only one way all the time. Sometimes a material may motivate someone to initiate their creative output without much forethought, a generative, creative process that can be powerful.

Some clients appreciate the opportunity to talk about their work as they are making it, voicing their process and choices while in action. In other cases, the art process is a silent journey, and discussion and meaning making happen afterwards. Again, there is not one right way. Taking your cue from the client is a great way to honor their creative process, and it can be a point of discussion later.

Questions to spark reflection or discussion

- How did you choose to represent boundaries or boundary issues in your art piece?

- How clear are your boundaries? (You might use words that convey clarity or a lack thereof, such as opaque, translucent, transparent, cloudy, visible, invisible, etc.)

- In what way does your artwork reflect boundaries that you have (or someone else has)? In what way does your artwork reflect boundaries as you wish they might be?

- Who has created your boundaries? How do you feel about this?

- Where is your boundary/boundaries firm, and where is it/are they flexible or permeable?

- How impassable is your boundary?

- How much do your boundaries vary in different relationships? In different circumstances within a single relationship?

- How are your boundaries helpful or hurtful to you?

Alternate art therapy project ideas
Alternate art therapy project idea 1: Personal map
Another approach to exploring boundaries is to make a personal map that examines where a client has delineated space (e.g., physical but also metaphorical space to exist, flourish, and develop), and where the boundaries are. This may include discussion of boundary lines that are flexible and permeable and boundary lines that are impassable; including a discussion about who created those boundaries and why they were created can be helpful. Referring to boundary lines on maps between countries can be useful for inspiration and reflection. Medieval European cultures classically built large stone walls enclosing their cities. Indigenous cultures in the American Southwest and in Western Asia often built cities within caves that afforded them a certain level of security from natural large stone walls. Infamous well-fortified boundaries include the Korean Demilitarized Zone and the Berlin Wall. In contrast, some countries have boundaries that are almost invisible and require a sign declaring their presence; in these cases you can often drive or walk right over the line.

Alternate art therapy project idea 2: Clear tape human figures
Using a technique of person-molded packing tape and clear plastic wrap, the "shell" of a body can be created that is completely transparent. Exploration of boundaries through transparency can provide a rich metaphor for how established and visible our own boundaries are or need to be. This technique is sometimes used in art therapy work (Bechtel, Wood, and Teoli 2020), and has been frequently depicted on social media. It is sometimes called *clear tape people* or *human tape sculptures*, and there are plenty of tutorials online.

PROJECT EXAMPLES

In *Holes in My Boundaries* (Figure 4), Savannah constructed a box using cardboard from a pizza delivery box. What the viewer can't see entirely is the intense and vibrant underlayer beneath the tattered but intact caution tape boundary, which creates the top of the box. The holes and tears that provide slight windows into the private underlayer are intentional.

Figure 4: *Holes in My Boundaries*, by Savannah (2023)

The art piece *Bound* (Figure 5) by Jacey Ludlam includes the use of paper, caution tape, magazine collage, trim, and notions. This piece is tied up, as the title and materials tell us, and there is a strong juxtaposition between the methodical wrapping and the frayed edges.

Figure 5: *Bound*, by Jacey Ludlam (2023)

REFERENCES

BBC News (2003) "Graffiti star sneaks work into Tate." October 17. http://news.bbc.co.uk/2/hi/entertainment/3201344.stm

Bechtel, A., Wood, L.L., and Teoli, L. (2020) "Re-shaping body image: Tape sculptures as arts-based social justice." *The Arts in Psychotherapy 68*, 101615. https://doi.org/10.1016/j.aip.2019.101615

Bray, R.S. (2014) "Rotten prettiness? The forensic aesthetic and crime as art." *Australian Feminist Law Journal 40*, 1, 69–95. https://doi.org/10.1080/13200968.2014.931900

Czerny, A.B., Lassiter, P.S., and Lim, J.H. (2018) "Post-abuse boundary renegotiation: Healing and reclaiming self after intimate partner violence." *Journal of Mental Health Counseling 40*, 3, 211–225. https://doi.org/10.17744/mehc.40.3.03

Fenner, L.B. and Gussak, D.E. (2006) "Therapeutic boundaries in a prison setting: A dialogue between an intern and her supervisor." *The Arts in Psychotherapy 33*, 5, 414–421. https://doi.org/10.1016/j.aip.2006.08.002

Fox, C.F. (1995) "The fence and the river: Representations of the US–Mexico border in art and video." *Discourse 18*, 1/2, 54–83. www.jstor.org/stable/41389403

Frame Blog, The (2023) "How artists have used the frame in the past, & how they can use it now." https://theframeblog.com/2016/06/09/how-artists-have-used-the-frame-in-the-past-how-they-can-use-it-now

Goldsmith, S. (2015) *The Art of Bereavement* [Exhibition/show].

Halpern, M.K. (2012) "Across the great divide: Boundaries and boundary objects in art and science." *Public Understanding of Science 21*, 8, 922–937. https://doi.org/10.1177/0963662510394040

Johnson, S.M. (2004) *The Practice of Emotionally Focused Couple Therapy*. Abingdon: Brunner Routledge.

Landgarten, H.B. (1994) "Magazine photo collage as a multicultural treatment and assessment technique." *Art Therapy 11*, 3, 218–219. https://doi.org/10.1080/07421656.1994.10759089

Ludlam, J. (2023) *Bound* [Collage]. Private collection.

MoMALearning (no date) "Maps, borders, and networks." www.moma.org/learn/moma_learning/themes/maps-borders-and-networks

Ramos Collado, L. and Álvarez Lezama, M. (2013) "Hollywood kills: Pepón Osorio and his 'Scene of the Crime'." Still Life With Keyboard, November 27. https://bodegonconteclado.wordpress.com/2013/11/27/hollywood-mata-pepon-osorio-y-su-scene-of-the-crime/#more-2691

Safeopedia (2018) "Caution tape." September 26. www.safeopedia.com/definition/6579/caution-tape

Savannah (2023) *Holes in My Boundaries* [Painting and sculptural collage]. Private collection.

Scott, A.L. (1988) "Human interaction and personal boundaries." *Journal of Psychological Nursing and Mental Health 26*, 8, 23–27. https://doi.org/10.3928/0279-3695-19880801-11

Scott, A.L. (1993) "A beginning theory of personal space boundaries." *Perspectives in Psychiatric Care 29*, 2, 12–21. https://onlinelibrary.wiley.com/doi/10.1111/j.1744-6163.1993.tb00407.x

Tripp, T., Potash, J.S., and Brancheau, D. (2019) "Safe place collage protocol: Art making for managing traumatic stress." *Journal of Trauma & Dissociation 20*, 5, 511–525. https://doi.org/10.1080/15299732.2019.1597813

Wulkan, R. (2017) "Across divides: Borders and boundaries in contemporary art." Derfner Judaica Museum + The Art Collection. https://derfner.org/2017/03/30/across-divides-borders-and-boundaries-in-contemporary-art

Chapter 8

LOCUS OF CONTROL

> Marissa dialed the number of her therapist, seeking some validation. She had just arrived home from lunch with her old friend, Janis. Marissa had spent the first half of their lunch catching Janis up about her husband's many affairs and their subsequent divorce. Janis, who had a rocky marriage herself, responded in full defense of marriage, and questioned Marissa's leaving. She seemed unmoved by Marissa's story. "Of all the people I know, Marissa, you're that last person I'd have pegged for giving up on your marriage," Janis said. "Did you two even try to work through it? Did you guys consider couples counseling?" It was all Marissa could do to get through the rest of the lunch. By the time she got in her car, she was crying. Why did things like this keep happening to her? First, her husband had abused and controlled her, and now, when she needed support the most, she was met with judgment from a friend. It felt like she had a big bull's-eye on her back and a sign that said, "Shoot here, easy target."

The term "locus of control" was originally defined by Rotter (1954) and related to social learning theory. Put simply, locus of control has to do with the place (either internal or external) where reinforcement for behavior is found (Flammer 2015). An internal locus of control is defined as having a belief that outcomes in a person's life are related to personal efforts (personal responsibility), whereas someone with an external locus of control believes that outcomes are largely due to factors outside of their personal control (faith in external resources) (April, Dharani, and Peters 2012). There may also be situations or occasions across time where we actually believe both internal and external factors influence outcomes in our lives, a state called *bilocal expectancy* (April *et al.* 2012). For example, someone might think that getting sick is outside of their control (external locus of control) but that the healing is something that they have influence over (internal locus of control). Someone might also have a more external locus of control in one area of their life (interpersonal relationships, for example) and a more internal locus of control in another (such as work). Locus of control is closely related to other types of control beliefs such as competency (related to ability), mastery (related to skill), and self-efficacy (related to belief in self) (Wallston 2015).

When applied to self-worth, locus of control is the degree to which a person's sense of self-worth is determined by internal or external factors (Czerny and Lassiter 2016). You can assess your own locus of control by asking yourself, do you feel good about yourself because others treat you well or when things work out to your benefit (external locus of control), or do you feel good about yourself regardless of how others treat you or when things don't work out the way you had hoped (internal locus of control)? In the case of Tanya, her self-worth was impacted by an external locus of control.

> Tanya's husband came in from the garage, sweaty and covered in grease. "You keep riding those brakes like you do and we'll need to replace them or the car before the year is out," he said. "I've told you over and over to stay off those brakes when you're driving. You cost us more money than anything else in life." Tanya's mood plummeted. She had woken up happy; she and her husband had been out on a date the night before. Now he was upset about having to fix the car again and it was all her fault; she was a bad driver and a bad wife. She felt worthless, and suddenly it seemed like nothing she ever did was good enough.

Most of us are somewhere on a continuum between internal and external locus of control related to self-worth; many of us are not completely on one or the other end of this continuum. Someone who is wholly external might come across as lacking authenticity, and someone who is wholly internal might come across as uncaring. However, research tends to suggest that individuals who have an internal locus of control related to self-worth feel good about themselves and may also have higher levels of competency, mastery, and self-efficacy as well, resulting in the ability to take on new challenges and deal with life stressors that inevitably occur for all of us (April *et al.* 2012).

DIFFERENCES BY CULTURE AND GENDER

Locus of control can vary based on someone's cultural background (Miller and Källberg-Shroff 2015) and gender (Adams 2010). Cultural background is often categorized into one of two rather broad categories: collectivist or individualist. Collectivist societies tend to consider and even prioritize the greater good of the social group, and thereby may limit personal freedom or perceived control over someone's autonomy. Individualists, in contrast, tend to consider themselves independent of social collectives or groups, and thus place emphasis on their personal preferences, rights, and needs over and above the social group they may be affiliated with (Stocks, April, and Lynton 2012). Individuals from collectivist cultures might value an external locus of control and find greater sense of worth when fulfilling obligations to friends and family. Conversely, someone from an individualist culture might find a greater sense of self-worth when paying more attention and prioritizing their own needs and desires. While the idea of collectivist versus individualist cultures can be helpful constructs in considering tendencies, they are, in fact, not so easily delineated from each other in that people are more nuanced than simply fitting neatly into one or another category. This is true of cultural backgrounds in general; we cannot simply categorize individuals based on broad hypothetical traits of their larger society. In today's modern world, the blending of cultures and the reality of intersectional identities means that tribal alliances and territorial delineations look different than they historically did. Supporting the premise that neither internal nor external are better or worse for an individual, April and colleagues (2012) found that greater levels of happiness occurred in individuals who demonstrated bilocal expectancy.

> **Breakout box: Feedback vs. criticism**
>
> Locus of control can influence how we respond to feedback. Keep in mind that feedback should be formative, in that it is meant to help you grow. Criticism, on the other hand, is looking for fault and will feel very different than formative feedback (although sometimes it is couched as *constructive criticism*). Feedback is common in education and training and self-help processes. While victims of relationship abuse are usually very familiar with criticism, they may have a difficult time understanding and accepting feedback because they are very sensitive to information that *feels* like criticism.
>
> Additionally, someone with an external locus of control around self-worth might find it very difficult to accept any feedback; they may become defensive when feedback is offered. In contrast, someone with an internal locus of control around self-worth might be more receptive to receiving feedback and acting on it without feeling overly defensive or shutdown.
>
> The distinction between formative feedback and personal criticism can be difficult to discern. When in a situation where you are faced with feedback that may not feel good, we encourage you to pause and evaluate if the person you are interacting with (e.g., romantic partner, boss, or supervisor, etc.) has your best interests and optimal development at heart. Is this person trying to guide your growth, or are they shaming you? This may help you assess what feedback you want to incorporate into your growth, and how you want to respond.

INTERNAL VS. EXTERNAL LOCUS OF CONTROL

An internal locus of control related to self-worth isn't necessarily better than an external locus of control. In fact, depending on the situation, one or the other might be needed or more helpful. For example, in their review of the literature on locus of control, Galvin *et al.* (2016) pointed out that some studies showed that those with an external locus of control were more receptive to workplace assistance than internal counterparts and, conversely, that internal counterparts tended to be more action-oriented at work versus their external counterparts.

Victims of relationship abuse learn very quickly to gauge and assess their partners for signs of escalating tension that might indicate a build-up toward violence; they tend to have a more external locus of control in that external forces often provide the impetus for their behaviors. The goal of treatment is not necessarily to change someone's locus of control, but rather to bring awareness to where a person falls on the continuum between internal and external, and to increase awareness of the factors that might influence their tendency. There is benefit to thoughtfully incorporating both an internal and external locus of control in different situations and relationships. Ultimately, the goal is to increase the flexibility someone is able to demonstrate between the two based on need and situational circumstances.

> Serenity stood in front of the cashier at the grocery store, watching as the woman at the register scowled and threw her items down to the young man bagging. Serenity could tell that the woman (her name badge said "Norma") was in a foul mood. When Norma didn't even greet her, Serenity had an immediate flash of guilt, as if she had done something wrong. It was an old, familiar feeling. But then she realized that Norma was probably having a bad day. Maybe working as a cashier in a busy grocery store wasn't her dream job. Serenity felt some compassion for Norma. It wasn't that long ago that Serenity had felt trapped and angry too.

Suddenly it dawned on Serenity that, a year ago, Norma's treatment toward her would have triggered a chain reaction of spiraling mood and self-doubt. Thank goodness for all of that work she had done with her therapist using the Empowerment Wheel model. Now, she could clearly see that Norma's behavior had nothing to do with her. Serenity looked up at Norma and smiled. "I hope your day gets better. I hope they let you take a break soon." Norma's shoulders dropped. She looked up at Serenity and smiled. "Thank you," she said. "It's been crazy all day and I've been on my feet since 8am."

"Well, they don't know what a great worker they have in you," said Serenity. Norma grinned from ear to ear. "Thank you," she said.

Serenity left the grocery store feeling great about not letting Norma's bad mood impact her self-worth, and for giving Norma a bit of positive feedback. She remembered how much that had helped her.

Easing into reflection: Locus of control

- How does the way others treat you affect you? Take a moment and reflect on your relationships with others. What is it like for you when others treat you well? What is it like for you when others treat you poorly? Write down a few thoughts.

  ....
  ....
  ....
  ....

- Now write down a few thoughts about how it feels when someone gives you feedback about you. How do you respond? Do you immediately agree? Are you defensive or do you shut down? Can you hear what they say and reflect on it?

....
....
....
....

LOCUS OF CONTROL ART THERAPY PROJECT: CREATING STORIES
Purpose
The purpose of this art project is to invite the client to visually explore the concept of locus of control in their life through the use of graphic storytelling. Most western-based researchers promote an internal over external locus of control, and many promote changing a client's locus of control as a therapeutic goal (Rosal 1985, 1993). We feel strongly that the goal of therapy is to help the client identify and assess their own locus of control, and exercise agency over whether that best suits them. This project provides a container for exploring the way things happen in our lives: what can happen, and who or what are the influential factors impacting what can happen.

History
In art therapy, locus of control is explored through clinical intervention and research. Rosal (1993) presented a study that used art therapy, specifically with a cognitive-based approach, as an intervention to modify the locus of control in children identified with behavior disorders. The premise in this study was that an internal locus of control is more optimal for children in the educational setting.

In another study, HIV-positive, gay, Latino men participated in a six-week arts-based workshop where they created their own retablos; the author hypothesized that this intervention would help to foster an increase in the internal locus of control (Rangel 2006). (Retablos are ornate paintings from the Mexican tradition that are frequently done on tin or wood, and displayed behind an altar, or within a frame that functions as a sacred and inspiring monument.)

Robey and colleagues (2016) set out to find evidence of a correlation between locus of control or self-determination and participation in art making. While they were not able to demonstrate this evidence in their study, they did reveal findings that demonstrated that participation in art making may be a practical and effective domain for exploring constructs related to self-determination, agency, and locus of control. Their qualitative results suggest that non-participants in art making were more likely to emphasize ideas such as luck, while art participants were more likely to value effort and ambition in regard to their circumstances (Robey *et al.* 2016).

Some research in art therapy has looked at populations with issues pertaining to locus of control, and the consideration of art therapy as an intervention for those identified. Holt and Kaiser (2001) utilized the Kinetic Family Drawing art therapy assessment with children to determine differences between those whose parents had substance abuse problems and those who did not. Among other issues that children of alcoholics are at risk for developing, external locus of control is thought to be one that does not serve them well.

One study examined the impact of art therapy on imprisoned men and women. The hope was to assess change and possible improvement of depression, locus of control, and behavior after 15 weeks of treatment. Gussak (2009) implemented the Adult Nowicki-Strickland Locus of Control Scale (Nowicki and Duke 1974) as one of several pre- and post-intervention assessments. While the prison population is believed to generally have an external leaning locus of control, an internal locus of control is considered a deterrent to criminal behavior and recidivism. The study revealed that both men and women demonstrated a significant decrease in external locus of control (Gussak 2009).

Salmon and Gerber (1999) looked at the role that expectations play in depression and dependency through the use of a three-panel graphic drawing examining the present, past, and future. Expectancy, or the likelihood that something will occur, is a topic that includes locus of control, which also considers someone's own role in what will occur. The study concluded that the graphic stories of airplanes developed by Air Force participants demonstrated an external locus of control; the authors considered the relationship of this to depression and feelings of helplessness (Salmon and Gerber 1999).

Some therapeutic techniques are designed to highlight the issue of locus of control. One of these was called *create a fairytale*, whereby the authors encouraged the use of power and magic as a means of representing a person's locus of control (Bradley *et al.* 2023). McCormick, Rosenblad, and Newmeyer (2021) described the use of sandtray therapy as a tool to help clients increase their internal locus of control. Scott and Ross (2006) named balancing locus of control as one of their identified essential processes that occur when using creative arts techniques with clients coping with trauma and addiction.

Locus of control, expectancy, and agency are all explored in visual art. In fact, agency, often considered a synonym for internal locus of control, is often the process by which artwork is generated. Locus of control was the theme of a recent art exhibition, and referenced "the endless tension experienced in the painting process, between the sense of total mastery that we have when we are in control of the painting, and the abyss of disempowerment when the painting refuses to obey" (art.b 2022, para. 2). Artists sometimes muse over where a piece of art that they made came from; some believe that there is great individual agency involved, while others describe being a vessel for delivering a piece of art to the world (Milner 2010).

In this art project we invite you or your client to create a multi-paneled graphic story (similar to the type frequently seen in comic strips and cartoons) as a way of exploring the concept of locus of control. There is a benefit for the client in trauma treatment to tell their story (Rankin and Taucher 2003). Through the use of graphic stories we have the opportunity to slow down time, and to consider our reactions and responses in a more concerted way. If you grew up in the era of newspapers, you may remember the popularity of the Sunday comics that could deliver you into a new world with just a few panels of information. Bil Keane (2001) did this expertly in the single-paneled Family Circus drawings when he used a dotted line to convey the lengthy journey that his children would go on through the house or yard. He demonstrated both the agency that each child would take, and also the happenstance of where they ended up, fueled by curiosity and opportunity (Weldon 2011). Graphic novels have increased in popularity in teen and adult literature over the years; people of all ages can appreciate the way a story can be told simultaneously, with both words and images. Rachel Lindsay (2018) does an outstanding job of representing her struggles with mental illness, including incidents of mandatory hospitalization, medication maintenance, and family involvement. Sometimes she narrates a whole strip of events and communication. On some pages a single image fills the whole page and speaks volumes.

For this art project, consider an idea that may benefit from being explored through a graphic story. It may be based on a relationship, a memory, a feeling, or any part of an experience. This idea can be the inspiration for a graphic story. Don't worry about the quality of the artwork. Some graphic strips are teeming with details, while others convey strong ideas with only stick figures. Graphic stories are powerful because of the ideas that they convey, and to that end, the art supports those ideas. Graphic stories are often relatable because they capitalize on the use of symbols that are universal to our experience.

Project goals

1. To consider someone's locus of control, and how much impact they feel that they may have on what happens in their life.
2. To explore what and who are the internal and/or external factors that may exercise control in someone's life.

3. To provide a story or narrative that can serve as a tool for reflection that someone can explore, consider, reframe, or rewrite as needed in deciding if the locus of control depicted fits them.

Warm-ups

Idea 1, Circle of control: Ask the client to draw a large circle on a piece of paper. It can be drawn by tracing a plate or a pot lid, or it can be free hand, even if it is imperfect. On the inside of the circle they should write "Things I can control" and on the outside "Things I cannot control." Now, using any writing or drawing materials, they should fill in as much of the page as they can. Ask them to try to come up with at least five things for inside the circle, and five things for outside the circle. They can use words, images, colors, or anything that conveys their ideas.

Idea 2, Personal roadmap: Maps are enormously useful for getting us to where we need to go. In modern times, we often rely on Google Maps, or Waze, or similar apps to get around. Sometimes GPS saves the day. In previous eras we relied on printed MapQuest directions, or maps sourced from the American Automobile Association (AAA). You might still be a fan of unfurling the large paper maps to hone in on where you are and where you need to go. This warm-up is a simplified version of map making. Ask the client to draw a line across the paper that goes off the edges in two places. Their line can go directly across the paper, or it may jut and jag or curl around in a circuitous fashion. This is their path. Next ask them to create a symbol that represents where they are on this path, and also some obstacles that could hamper their progress on this path (e.g., potholes, traffic) and some opportunities that may accelerate their progress (e.g., detour, shortcut). Alternate routes can also be considered, since there is rarely only one way to get where we are going. They should consider what is the best route for them, and what options they can see on their path.

Materials suggested

- White paper, 8½ x 11 inches, or 14 x 17 inches

- Graphite pencil and eraser
- Marker pens
- Colored pencils
- Scissors
- Glue sticks

Preparation

Ask the client to consider what size and shape of a panel they want to start with. They should draw a square, circle, or rectangle that is big enough to make something happen in; this shape is their graphic story panel. They should then create a series of three squares or circles, so that they have a path to let their story grow. They can always add in more panels if they need them. Similarly, if they have more than they need, they don't have to use them all. The story is done when the artist says it's done.

Sometimes the shape of the panel helps convey a piece of the story. For example, a jagged star-like shape might convey something exciting or jarring. A soft, organic bubble shape may convey that something is vague, or even dreamlike. In this way, graphic artists can use the lines that define their space to help convey ideas about the story.

Process

There is not only one way to build a graphic story; many formulaic ideas can be helpful, particularly if new to this art technique. For the purpose of this exercise, and particularly with a new graphic artist, we suggest starting with three panels, and following one of these suggested prompts:

- Prompt 1: Fill in your three panels by drawing in order (1) what used to be; (2) what is now; (3) what will be in the future.

- Prompt 2: Fill in your three panels by drawing in order (1) an event that happened; (2) how you felt about it at first (or what you did); (3) how you felt about it later on (and what you did later).

- Prompt 3: Fill in your three panels by drawing in order (1) the first day of the relationship; (2) a day in the middle of the relationship; (3) the last day of the relationship.

- Prompt 4: Fill in your three panels by drawing in order (1) an event that happened; (2) what you did afterward; (3) what you wished you had done instead.

- Prompt 5: Fill in your three panels by drawing in order (1) an interpersonal encounter; (2) a dramatic escalation; (3) the resolution you would like to see.

Questions to spark reflection or discussion

- What was your graphic story about?

- What did you learn or affirm about yourself from this story?

- What internal factors (e.g., felt sense, intuition, sixth sense, motivation, desire, need) did you explore in this project?

- What external factors (e.g., another person or people, faith, destiny, God, karma, the universe, divine intervention, ghosts or other worldly beings, time) did you explore in this project?

- What did you learn or affirm about your belief in how and why things happen?

- After making art, how do you feel about your own locus of control?

Alternate art therapy project idea
Tarot cards
Tarot cards have a rich history in art, in therapy (Bouchard 2020), and also in certain pagan and occult traditions (Place 2005). At their root, they are symbols that many people believe have some sort of universal meaning and tap into our collective unconscious

(Chevalier and Gheerbrant 1996; Jung 2014). In art therapy, there are many uses for symbolic cards that are inspired by the Tarot, including SoulCollage® cards (Frost 2001, 2010), Spirit or Oracle cards (Boley 2021), and Affirmation cards (Keithley 2023). Thomas (2011) suggests that clients could create a deck of cards that would encourage them to meet their daily challenges: "These cards can contain mantras, affirmations, or reminders about who you are or your personal strengths" (Thomas 2011, p.66).

In this book, we are not promoting any specific card tradition or usage, and if you are a believer of a tradition or usage, we urge you to follow it. Many artists recreate the traditional Tarot cards with their own artwork. Some artists also reimagine or recreate cards with images or ideas that they feel need to be represented. In the pulling of Tarot cards, the question of agency could be posed, and is sometimes looked at in contrast to divinity. Yet cards can be pulled from any perspective. A card may be viewed as something you choose, or as something that was chosen for and delivered to you. We do not espouse either of these as the universal truth, but encourage you to consider what you believe and to explore your truth. Consider creating your own cards that have a symbol or idea that is important to you. What do the cards mean to you? What might be conveyed if you pulled that particular card?

PROJECT EXAMPLES

Figure 6: *Where We're Headed*, by an anonymous artist (2023)

You can see an example of a locus of control graphic story in *Where We're Headed* (Figure 6). The artist drew a three-panel story in free-form square blocks. In the first panel, the artist is reflecting on how things were in the beginning. Her partner was passionate and charismatic, and she was taken with his rugged good looks and charm. In the second panel we see an image of how things were in the middle of their relationship. She drew what she described as a typical scene in their relationship—she had just got home from a double shift at work on her feet all day while her unemployed and domineering partner was already sitting with his feet up drinking beer and shouting demands at her. In the last panel she depicted a foretelling of the future. She stated that this was where she expected they would get to. In this future panel, she is serving her partner as his literal table, and being treated as such. While she put lots of small details into her depiction of the first and second panel, she noted that she couldn't even finish the third panel, imagining it made her feel sick. She also noted that she omitted drawing any identifying details on herself in the third panel—no eyes or face even. She described that continuing with her partner would have meant losing her personhood. This story provided an opportunity to talk about alternate endings, or building in a new storyline.

Figure 7: *The Unloved*, by Rachel Woerner (2023)

In Figure 7, we see an acrylic on canvas painting of a spider, inspired by the Tarot card project. Spiders are a symbol commonly represented in various Tarot and Oracle decks, but their meanings vary. Sometimes their legs represent various paths, or their bodies can represent traveling vast distances, as spiders often do on their silken threads. Spiders may also represent weavers, healers, and have associations with fire. Some believe that the spider represents new beginnings, and in some cultures they symbolize good luck.

REFERENCES

Adams, P.E. (2010) "Understanding the different realities, experience, and use of self-esteem between black and white adolescent girls." *Journal of Black Psychology 36*, 3, 255–276. https://doi.org/10.1177/0095798410361454

Anonymous artist (2023) *Where We're Headed* [Drawing]. Private collection.

April, K.A., Dharani, B., and Peters, K. (2012) "Impact of locus of control expectancy on level of well-being." *Review of European Studies 4*, 2, 124–137. https://doi.org/10.5539/res.v4n2p124

art.b (2022) "Locus of control." www.artb.co.za/exhibitions-locus-of-control/#:~:text=The%20theme%20of%20the%20exhibition,the%20painting%20refuses%20to%20obey

Boley, M. (2021) "Oracle decks: What they are and how to use them." *Medium*, May 17. https://link.medium.com/NjZ852FFDzb

Bouchard, C. (2020) "Therapeutic Practice of Artistically Manifesting a Tarot Pull to Facilitate Personal Insight: An Arts-Based Self Study." Dissertation. www.proquest.com/dissertations-theses/therapeutic-practice-artistically-manifesting/docview/2626888954/se-2

Bradley, L., Mendoza, K., Hollingsworth, L., Johnson, P., Duffey, T., and Daniels, J. (2023) "Creative supervision: Ten techniques to enhance supervision." *Journal of Creativity in Mental Health*, 1–13. https://doi.org/10.1080/15401383.2023.2176391

Chevalier, J. and Gheerbrant, A. (1996) *A Dictionary of Symbols*. Harmondsworth: Penguin.

Czerny, A.B. and Lassiter, P.S. (2016) "Healing from intimate partner violence: An empowerment wheel to guide the recovery journey." *Journal of Creativity in Mental Health 11*, 3–4, 311–324. doi: 10.1080/15401383.2016.1222321.

Flammer, A. (2015) *International Encyclopedia of the Social and Behavioral Sciences* (2nd edn). Elsevier.

Frost, S.B. (2001) *SoulCollage: An Intuitive Collage Process for Individuals and Groups*. Santa Cruz, CA: Hanford Mead Publishers, Inc.

Frost, S.B. (2010) *SoulCollage Evolving: An Intuitive Collage Process for Self-Discovery and Community*. Santa Cruz, CA: Hanford Mead Publishers, Inc.

Galvin, B.M., Randel, A.E., Collins, B.J., and Johnson, R.E. (2016) "Changing the focus of locus (of control): A targeted review of the locus of control literature and agenda for future research." *Journal of Organizational Behavior 39*, 7, 820–833. https://doi.org/10.1002/job.2275

Gussak, D. (2009) "The effects of art therapy on male and female inmates: Advancing the research base." *The Arts in Psychotherapy 36*, 1, 5–12. https://doi.org/10.1016/j.aip.2008.10.002

Holt, E.S. and Kaiser, D.H. (2001) "Indicators of familial alcoholism in children's Kinetic Family Drawings." *Art Therapy 18*, 2, 89–95. https://doi.org/10.1080/07421656.2001.10129751

Jung, C.G. (2014) *The Archetypes and the Collective Unconscious*. Abingdon: Routledge.

Keane, B. (2001) *The Family Circus by Request*. Nashville, TN: Ideals Publications.
Keithley, Z. (2023) "How to use affirmation cards (with recommendations)." https://zannakeithley.com/how-to-use-affirmation-cards
Lindsay, R. (2018) *RX: A Graphic Memoir*. New York: Grand Central Publishing.
McCormick, R., Rosenblad, S.R., and Newmeyer, M. (2021) "Untapped therapeutic potential: Using sandtray in substance abuse treatment groups." *Journal of Creativity in Mental Health 16*, 4, 522–536. https://doi.org/10.1080/15401383.2020.1789016
Miller, J.G. and Källberg-Shroff, M. (2015) *International Encyclopedia of the Social & Behavioral Sciences* (2nd edn). Oxford: Pergamon.
Milner, M. (2010) *On Not Being Able to Paint*. Abingdon: Routledge.
Nowicki, S. and Duke, M.P. (1974) "A locus of control scale for noncollege as well as college adults." *Journal of Personality Assessment 38*, 2, 136–137.
Place, R.M. (2005) *The Tarot: History, Symbolism, and Divination*. London: Jeremy P. Tarcher/Penguin.
Rangel, A. (2006) "Internal Locus of Control and Retablos: The Application of Art Therapy with HIV Positive Gay Men." Art Therapy, Master's Theses in Print, 137. https://scholar.dominican.edu/art-therapy-print-theses/137
Rankin, A.B. and Taucher, L.C. (2003) "A task-oriented approach to art therapy in trauma treatment." *Art Therapy 20*, 3, 138–147. https://doi.org/10.1080/07421656.2003.10129570
Robey, K.L., Reed, M.D., Steiner, P.L., and Fader Wilkenfeld, B. (2016) "Fine arts participation, self-determination, and locus of control among persons with developmental disabilities." *Arts & Health 10*, 1, 45–56. http://dx.doi.org/10.1080/17533015.2016.1247900
Rosal, M.L. (1985) "The Use of Art Therapy to Modify the Locus of Control and Adaptive Behavior of Behavior Disordered Students." Unpublished doctoral dissertation, University of Queensland, Brisbane, Australia.
Rosal, M.L. (1993) "Comparative group art therapy research to evaluate changes in locus of control in behavior disordered children." *The Arts in Psychotherapy 20*, 3, 231–241. https://doi.org/10.1016/0197-4556(93)90018-W
Rotter, J.B. (1954) *Social Learning and Clinical Psychology*. Hoboken, NJ: Prentice-Hall, Inc.
Salmon, P.R. and Gerber, N.E. (1999) "Disappointment, dependency, and depression in the military: The role of expectations as reflected in drawings." *Art Therapy 16*, 1, 17–30. https://doi.org/10.1080/07421656.1999.10759347
Scott, E.H. and Ross, C.J. (2006) "Integrating the creative arts into trauma and addiction treatment: Eight essential processes." *Journal of Chemical Dependency Treatment 8*, 2, 207–226. https://doi.org/10.1300/J034v08n02_11
Stocks, A., April, K.A., and Lynton, N. (2012) "Locus of control and subjective well-being—A cross cultural study." *Problems and Perspectives in Management 10*, 1, 17–25.
Thomas, B. (2011) *Creative Expression Activities for Teens: Exploring Identity Through Art, Craft, and Journaling*. London and Philadelphia, PA: Jessica Kingsley Publishers.
Wallston, K.A. (2015) *International Encyclopedia of the Social & Behavioral Sciences* (2nd edn). Elsevier.
Weldon, G. (2011) "Bil Keane's dotted line: An appreciation." NPR, November 11. www.npr.org/2011/11/11/142218444/bil-keanes-dotted-line-an-appreciation
Woerner, R. (2023) Untitled [Painting]. Private collection.

Chapter 9

RELATIONSHIP AUTHENTICITY

Imani stopped in front of the bookstore and stared at the display in the window. Front and center was the book that everyone was talking about, *Love Wars*, written and published by her childhood best friend, Jada Jones. Imani and Jada had gone to elementary and middle school together, both dreaming of becoming writers and journalists one day. They dreamed they would share an apartment together in New York while climbing their respective ladders of success. Imani and Jada had started drifting apart in high school, when Imani began dating her high school sweetheart, Joe. Joe was controlling and jealous, and he didn't want Imani hanging out with her girlfriends. At first, Imani was reluctant to give up her "girl time," but her friends were busy with activities too (Jada had become editor-in-chief of the school newspaper) and Joe was so in love that he wanted them to spend all of their time together. It became too difficult to resist Joe's desires, and easier to keep him happy; she stopped hanging out with her girlfriends and spent time with Joe or at home doing schoolwork. Somewhere along the way she stopped dreaming about her future too. As Imani stared at the bookstore window, she wondered about other things she had given up to keep Joe happy. She used to sing in the church choir and she had loved that. But Joe didn't like that the choir practice was on Friday nights and sometimes ran late. So she stopped singing. She stopped dreaming of moving to New

York, of pursuing journalism and being a writer, and really of any future at all. Staring at the bookstore window, Imani was struck by how much she had given up over the years. Giving up dreams that she had held for so long made Imani feel like she didn't even recognize herself.

Relationship authenticity is someone's ability to remain true to their self (thoughts, feelings, actions) while in relationship with a partner or potential "other." In other words, relationship inauthenticity occurs when the desire for a relationship is so strong that someone is willing or forced to compromise parts of self (thoughts, feelings, actions) in order to stay in the relationship. To be clear, no one chooses intentionally at the start of a relationship to let parts of their self go; rather, relationship inauthenticity evolves over time, as anxiety about the relationship increases. This could happen in response to someone's fear that maintaining relationship authenticity might damage the integrity of the partnership or increase conflict in the relationship. Also, prioritizing the relationship by ignoring or minimizing parts of self may be interpreted as an act of compromise.

Did you know?
Compromise vs. control

Differences between individuals in a relationship are inevitable. No matter how closely connected you are to another person, or how healthy you consider your relationship to be, you will find that the differences between you can sometimes cause friction or disagreements. As a result, compromise becomes an important part of any relationship. For survivors of relationship abuse, however, it can be difficult to discern the difference between compromise and control. In fact, there are distinct differences between the two that you can learn to recognize.

First, it is important to understand that compromise is finding a middle ground, and that might mean that neither party really feels like they have "won;" rather, a solution has been found that each partner can live with. This implies that both partners give a little. As a six-year-old client in an art therapy group once said, "Compromise is when red and blue make purple." In other words, both colors were willing to change a little to create something new and pleasing to each of them. The changes were mutual and not one-sided.

Compromise also involves good will from both parties, even in situations where one or both don't really want to give in. It's okay to feel passionate about your viewpoint or position. It is also okay to recognize that you both care for each other and that you want to find a tenable solution for both of you. This also implies that both parties value finding mutually acceptable solutions, and that doing this is more important than winning or being right.

Finally, compromise allows each of you to remain uniquely you; your identities are not minimized, belittled, or victimized. Your values are still intact. Unhealthy compromise might require that one of you is always giving in, or that values are consistently questioned or ignored. Healthy compromise is mutual, reciprocal, and respectful of each individual's identity and deeply held values or beliefs.

THE TRUE SELF

We are primarily relational and social human beings, and part of living authentically is living within a social environment where there is constant and ongoing negotiation between our true self and our relational self. To be fully authentic means that we risk social disapproval by being willing to speak out and remain true to our own thoughts, feelings, and values. Conversely, inauthenticity occurs when someone is overly concerned with social disapproval and attempts to silence or deny their true self with the ultimate hope of social approval or acceptance, or to avoid conflict (Wang 2016).

Winnicott (1960) wrote about the true self as the part of ourselves that we hide away from the world in fear, and the false self as the one that we promote and display. He theorized that this is a learned strategy built off of shame and prior experience, whereby we are socialized to feature a version of ourselves that we don't always identify with as a means of self-protection (Cresci 2019). This psychoanalytic phenomenon explains why people often showcase the best of themselves and their experiences on social media (Gil-Or, Levi-Belz, and Turel 2015), and why we conform ourselves in relationships in a way that can feel like a denial of authenticity.

Victims of relationship abuse are prone to fluctuations in relationship authenticity primarily because of the constant threat they are exposed to, but also as a means to "please" their partner and avoid conflict in the relationship. In fact, authenticity will most likely not occur in a dangerous or unsafe relationship, in that partner inequality has been shown to inhibit the capacity for authentic self-expression in relationships (Neff and Suizzo 2006). A complicating factor that contributes to victims of relationship abuse demonstrating low authenticity in relationships is the correlation between experiencing childhood abuse and relationship abuse later in life (Dube *et al.* 2005; Fleming *et al.* 1999), and the resulting splitting or fragmenting of self that can occur. When an individual experiences the terror of abuse or neglect, especially at the hands of someone they love, they need enough distance from the event in order to remain somewhat intact and whole. Distance is created through splitting or fragmentation of self. This distancing ultimately results in splintering off the "bad" (victim) self that experienced the trauma, because holding that memory as part of self is too difficult and overwhelming (Fisher 2017). The "good" self that remains often feels not fully real or authentic. This, coupled with the threat of danger or abuse in the adult relationship, makes authenticity almost impossible and inauthenticity extremely easy to slip into, and at times even useful and helpful in minimizing the level of threat.

In a study of 123 survivors of intimate partner violence (Flasch, Murray, and Crowe 2015), researchers found that a central theme to the healing and recovery journey included regaining and recreating a person's identity through the process of reclaiming lost parts of self and learning to love their self again. Some participants in this study described completely losing any sense of self during the abuse, as if the violence obliterated any knowledge or understanding they had previously had about who they were prior to the abusive relationship. As a result, the healing journey was a gradual rebuilding and rediscovery of self and of the parts that had been lost.

VARIOUS OUTCOMES

Relationship inauthenticity can look different for each individual; the controlling nature of perpetrators of relationship abuse can exacerbate the victim's need to compromise parts of self. In addition, some abusive or controlling behaviors can actually seem flattering in the early stages of a new relationship. For example, being pulled into the center of someone's life and wanting to spend every moment with a new partner can feel good and even loving in the beginning, but smothering and controlling months later. Imani gave up time with friends and ceased to develop those relationships. She also foreclosed on her postgraduate career goals. Imani's story is one example of relationship inauthenticity; for others, relationship inauthenticity can occur through the loss of hobbies, cherished activities, values, beliefs, or spiritual practices. It can also involve the loss of statuses or roles, such as when an individual is forced to take on a parenting role or, conversely, forfeiting the dream of being a parent one day.

Relationship authenticity is enhanced when we are present-focused and open to revealing our true selves within a relationship. In order to do this, we must, first, know ourselves well and be comfortable with who we are. Second, we must be willing to embrace relationship vulnerability and not shy away or view vulnerability as a weakness. And it helps to find a partner who is emotionally available and responsive to our needs (and their own) as well. The good news for an individual who does not know their true self is that it's never too late to start. People continue to develop throughout life, so knowing your true self is a process, and one that can start at any time.

> **Did you know?**
> **Authenticity and red flags**
> Being open and vulnerable in our relationships can sound risky and even terrifying for survivors of relationship abuse. Because victims of relationship abuse are sometimes low on authenticity, they may easily miss cues that signal red flags in a relationship, resulting in unsafe relationships and potentially new experiences of control or abuse. The safest place to begin this process is with a therapist. A therapist can help survivors of relationship abuse experience the intimacy of a safe relationship that is appropriately boundaried and non-sexual. For many survivors, this will be a new experience. But it is an essential experience and a necessary step in the healing journey. Once a client can experience a safe, secure attachment in therapy, they can begin to generalize that experience and knowledge to their outside relationships. Over time, survivors can learn to show up in their relationships differently than they have in the past, more fully present, more open to being fully seen, more able to respond to red flags, and more willing to express their needs in a reciprocal and engaged relationship.

Another aspect of relationship authenticity is self-acceptance. The same way that healthy romantic relationships grow when love is nurtured, so, too, does our own self-acceptance. In order to truly achieve authenticity within ourselves and within our relationships, we must first *like*, and eventually *accept*, ourselves. The act of self-acceptance engenders feelings of self-worth, which, in turn, provide a preventive force against relationship abuse. If you accept yourself, and believe you are worthy of love, then accepting any behavior that minimizes, destroys, berates, or disrespects that worthy self becomes untenable.

> Sofia knew what she needed. She knew that time alone was one of the ways that she refueled and grounded herself,

especially given the pressures and demands of her job as a social worker. After talking to hurt and wounded people all day, she frequently needed time alone to unwind and reconnect with herself before engaging in social activities. Her new boyfriend, Marco, understood this, and went out of his way to create space for her to be alone and uninterrupted at the end of the day. Sofia was incredibly grateful and cherished their relationship more because of it. It had not always been this way for Sofia. Learning to ask for what she needed did not come easily. Over time, however, she had learned that not speaking out or expressing her needs actually made things worse. It also took some time to find someone who could return that respect. After her relationship with Alfonso had ended, she was initially frightened of dating and didn't trust herself to "pick" the right person. The men she dated were at times a milder version of Alfonso, but still over-controlling; she didn't want to end up in an abusive relationship again. It wasn't until she started investing time in her own development and growth that things changed. She stopped focusing on "getting a man" and decided to find her own happiness, regardless of whether she was with a man or not. That was when things started to change. She went back to school to get her Master's degree in social work, and she met Marco at the graduate student orientation. They connected and had common interests, but she was interested in being patient and seeing what might evolve between them. She enjoyed talking to him and didn't push herself to analyze where the relationship was going. In the past, she might have been scared by the ambiguity of their status. Now, she stayed focused on each moment, and simply enjoyed the budding relationship for what it was. She didn't feel pressured to always say "yes" to Marco, ignoring her own needs and setting aside her own priorities. Instead, she was honest with him, and to her delight, he respected that in her. Sofia felt good about the relationship, and she felt good about herself too. She liked this new version of herself. It felt like she was finally coming home.

Easing into reflection: Relationship authenticity

- Reflect on the relationships in your life, both past and present. What kinds of things have you given up or compromised on in order to be in a relationship? Take a moment and write these things down.

  ....
  ....
  ....
  ....

- As you look at the list you made, are the items internal (parts of you) or external (activities, hobbies, friends)? Take a moment to categorize your list.

  ....
  ....
  ....
  ....

- Now look at your list and consider the following: are there things on your list that you would like to reclaim? Are there losses that you need to grieve?

  ....
  ....
  ....
  ....

ACCOMMODATING SELF ART THERAPY PROJECT: AUTHENTIC SELF SCULPTURE
Purpose
Since relationship authenticity has to do with an individual both knowing who they are, and then living in congruence with their own values, this art activity is designed to help discover, confirm, and clarify aspects of the self. For this project, invite your client to make a piece of art using beads, and some sort of core that will hold things together; this could be wire or string, pipe cleaners or fabric. The beads will be strung or knotted on the core material, and may create some sort of charm, ornament, bracelet, fidgit, zipper pull, or other decoration that can serve as a reminder of qualities that promote authenticity.

This art project is not intended to be a bracelet specifically, but in working with beads, wire, string, and yarn, it often develops into something resembling a bracelet. It is fine to make a bracelet out of their materials, either intentionally or by accidental design. Bracelets have long held significance in many cultures, have been worn by all genders, and have often served as reminders. In recent times, bracelets often hold special personal significance for the wearer. The popularity of bracelets can be traced back to at least 5000 BCE, in Egypt. Throughout history, bracelets have been recorded for use in secular and religious interests, and more specifically for use in marriage contracts, military uniform, personal health, displays of wealth, group identification, and superstitions (Wheat 2023).

In the earlier vignette we saw Imani slowly let go of the things that were important to her and that helped to define her identity. First, she stopped seeing her friends. Then she let go of her career goals, and the educational steps that could have helped to take her there. She stopped singing in the choir, something she loved and that connected her to the arts, her faith, and her community. While no one activity or hobby or even our career defines us completely, they are significant parts of who we are, and speak to underlying values and beliefs that connect us to our authentic selves. If Imani was creating an authentic self sculpture, we might suggest that she choose a bead to represent qualities that she sees in herself, or qualities that she wishes to see. Alternatively, we could ask her to choose a bead that represents each of the things that she gave up in her life (e.g., friends, career goals, choir singing, etc.), things that in some way represented or connected her to her authentic self.

In this project, the beads represent identified facets of self that are woven into the thread of someone's being. We are encouraging survivors of relationship abuse to begin to identify their own needs, and acknowledge what has been sacrificed. In healthy relationships people can often accommodate their partner without denying themselves what they need or repressing who they are. In this project, your client can begin to see what was sacrificed, and assess whether that still holds value for them. They can then decide what they may want to reincorporate.

The authentic self sculpture project consists of beads that represent values or aspects of self; collectively this sculpture serves as a reminder to hold true to those values. The sculpture is a manifestation of the authentic values and aspects of the maker.

Project goals

1. To explore aspects of one's authentic self.
2. To identify pieces of the self that may have been denied, repressed, or sacrificed (by choice or force) in order to optimally maintain the relationship.
3. To evaluate the sacrificed parts of self, and assess if there is value or interest in reincorporation; to mourn the loss of parts of self if necessary (which could be activities or characteristics).
4. To identify values that represent one's authentic self, and eventually activities and pursuits that will have them living in congruence with these values.

Warm-ups

Idea 1, Seven levels deep: Ask the client to draw a line representing the ground across a piece of paper, near the top of the page. Floating in the air above the ground, they should write their question.

This should be a big and important question, such as "What do I want to do next?" or "What is the most important thing now?" or "What do I want out of life?"

Next, on top of the ground (underneath where the question is), they should write the answer to this question. Then they should reframe their answer in the form of a question, and ask themselves that new question. On their piece of paper they next "dig" down underground and write an answer to this new question. When they have that answer, they should reframe it into a new question, and then "dig" down in their drawing to find the answer to that. Ultimately they should have seven levels' deep of questions and corresponding answers that get them closer to the root of the issue.

For example, let's imagine that a person answered the question "What is the most important thing now?" by saying "Safety." The next question may become "Why is safety the most important thing now?" The person's answer to that may be "So that I can be healthy and strong." A new question may emerge asking, "Why is it important to be healthy and strong?" And then the person may answer, "I don't want my kids to see me mistreated or as a victim." This might lead to the question "Why is it important for your kids to not see you mistreated or as a victim?" And that may lead to the answer that "I want to model healthy relationships with myself and others for my kids, and I don't want them to learn that it's okay to let people treat them this way." The goal is to encourage six layers deeper beyond the initial question to help in understanding more of our ultimate "why?" This can be an effective warm-up, but it can also be used as a fuller project.

Idea 2, Discovering the new me: Ask the client to draw three linking rings that overlap, as in the graphic to the right. One of the circles is labeled "Past me," one of the circles "Present me," and one of the circles "Future me." The circle that represents "Past me" should be filled with things that they enjoyed and engaged

with, and that helped them express their authentic self and live in congruence with their values. Imani might include a degree in journalism or singing in the choir. The things listed here may still be a part of their experience, or may have been sacrificed for the relationship. For the "Present me" circle, they should write or draw things that are currently in their life that are representative of who they truly are and what they value. For the "Future me" circle, they should fill the space with writing or drawing about things that they want to pursue or that they would like to try. If they've always wanted to do something, and they're not sure if they'd like it, they should write it down anyway. Maybe they want to learn to play the piano, or get a job, or switch careers, or move to another country. Anything that they've fantasized about that might be a part of their authentic self has a place here. This is not a contract; it's an exploration. Notice that there may be some overlapping of the circles. Is there anything that belongs in more than one circle?

Materials suggested

- Beads
- Wire: 14, 16, or 18 gauge are relatively easy to manipulate
- Needle nose pliers, or jewelry pliers
- Wire cutter (often sold in a set with jewelry pliers)
- String, yarn, or fishing line
- Chenille stems (also called pipe cleaners)
- Scissors

Preparation

Very little preparation is needed, as the process of choosing materials is a significant part of the project. Additionally, inviting your client to assemble their own materials is an opportunity to foster as much agency as possible for this piece. Choosing items to use based on color, size, shape, texture, or patterns can have enormous significance. One of the fascinating aspects of the art-making process is the way that individuals assign meaning to various items that they choose.

Beads are sold in a variety of different materials (e.g., plastic, wooden, glass, metal), sizes, and amounts (e.g., individually, small packages, bags, large tubs). You can buy beads at art supply stores, but also at large chain home goods retailers, and online. Some drug stores and dollar stores have a craft section where you may find beads. You can even make beads somewhat easily out of polymer, air dry clay, noodles, or aluminum foil. If you have the means, including budget and storage, consider buying a 3lb or 5lb tub, which will give you an ample variety of beads including various colors, textures, sizes, and possibly materials.

For the core of the project, the client will want to choose something that is both sturdy and flexible (another great metaphor for a healthy person). We recommend using copper wire if possible. Copper has a color that makes it feel precious and valuable (you can also buy copper-colored wire, which is a cheaper wire made to look like copper). Art wire is now sold in a variety of colors, such as pink, red, blue, and green. Wire is sold by the gauge, which indicates the thickness of it; the thicker the wire, the sturdier it may be, but also more difficult to manipulate. A higher number gauge indicates a thinner wire, while conversely, a lower number gauge indicates a thicker wire (Barst 2013).

The best preparation for this project is having a sufficient variety and display of materials that fosters creativity without being overwhelming. Have a display arranged in an attractive way, and give your client license to make choices in materials freely.

Process

Invite your client to choose five beads that represent aspects of their authentic self. If five beads feels too limiting, allow for a few more. If a client seems overwhelmed by needing to choose five beads, invite them to start with just two. The amount is not the most important factor here—what matters is to foster a sense of agency and confidence. Having the client make a specific and intentional decision about any amount of beads, however that decision is made, is a success. The goal is to help them make that decision and feel a sense of pride in having made it. Varying the amount of chosen materials is an easy way to help the client feel a sense of successful and meaningful decision-making power. They will then ascribe some meaning to each bead, which may come quickly, or with careful deliberation. These may include things that they like and prefer, characteristics of themselves, or relationships that are healthy and supportive. They may also use a connector that has certain qualities and meaning for them. Wire can be shiny or dull, and can be easy or more difficult to bend, cinch, and twist. Beads can be large or small, heavy or light, shiny, round, flat, multifaceted, and many other things. The properties of the beads can often correlate to the properties of the person or become descriptors of their authenticity.

Questions to spark reflection or discussion

- How did you choose your beads and core material?
- Did you have a plan for your sculpture, and work towards that vision, or did you create spontaneously?
- What challenges did you face in creating this piece? In what ways did the art flow more effortlessly?
- What do the beads you chose represent?
- What have you given up in your life in order to please others?
- How have you made yourself small or silent so that others could be big or important?
- What is the significance of your sculpture?

Alternate art therapy project ideas
Alternate art therapy project idea 1: Found object, authentic self sculpture
Authentic self sculptures can be made with almost any material. One approach to 3D art making that we encourage is the use of found objects (including recyclables!). Ask the client to consider

forming a box or bin that includes scrap paper, toilet paper rolls, paper towel cardboard inserts, bottle caps, can tabs, popsicle sticks, or any other miscellaneous materials. If they use things like jar lids or soda can tabs that come off of food materials, they should make sure to wash them first. The rubber bands that come around mail delivery can be recycled. All of these items can be repurposed into a sculpture, with or without the addition of paint. The value of art frequently comes from the meaning we ascribe to it, and humans are exceptional at ascribing meaning to everything! Also, working with found and recycled objects provides a wonderful metaphor for individuals who are coping with trauma and coming out of relationship abuse situations; like the trash materials used here, people frequently feel discarded, devalued, and unwanted. Using recycled materials and giving new meaning and value to objects helps create the powerful metaphor that people, too, are not disposable and can grow anew.

Alternate art therapy project idea 2: Nature-made, authentic self sculpture

Authentic self sculpture making can also be made with natural materials. The client should spend 5–10 minutes walking around outside collecting materials. If they have a yard or a park it is probably full of materials, but even a walk around the block can usually yield plenty of small stones, twigs, leaves, grass, and flowers. They should collect anything that may seem of interest and useful. Discarded materials like bubble gum wrappers and bottle tops may be treasures for this sculpture. Then give the client time to assemble the items outside. Encourage taking a picture of the piece before returning nature to its purest form. Sometimes art is not intended to last forever, but only to remain in our memory (and cell phone cameras).

PROJECT EXAMPLES

In *Hidden* (Figure 8), the artist used a thin 20-gauge wire to string a series of beads with clear and deep purple tones. Importance was given to an inner authentic self and an outer authentic self—one known to the world, and one shown more selectively.

Figure 8: *Hidden*, by Melissa Paolercio (2023)

Pull and Flow (Figure 9) is a sculpture made of woven fabric, string, beads, chenille, and trim. It is amorphic and lacks symmetry, but does not lack organization. In fact, it represents well the deliberate creative and unique authentic self of the artist who chose these contrasting colors of blue and orange, which, in this piece, seamlessly fit.

Figure 9: *Pull and Flow*, by Betsy Weiss (2023)

The artist who made the piece called *Authentically Me* (Figure 10) spoke about her method of choosing beads that reflected aspects of herself. Some of these characteristics were present in her life both during and after her abuse, while others reflected old ways of being, or new skills learned. She chose a mirrored bead that represented learned ways of functioning in relationships that helped her manage stress and conflict. The large, twisted, pink bead reminded her of both clouds and cotton candy; this bead represented a certain dreaminess and a penchant for fantasizing about *what ifs*, and it also represented a certain childlike playfulness and whimsy that she felt and strived to hold on to. The organic brown bead was not completely round and represented a move away from perfectionism, unattainable standards, and harsh judgment.

Figure 10: *Authentically Me*, by an anonymous artist (2018)

REFERENCES

Anonymous artist (2018) *Authentically Me* [Beaded wire bracelet]. Private collection.

Barst, J. (2013) "All about jewelry wire—wire gauge sizes explained." JTHQ (Jewelry Tutorial Headquarters), October 16. https://jewelrytutorialhq.com/jewelry-wire-gauges-explained

Cresci, M.B. (2019) "Winnicott's True Self/False Self Concept: Using Countertransference to Uncover the True Self." In B. Willock, I. Sapountzis, and R.C. Curtis (eds) *Psychoanalytic Perspectives on Knowing and Being Known: In Theory and Clinical Practice* (Chapter 10). Abingdon: Routledge.

Dube, S.R., Anda, R.F., Whitfield, C.L., Brown, D.W., *et al.* (2005) "Long-term consequences of childhood sexual abuse by gender of victim." *American Journal of Preventive Medicine 28*, 5, 430–438. https://doi.org/10.1016/j.amepre.2005.01.015

Fisher, J. (2017) *Healing the Fragmented Selves of Trauma Survivors*. Abingdon: Routledge.

Flasch, P., Murray, C.E., and Crowe, A. (2015) "Overcoming abuse: A phenomenological investigation of the journey to recovery from past intimate partner violence." *Journal of Interpersonal Violence 32*, 22, 3373–3401. https://doi.org/10.1177/0886260515599161

Fleming, J., Mullen, P.E., Sibthorpe, B., and Bammer, G. (1999) "The long-term impact of childhood sexual abuse in Australian women." *Child Abuse & Neglect 23*, 2, 145–159. https://doi.org/10.1016/S0145-2134(98)00118-5

Gil-Or, O., Levi-Belz, Y., and Turel, O. (2015) "The 'Facebook-self': Characteristics and psychological predictors of false self-presentation on Facebook." *Frontiers in Psychology 6*. https://doi.org/10.3389/fpsyg.2015.00099

Neff, K.D. and Suizzo, M.-A. (2006) "Culture, power, authenticity and psychological well-being within romantic relationships: A comparison of European American and Mexican Americans." *Cognitive Development 21*, 4, 441–457. https://doi.org/10.1016/j.cogdev.2006.06.008

Paolercio, M. (2023) *Hidden* [Beading]. Private collection.

Wang, Y.N. (2016) "Balanced authenticity predicts optimal well-being: Theoretical conceptualization and empirical development of the authenticity in relationships scale." *Personality & Individual Differences 94*, 316–323. https://doi.org/10.1016/j.paid.2016.02.001

Weiss, E. (2023) *Pull and Flow* [Beaded fabric]. Private collection.

Wheat, M. (2023) "The history and cultural significance of the wrist bracelet." WristCo. www.wristco.com/wristband-articles/history-cultural-significance-of-wrist-bracelet

Winnicott, D.W. (1960) "Ego Distortion in Terms of True and False Self." In D.W. Winnicott (ed.) *The Maturational Processes and the Facilitating Environment: Studies in the Theory of Emotional Development* (pp.140–152). New York: Karnac Books.

Chapter 10

SELF-TALK

Lissa sat down on the edge of her bed and sighed. She looked down at the peach comforter, and recalled how much she had loved it on sight in the store, and how Jack had belittled her when she brought it home. "You actually spent money on that?! You have no taste," he had said. It was just another thing she had gotten wrong.

Now, as she sat and reflected on the latest incident, the conflict she had had with her supervisor at work, she could hear Jack's voice in her head, "You're a stupid woman, Lissa. You just don't know how to handle people." She had hoped to get some support from him, but it didn't come. Nothing she did was ever good enough. She could feel the sting of familiar tears and that same old ache in her chest. She knew she should try just a little bit harder; he was right that she didn't know how to handle people. But no matter what she did, she always had these situations that caused her distress and he was often reminding her of how inept she was in navigating these interpersonal relations. "If you didn't have me helping you, you would never be anything," he would say. Jack was right. "I just mess stuff up!" she muttered as she hung her head and began to cry.

A common outcome of experiencing relationship abuse is the internalization of the abuser's negative messages about the victim, resulting in severe or extreme negative self-talk. Self-talk, sometimes called inner speech or verbal thinking, has been linked to self-regulation, and can impact behavior and emotion (Beck,

Steer, and Brown 1996; Ellis and Maclaren 2005; Meichenbaum 1977; Vygotsky 1986). Long-term exposure to negative self-talk can have a profound impact on emotional wellbeing (Latinjak *et al.* 2019).

Internalized negative messages often become deeply embedded in the psyche, and tend to run automatically or exist outside of an individual's conscious awareness. Negative self-talk can erode self-esteem and damage someone's sense of self and individuality. The insidious nature of such internalized messages can be challenging to address, especially when they are related to traumas that occurred during key developmental periods in an individual's life. Bringing awareness to the nature of such messages is essential to the healing and recovery journey from relationship abuse. We do this by, first, learning to recognize them, and second, by challenging or reframing them into more adaptive, positive messages.

The concept of self-talk, however, is more profound than the act of identifying and challenging negative messages. It is also connected to the use of voice as a means of reclaiming empowerment. The shift from listening to "other" to listening to "self" is in itself empowering in that it helps us connect to self-wisdom, intuition, and inner resources that have been untapped, ignored, or left unattended due to the abuse. It is the move toward subjective knowing, as described by the authors in *Women's Ways of Knowing* (Belenky *et al.* 1986). It is a move away from silence or passive absorption of "externally oriented perspective on knowledge" to a "new concept of truth as personal, private, and subjectively known or intuited" (1986, p.54). It is a self-driven renegotiation of identity in which the individual becomes their own authority.

Did you know?
Learning self-talk
We learn so much from our primary caregivers; indeed, some of our negative self-talk messages may originate there. Many messages that we hear as we learn, grow, and develop are internalized. It often starts from people who hold a place of power or authority in our life, but we may

> internalize messages from anyone we see as valid, valuable, or espousing a truth: a teacher, a doctor, a playground bully. Depending on how much authority a message is delivered with, and how much self-worth is held by the person it's delivered to, that message may live long in the psyche. Internalized messages are not always negative, and self-talk can promote positive messages, too.
>
> We can grow into a deeper level of self-acceptance by being in a relationship that is validating, affirming, and where love is given freely. For some, this might be a therapeutic relationship, and for others an intimate partnership. The expectation that we must challenge and change our negative self-talk in order to love and accept ourselves might ignore the fact that many of us can learn positive self-talk through the loving acceptance we experience in relationships with other individuals who are safe and validating. Working on self-talk in therapy through the use of the Empowerment Wheel model can help promote internalization of positive messages.

Survivors of relationship abuse would benefit from more research that examines the impact of negative self-talk, and related concepts such as self-compassion, on their experience and their subsequent move toward empowerment. One study that examined the impact of self-compassion support groups on outcomes such as autonomy, emotional restoration, and safety found that depression and anxiety decreased, and that there was an increase in autonomy, ability to obtain resources, and overall wellbeing for the 251 shelter residents in their study (Allen, Robertson, and Patin 2021). Self-compassion consists of three interrelated components: self-kindness, common humanity, and mindfulness. This was the first study to look at the impact of self-compassion for survivors of relationship abuse living in a shelter setting. Self-talk is a related concept to self-compassion in that self-kindness would not be possible without some awareness and redirection of negative self-talk. We can apply insight from this research to Lissa's case.

> Lissa's awareness of her inner critic increased as she spent time in therapy detailing her difficult and traumatic past. With the help of her therapist and the Empowerment Wheel model, she began to connect key experiences with the development of blocking beliefs about herself that had been at the core of many of her relational experiences. For example, Lissa was able to connect the belief that she was worthless to several of her adult relationships and to the fact that her mother had divorced her father and moved out of the home when Lissa was six years old. Lissa's father then began drinking, resulting in Lissa being raised by her paternal grandmother, who was also taking care of her adult, intellectually disabled, uncle. Lissa's needs were often secondary to everyone else's in the family, and Lissa spent a lot of time wondering what she had done wrong that had resulted in her being treated so poorly. Her adult relationships echoed this theme, and many of the men she dated and committed to eventually treated her as disposable and unworthy of their time and attention. Even though Lissa began to understand the connection between her relational experiences and her beliefs about herself, shaking the belief that she was disposable was difficult for her to do. For several years, Lissa struggled to redefine this belief about herself. She often heard Jack's words in her head. She ruminated on the words of her grandmother, telling her, "It's not all about you, you know." In therapy, Lissa learned to acknowledge these messages when they arose, but not to give them additional power by reinforcing them with her own voice. Dismantling these messages took time, but eventually Lissa learned to challenge her negative self-talk. Slowly, over time, she developed more compassion and understanding for herself as well.

Easing into reflection: Self-talk

- Take a moment and think about a time when you felt anxious. Listen to the automatic thoughts that run through your mind as you reflect on that time. What are you telling yourself? Write the thoughts you had about yourself down.

  ....
  ....
  ....
  ....

- Now take a look at your list and ask yourself: Whose voice do you hear when you read these thoughts? How does it feel to read these thoughts? Where in your body do you feel those feelings?

  ....
  ....
  ....
  ....

- Choose the most distressing thought and restate it in a positive way. How does it feel to read this new thought? Where in your body do you feel this feeling?

  ....
  ....
  ....
  ....

SELF-TALK ART THERAPY PROJECT: FINDING OWN VOICE
Purpose

Making art is an effective way to externalize our internal dialogue. Self-talk is often unconscious and so pervasive that individuals may not realize how ingrained toxic messages have become. Giving form to this self-talk brings these messages into consciousness and helps someone better understand the way that they are communicating with themselves.

The art therapy literature generally advocates for helping clients to find their voice through art, including the externalization of inner dialogue. One study gave form through interviews and artwork to elderly Japanese-Americans held in US internment camps during World War II. Participants had internalized the negative message that they were enemy aliens, which, over time, evolved into personal concern for the discrimination of other minority groups marginalized by war. In this study, art therapy helped give voice to the burdens carried by these Japanese-American survivors of internment camps, as well as to the actions launched by it (Yates *et al.* 2007).

Carr (2020) helped to give voice to fragile, terminally ill patients through the art of portraiture, when they were too weak to make their own art. Lark (2005) discussed the limitation of spoken English faced by clients in therapeutic groups addressing racism. She included art making in the large group dialogue technique to promote greater accessibility for clients. She suggested that art making as an expressive tool may present more equality of voice for participants (Lark 2005). Another group of authors led a series of art therapy groups that developed and resulted in the creation of a collaborative zine. Houpt *et al.* (2016) asserted that participation in the zine art therapy group increased creative development and connection among the elderly clients, and ultimately gave voice to the undervalued and overlooked members of the nursing home community. A similar goal, but a different art therapy process, led Majaj and colleagues (2020) to use an embodied art therapy process to promote autonomy, self-awareness, and an assertion of voice in a single child client. A common thread in these studies is the goal of promoting voice in the clients. The use of someone's voice is generally equated in therapy with positive self-esteem, good self-awareness, and feelings of competence and empowerment.

Our inner voice and dialogue can also appear as an inner critic. Self-talk can be affirmative, but this is not unusually the self-talk that gets attention in therapy. While criticism can be helpful and formative, it is generally powerfully negative when contextualized by the inner critic. Haeyen and Heijman (2020) incorporated an inner critic-targeted intervention into their compassion-focused art therapy treatment protocol. In this intervention, clients were invited to create visual replies to textual inner critic messages. Another author suggests writing with the non-dominant hand as both a warm-up and an exercise in challenging the authority of the inner critic (Martinez Barrio 2020). One thesis proposes using self-portraiture with older adults as a tool that helps to identify and overcome the judgment of their inner critic (Echeverry 2023). Ricks (2014) conducted an arts-based study with 12 female adults over 55 years old where she encouraged meaning making from experiences with their inner critic and their sacred voice (an inner source of wisdom that is suppressed to accommodate a culture that marginalizes women's inherent knowledge). Participants were guided in a process of self-reflection and analysis toward a goal of confronting their inner critic (Ricks 2014).

There are many books, articles, and workbooks that espouse the benefits of identifying, understanding, and overcoming the inner critic. It is seen in therapy as a beneficial, if not essential, task to promote wellness, positive self-talk, and ultimately raise self-esteem. Stinckens, Lietaer, and Leijssen (2013) promote a flexible approach that considers the nature and intensity of that individual critic as the optimal way to promote successful negotiations.

Survivors of relationship abuse often experience having internalized the voice of their abusive partner. In many cases, things that they have been told continue to play in a continuous loop inside their head, sometimes outside of their active awareness. Art making can help facilitate cognitive processing and reframing, so that a person can contextualize the messages they are constantly subjected to, and develop a sense of control and empowerment.

Project goals

1. To identify the messages associated with self-talk.
2. To understand the origin of the messages in self-talk, as well as contextualize them.
3. To begin the procedure of reprocessing and reframing the self-talk messages one hears.

Warm-ups

Idea 1, Draw your inner critic: Invite your client to give form to their inner critic by drawing it. Have them create an image of that being whose voice they hear in their head. Using any 2D art materials (or sculpt with 3D art materials), ask them to consider what the maker of that voice inside them looks like. This can be a great way to externalize that voice and underscore that a person is not the messages that they give to themselves. Some clients find benefit in depicting their critic as nasty, or scary, or even silly. This can be a time to highlight that the critic who is always judging is also not a depiction of perfection. Some clients may notice a resemblance between the critic they create and those they know from real life. This could be a point of reflection, discussion, and can even spur some journaling or further artwork. If your client is ready for confrontation, you might invite them to talk back to this inner critic that has fed them such harsh messages.

Idea 2, Draw with limitation: Invite your client to make a drawing with their eyes closed. If this is uncomfortable for them, suggest that they use their non-dominant hand in drawing. The idea here is to create some amount of tolerable discomfort. Allow 3–5 minutes to create a piece of art in this personally altered state. Encourage the client to pay close attention to how it feels in their body to create with this new change, and what messages they are noticing in their mind. The goal is not to steer a particular kind of thought at this time, but to notice what thoughts arise. Suggest that the client tune in to hone their understanding of the sort of messages that they are telling themselves, both constructive and critical.

Materials suggested

- White paper, 8½ x 11 inches, or 14 x 17 inches
- Graphite pencil and eraser
- Marker pens
- Colored pencils
- Scissors
- Glue sticks
- Magazines, cut paper, and miscellaneous collage material (old brochures, marketing material, maps, and junk mail can sometimes provide great tools for collage)

Preparation

This project is about inviting reflection on those internalized messages, the self-talk loop that plays in the client's head, and the inner critic whose judgment has been inescapable. With these ideas as a catalyst, the client is invited to create a drawing and/or collage that explores what self-talk looks like for them. While the experience of self-talk may be universal, the way it manifests in each person is highly individual. The person may want to examine the nuance of their own self-talk by considering frequency, intensity, variation of voice or message, volume, quotations, and subliminal messaging. While this piece could have greater structure imposed on it, there is also great benefit in the creative process of having directives that are broad in nature and allow for the maximum personal choice and direction.

This project has been proposed with limited materials here, but given the space, time, and budget could involve a greater choice of materials. Some clients may benefit from more complex or simply different materials. In Figure 12 we see an example that was made with acrylic paint on canvas, a medium with which this particular artist was comfortable. This may be a point of discussion if you are not sure what material may best spark your client's comfort and creativity.

Process

Assemble your materials in an attractive presentation. Invite your client to reflect on the inner messages that they hear. The short warm-ups may help stimulate consideration of their own self-talk. Let the client know that this artwork is about giving form to the self-talk that they hear. They can also give form through image making of the feelings that come up for them when they hear their internal self-talk. Some individuals can easily access their self-talk and internal messages; this internal discussion may be so prolific in them that it does not take too much time to get there. If your client is experiencing a hard time accessing their self-talk messages, encourage them to sit in silence for a few minutes. Closed eyes or downcast gaze may help this. Sometimes feeling like you are supposed to be doing something, and not knowing what to do, can generate the perfect circumstances for negative self-talk and inner critic messages to arise. When that happens, it is good fodder for the therapeutic space; encourage discussion about this with your client.

Questions to spark reflection or discussion

- How did you start your art making?
- At what point in your creative process did you notice self-talk, your inner voice, or an inner critic? How pervasive was this voice/talk? What messages were being conveyed?
- What challenges did you face in creating this piece?
- Does your inner critic or inner voice resemble any person or people that you know or knew?
- Can you think of a person or people in your life whose voice has been supportive, or even buoyant? What kinds of things does that person/people say?

Alternate art therapy project ideas
Alternate art therapy project idea 1:
Blind contour drawing
Ask your client to try creating a drawing using the "blind contour" technique. This is a form of drawing from life where you look only at the object or person that you are drawing, and not at your paper (Hill 2019; Skill Share 2021). This technique was made famous in art therapy through the work of Elizabeth "Grandma" Layton (n.d.), a chronically depressed woman from Kansas who did not start making art until she was 68 years old. After years of futile attempts to address her major mental health issues, she worked with an art therapist and developed a love for blind contour drawing, and specifically self-portraits. She described rough beginnings with this technique, as her hand–eye coordination developed, but ultimately became a celebrated artist, and credited art with saving her life (Layton *et al.* 1984). Layton's work and story have inspired many to try blind contour drawing and to consider the benefits of incorporating art making in therapy. Layton's work can be a great stimulus, since her drawings and paintings are so rich with detail and emotion. Remind your client if they are frustrated by the blind contour drawing process that expecting perfection or even success on first tries may negate the learning process. Hand–eye coordination is a neuromuscular process that is strengthened with exercise.

Alternate art therapy project idea 2: Speech and thought
Another idea that you might consider for making artwork that will examine self-talk and inner critic messages is artwork that includes speech and thought bubbles. Made famous in the art world by artist Roy Lichtenstein (2022), speech and thought bubbles correlated with the pop art movement, and the rise in popularity of graphic novels and cartoon storytelling. Invite your client to create a depiction of themselves—it could be a stick figure, a full person, or a magazine cut-out, or they can use a metaphor to depict themselves as an animal, object, or action. Consider how self-talk could arise through the use of speech and thought bubbles. Look at the relationship between the artwork and the speech and thought bubbles. Invite your client

to consider a response to the speech and thought bubbles, or to identify if there is a response apparent in the image.

PROJECT EXAMPLES

In Figure 11, we see a bold piece that includes drawing, text, and collage. The artist here incorporated caution tape as a collage item (see Chapter 7). She also used black tape to delineate messages that she sends herself ("I am beautiful") from messages that were said to her ("No one will ever want you!"). She described the struggle of carrying this burden and the unlearning of unconsciously internalized messages.

Figure 11: Untitled, by Makeiah Milbourne (2023)

Figure 12 is an acrylic on canvas painting that exemplifies the physical and figurative pain of finding your voice. In this painting, the uvula (the pink fleshy ball that hangs in the back of the throat), which is an organ of speech, is visibly stitched up, promoting the assumption that it was previously lacerated. The uvula here is stylized as a heart, and has a drop that evokes a tear rolling down it. The viewer is looking into the void of an open mouth, perhaps staring at a scream, or maybe silence. Or maybe of an individual who is just finding their voice.

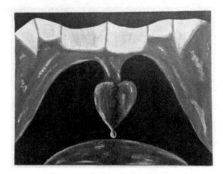

Figure 12: *Finding Your Voice*, by Rachel Woerner (2023)

REFERENCES

Allen, A.B., Robertson, E., and Patin, G.A. (2021) "Improving emotional and cognitive outcomes for domestic violence survivors: The impact of shelter stay and self-compassion support groups." *Journal of Interpersonal Violence 36*, 1–2, NP598–NP624. doi: 10.1177/0886260517734858

Beck, A.T., Steer, R.A., and Brown, G.K. (1996) *Manual for the Beck Depression Inventory-II*. New York: Psychological Corporation.

Belenky, M.F., Clinchy, B.M., Goldberger, N.R., and Tarule, J.M. (1985) *Women's Ways of Knowing*. New York: Basic Books, Inc.

Carr, S.M.D. (2020) "Portrait therapy: Supporting client voices of self-identity." *Art Therapy 37*, 4, 177–184. https://doi.org/10.1080/07421656.2020.1827879

Echeverry, B. (2023) "Overcoming the Inner Critic: The Therapeutic Use of Self-Portraits with Older Adults." Expressive Therapies Capstone Theses, 754. https://digitalcommons.lesley.edu/expressive_theses/754

Ellis, A. and Maclaren, C. (2005) *Rational Emotive Behavior Therapy* (3rd edn). Oakland, CA: Impact Publishers.

Haeyen, S. and Heijman, J. (2020) "Compassion focused art therapy for people diagnosed with a cluster B/C personality disorder: An intervention mapping study." *The Arts in Psychotherapy 69*, 101663. https://doi.org/10.1016/j.aip.2020.101663

Hill, E. (2019) "How blind contour drawing can help you become a better artist." Creativity, January 17. www.artsy.net/article/artsy-editorial-blind-contour-drawing-help-better-artist

Houpt, K., Balkin, L.A., Broom, R.H., Roth, A.G., and Selma (2016) "Anti-memoir: Creating alternate nursing home narratives through zine making." *Art Therapy 33*, 3, 128–137. https://doi.org/10.1080/07421656.2016.1199243

Lark, C.V. (2005) "Using art as language in large group dialogues: The TRECsm model." *Art Therapy 22*, 1, 24–31. https://doi.org/10.1080/07421656.2005.10129458

Latinjak, A.T., Hatzigeorgiadis, A., Comoutos, N., and Hardy, J. (2019) "Speaking clearly...10 years on: The case for an integrative perspective of self-talk in sport." *Sport, Exercise, and Performance Psychology 8*, 4, 353–367. https://doi.org/10.1037/spy0000160

Layton, E. (no date) "Elizabeth 'Grandma' Layton: Accomplished friend, sister, wife, mother, social activist, and artist." www.elizabethlayton.com

Layton, E., Lambert, D., Bretz, L., and Burdick, S. (1984) *Through the Looking Glass: Drawings by Elizabeth Layton*. Kansas City, MO: Mid-America Arts Alliance.

Majaj, L., Lay, R.P.M.H., and Iyer, M. (2020) "The Embodied Art Therapy Process (TEATP): A single case study surfacing a young child's voice." *Art Therapy 37*, 4, 201–207. https://doi.org/10.1080/07421656.2020.1823784

Martinez Barrio, B. (2020) "Peace Treaty: A Dialogue Between the Critical Voice and the Creative Voice." In E. Maisel (ed.) *The Creativity Workbook for Coaches and Creatives: 50+ Inspiring Exercises from Creativity Coaches Worldwide* (Chapter 18). Abingdon: Routledge.

Meichenbaum, D. (1977) *Cognitive-Behavior Modification: An Integrative Approach.* New York: Springer.

Milbourne, M. (2023) Untitled [Drawing with collage]. Private collection.

Ricks, C.F. (2014) "Voices of the Heart: A Woman's Journey into the Mirror of Self to Embrace the Gifts of Her Inner Critic." ProQuest Dissertations & Theses Global, 1641121023. www.proquest.com/dissertations-theses/voices-heart-womans-journey-into-mirror-self/docview/1641121023/se-2

Roy Lichtenstein Foundation (2022) "Biography." https://lichtensteinfoundation.org/biography

Skill Share (2021) "How to make blind contour drawings (and why you should)." Skill Share Blog, March 26. www.skillshare.com/blog/en/how-to-make-blind-contour-drawings-and-why-you-should

Stinckens, N., Lietaer, G., and Leijssen, M. (2013) "Working with the inner critic: Therapeutic approach." *Person-Centered & Experiential Psychotherapies 12*, 2, 141–156. https://doi.org/10.1080/14779757.2013.767751

Vygotsky, L.S. (1986) *Thought and Language.* Cambridge, MA: The MIT Press.

Woerner, R. (2023) Untitled [Acrylic on canvas]. Private collection.

Yates, C., Kuwada, K., Potter, P., Cameron, D., and Hoshino, J. (2007) "Image making and personal narratives with Japanese-American survivors of World War II internment camps." *Art Therapy 24*, 3, 111–118. https://doi.org/10.1080/07421656.2007.10129422

Chapter 11

INTEGRATED SELF

Zoe woke up early, grabbed a few clothing items, and quietly tiptoed out of the bedroom. She didn't want to wake Billy, her boyfriend of several years. In the hall she put on a light jacket, leggings, and running shoes. She did some light stretches, put in her earbuds, grabbed her phone, and turned on some music. Then she quietly left the house and headed out for a run.

It was a glorious morning, the trees were budding after a long winter, and the smell of blossom and new growth was in the air. Zoe could hear her feet slapping out a rhythm on the pavement. She focused on the sound of her feet and the light, breezy music on her phone. She pushed out the memories from the last week, the tension she felt about Billy—when he was there or gone, the argument with her co-worker Jill, and the way her boss frowned when she submitted that last report. She needed all of that, including the guilt and blame of it, which was always nipping at her heels, to be far away and behind her. With every slap of her feet, she felt further removed from it. She picked up her pace and tried to focus on her breathing, the slap of her feet, the music. She lost herself in the running and everything else started to fade. She felt the burning in her lungs and legs, but ignored it and pushed harder. A little pain in her legs would not stop her. "It's normal to be out of breath when you run," she rationalized. "Pick up the pace," she told herself. A faster song came on and she used that to push her body into higher gear.

"You can't outrun your past Zoe," she heard in her mind.

It was the same thing she had said to her therapist in session last week. She tried to push it away. She pushed her legs harder still. With a sharp cry, the emergency brake on her legs was activated. She skidded to a stop as it all came crashing in on her. Zoe bent over, breathing, panting, hands on her knees. She was shaking, on fire, and tired. But she would not stop today.

Zoe stood up. "I don't have time for this right now," she thought. She steeled herself, started running again, and picked up her pace. "Not now" was all she could think. "Not now, not now, not now." Zoe pushed herself again. "Keep going," she thought. "Just keep going."

The correlation between childhood abuse and adult relationship abuse has been firmly established (Coid *et al.* 2005; Dube *et al.* 2005; Fleming *et al.* 1999; Ørke, Bjørkly, and Vatnar 2022). In fact, adult revictimization is one of the more common, long-term consequences of childhood abuse. Victims of abuse, and especially those who experienced early childhood abuse in addition to revictimization as adults, often experience the fragmentation of ego states that can make feeling whole or integrated extremely challenging. The very experience of trauma is the experience of fragmenting parts of the self. Herman (1992, p.158) said it best when she stated, "While patients with simple posttraumatic stress disorder fear they may be losing their minds, patients with the complex disorder often feel they have lost themselves." We fragment or compartmentalize those experiences that are too burdensome to hold by splitting the "self" into "good" and "bad" parts. Fisher (2017, p.19) explains:

> Preserving some modicum of self-esteem, attachment to family, and hope for the future requires victims to disconnect from what has happened, doubt or disremember their experience, and disown the "bad [victim] child" to whom it has happened as "not me". By holding out some sense of themselves as "good" disconnected from how they have been exploited, abused children capitalize on the human brain's innate capacity to split or compartmentalize.

The terms "fragmenting," "compartmentalizing," "shattering," and "splitting" all speak to this phenomenon. While they are often used interchangeably, we have chosen to use the terms "fragmenting" and "compartmentalizing" to describe the dissociation that occurs in the aftermath of severe distress or trauma.

Compartmentalization can be an effective coping strategy, but, like all coping strategies, it often outlives its usefulness once the crisis is over. Multiple coping tools allow for more optimal functioning, since not every situation calls for the same tool. In order to maintain the delicate balance of this fragmented state, victims must continue to deny or dissociate from the "not me" part long after the traumatic event has ended. Eventually they begin to feel that their presentation to the world in which they live and function is only a single part of who they truly are, with other, more distressing parts of self being relegated to outer consciousness. This, in turn, impacts their ability to be fully present in any given situation. It can also negatively influence learning trajectories as well as intra- and inter-personal relationship awareness and growth (Czerny, Lassiter, and Lim 2018; Fisher 2017).

The fragmentation of self as a coping strategy is a form of dissociation. Dissociation can occur in mild or more severe forms. For example, if you've ever had the experience of driving somewhere and realizing when you arrived that you really weren't paying attention to the road or directions at all, that you were on auto-pilot and somehow managed to get safely to your destination anyway, then you've experienced a rather mild form of dissociation. For survivors of relationship abuse, dissociation can provide much needed and welcome relief from suffering. We can dissociate from thoughts, feelings, emotions, or identity as a means of protecting ourselves from distressing experiences. In her book *What My Bones Know*, Stephanie Foo (2022) describes how for years she dissociated from her emotions as a way of protecting herself from the truth of her childhood. Her form of dissociation was adaptive; she used school, work, and accomplishment as a way to distract from years of abuse and neglect by her parents. When a therapist finally explained dissociation to her and asked if she recognized dissociation as one of her ways of coping, she answered "no." At the time, she did not understand how closed off her emotional experience was to her, and nor did she understand that being emotionally numb is also a form of dissociation. It was only when she engaged in eye movement desensitization and reprocessing (EMDR) in therapy that she began to understand how fragmented parts of herself had remained hidden as a means to survival and functioning.

What Foo experienced is a form of structural dissociation, which can be described as "a deficiency in the cohesiveness and flexibility of the personality structure" (van der Hart, Nijenhuis, and Steele 2006, p.4). Structural dissociation is understood on a continuum from mild (primary), to moderate (secondary), and severe (tertiary) forms of dissociation. Primary structural dissociation often results in a diagnosis of acute stress disorder or single-incident PTSD. Secondary structural dissociation might look more like CPTSD or having borderline tendencies. In severe cases, tertiary structural dissociation can result in a rigid demarcation of the ego, as can be seen in individuals diagnosed with dissociative identity disorder (APA 2022). In Zoe's case, she demonstrates behaviors that would likely indicate secondary structural dissociation. Before she started her journey toward recovery, Zoe's complex PTSD symptoms manifested in excessive behaviors.

> **Breakout box: Flow vs. dissociation**
> The concept of "flow" (Nakamura and Csikszentmihalyi 2002) is associated with wellbeing and positive emotional states, whereas dissociation is typically associated with poor emotional wellbeing (Wanner et al. 2006). Flow, or being in the "zone," occurs when we immerse ourselves so deeply in a task that we reach a state of optimal performance and, similar to a dissociative state, lose track of time and space (Gold and Ciorciari 2020). The similarities between flow and dissociation overlap enough that it might be difficult to distinguish whether you are experiencing flow or dissociation. In spite of the similarities, dissociation and flow seem to operate as different mental processes (Thomson and Jaque 2012). What delineates flow from dissociation is that flow requires a situation wherein skill and some

level of enjoyment of the task are necessary. Flow may be connected to states of curiosity and creativity (Schutte and Malouff 2020). There is a fair amount of literature supporting the experience of flow in sports, creative efforts, and even gaming (Csikszentmihalyi 1996; Jackson *et al.* 1998; Smith *et al.* 2017).

One difference between flow and dissociation is intention. Dissociation happens as a result of emotional and psychological overwhelm or by being triggered by something that reminds you of something distressing. Flow, on the other hand, results from engaging in an enjoyable activity and choosing to participate. The simple act of choosing to engage in a certain activity doesn't guarantee that you'll experience flow, however, and nor does experiencing psychological overwhelm always result in dissociation.

For those who can access flow states, there may be an added benefit to losing oneself in an endeavor that is pleasurable, rewarding, and all-consuming (Csikszentmihalyi 1996; Franklin and Siemon 2008). Being in flow can help develop and build inner resources, such as someone's ability to tolerate ambiguity and frustrations that are inherent in the creative process. Accessing flow states doesn't mean that problems won't emerge, but rather that the process of addressing problems happens more fluidly.

You may want to take some time to reflect on your own experiences of dissociation versus flow. Ask yourself the following questions: Is dissociation and flow familiar to you? If you have experienced a flow state, how did it feel? What was the context in which you experienced flow? What are some ways that might allow you to experience flow again?

Healing occurs when victims move away from fragmentation toward integration. It involves learning to love and accept all parts of the self, including those parts that led to structural dissociation. It includes finding one's voice again (or perhaps for the first time) and nurturing or developing inner wisdom as a resource to reconnect to your full self.

Depending on the age of onset, complexity, and duration of the traumatic events that occurred, the journey toward integration of self can take a significant amount of time. While we do not believe that the activities in this chapter are meant to replace the psychotherapy that victims suffering from PTSD, CPTSD, or developmental trauma may need, we do believe that activities that help victims reconnect with lost parts of self can be helpful to the healing journey and facilitate an increase in inter- and intrapersonal awareness that is a necessary part of the process (see also Chapter 12).

> For Zoe, who we met at the beginning of this chapter, healing came slowly. Zoe had had a difficult childhood, witnessing her parents' constant fighting. The arguments frequently escalated into physical violence. Zoe's mother was determined to leave her father, but that process took multiple attempts, and Zoe lived in various domestic violence and homeless shelters throughout her youth. By the time her mother finally managed to leave permanently, Zoe was a teenager and had started down her own path of self-destruction. She started drinking at an early age, and ended up being abused by her first boyfriend at age 17. At that point Zoe's mother was more stable and tried to help, but Zoe was angry and resentful and determined to make her own way in the world. By the time she was 20, Zoe was alone and scared and living in a domestic violence shelter on her own. A counselor at the shelter started talking to Zoe about recovery, and she went to her first Alcoholics Anonymous (AA) meeting at age 21. She also found a therapist, Diedre, who specialized in working with trauma. Zoe was finally taking steps toward her own healing journey. Diedre helped Zoe identify her anxiety and her need to push forward in spite of what she was feeling. Through Diedre, Zoe learned to develop more affect tolerance, and together they practiced grounding and containment techniques. Zoe continued to work on her recovery and found a job at a local coffee shop. She also took

up running, which she was surprised to learn that she really enjoyed.

It took almost two years of stabilization work before Zoe and Diedre could begin to process the trauma of her past. Through the use of EMDR and ego state therapy, Zoe was able to acknowledge and accept the pain of her childhood. The first time Diedre asked Zoe to imagine her younger self, Zoe had resisted, stating that she hated that version of herself. That little girl was partly to blame for everything. She was selfish and bad. If only she could have been better at mitigating her father's moods and protecting her mother, perhaps then her parents would have loved her more. With Diedre's help, though, Zoe was eventually able to see that a lot of the pain and guilt she carried wasn't really hers to own. She blamed herself for things that were not her fault. She began to make small adjustments in the way she engaged with others; she was less needy and more comfortable in her own skin. Now, when she thought of that younger version of herself, she felt compassion and love for her.

Zoe dated different men during this time. A lot of them weren't much better than her father. But with each relational experience, she learned more about herself, and about what she wanted and didn't want in a relationship. There came a point where Zoe began to see her own worth, and she rejected relationships that didn't conform to that.

Zoe continued to run as a way to de-stress, but she no longer pushed herself past pain or discomfort. She listened to her body and responded with gentleness. When a knee injury sidelined her from running for a month, she was frustrated, but she respected the limits of her body. She did this in her relationships, too; she paid attention to red flags and adjusted her boundaries accordingly. And she didn't feel bad about doing that either! Her emotions and reactions were her body's way of talking to her, and she listened. She didn't have to buffer or drown her emotions in alcohol. In AA meetings, Zoe often shared parts of her journey. Women would walk up to her after the meetings ended and talk with her, often amazed that she was capable of opening up with such honesty. She completed her own 12-step journey and became a sponsor for other women. Over time, Zoe began to see that her trauma didn't define her. It was one strand of a much larger collection of strands that, when combined, created her identity. She often envisioned these strands coming together to create a beautiful, colorful braid that encompassed all of her parts.

Easing into reflection: Integrated self

- Imagine a past version of yourself. Take a moment to allow a full image of your younger self to form. What do you see? How old is this person? What is this person struggling with? What are this person's strengths? What could help this person? What do you think this person needs most? Take a moment to write down a few things that you notice.

  ....
  ....
  ....
  ....

- Now that you have written a few things down, how do you feel about this younger "you?" Do you identify with this person? What feelings show up in you? What else are you noticing? Whatever you feel is okay; just take note of it.

  ....
  ....
  ....
  ....

INTEGRATED SELF ART THERAPY PROJECT: PUZZLING

Purpose

Assembling yourself is a lifelong process. The growth and change of the developmental process is an essential task in integrating the pieces of the self. This assemblage lends itself to metaphors exemplified in art making. Many art therapists discuss the process of identity formation or integration through art making.

Chilton and Scotti (2014) lauded the benefits of collage as a complementary process to the work of piecing together identity. In their study, "collage making furthered the development and construction" of the identities being explored (2014, p.169). In a different study that incorporated art therapy with adolescents dealing with trauma, phototherapy and storytelling techniques were used to achieve greater self-awareness and a sense of integrated identity (Settineri *et al.* 2019).

Hill (2013) promoted the use of photography and visual ethnography as effective tools in addressing identity development in youth. Beaumont (2012) espoused several art therapy techniques for adolescents exploring identity formation and integration issues, including journaling, collage, sociograms, altered books, mask-making, and box projects. Focusing-oriented art therapy (adapted from the work of Eugene Gendlin; see Rappaport 2008) has been utilized as a means of helping clients to accept all parts of themselves, a step on the road to integration (see the Appendix). Rappaport (2008, p.26) encourages clients to adopt the focusing attitude, which "is a stance of conveying to the inner self that all feelings, thoughts, emotions, and felt senses that are present within the body/mind are welcome."

After experiencing the trauma associated with relationship violence, many people feel fragmented, disoriented, and emotionally fractured. This art project is about figuratively identifying the pieces of self, and then exploring how to assemble them. To do this, we work with the metaphor of puzzles, an activity that creates order out of component parts. While some puzzles have just one right way that they can come together, others have multiple possible outcomes.

Puzzles have a history in game playing, relationship building, and therapy (Abbott, Shanahan, and Neufeld 2013; Hill and Lineweaver 2016). They are frequently used in play therapy (Breen and Daigneault 1998; Islaeli, Yati, and Fadmi 2020), education, and even in the workplace, as gamification has become a common phenomenon in our culture (Michalewicz and Michalewicz 2008). They are now also used in teletherapy (Snyder 2021). Puzzles are used to decrease anxiety, increase confidence, build mastery, improve motor skills, invite distraction, promote cognitive exercise, and to make learning fun (Kim 2008; Milah *et al.* 2022; Pribadi, Elsanti, and Yulianto 2018). They can also be profound tools in understanding the complexity of the self (Linesch 2016; Oaklander 1978).

Project goals

1. To provide a tool for clients to recognize and identify the pieces of self.

2. To encourage space for construction of the integrated self through the metaphor of puzzle pieces as component parts that can symbolize so many things (e.g., parts theory, likes/dislikes, hobbies and interests, social roles, support persons and relationships, therapeutic coping strategies, etc.).

3. To create and recreate the integrated self in the safety of the therapeutic space (a practice realm where clients can experiment with change and explore identity before generalizing it to their daily life).

Warm-ups

Idea 1, Describe you: Ask the client to think about how many words they can come up with to describe themselves—they should try to fill a page. They can make a list, or incorporate words into some kind of design. They could consider things that describe how they look, how they act, how they carry themselves in the world. Ask them to consider words that describe their values and what they believe in, words that others who know them (or think they know them) might use to describe them. How many words or phrases can they come up with that describe a piece of the complex and multifaceted person that they are?

Idea 2, Collage you: Invite the client to create a collage with words that describe them that are harvested from magazines. Using scissors and a glue stick, they can choose their words and assemble them onto a page. You might consider providing your client with a pre-cut collage word bin (something commonly done in art therapy) if you think that looking through magazines will be overwhelming or distracting for your client. Consider using magazines that have lots of positive and affirming words. You can encourage them to turn the collage into a poem, or into a sort of advertisement for themselves (reminding them that advertisements usually highlight the positive attributes of something).

Materials suggested

- Paper, 8½ x 11 inches or larger
- Graphite pencil and eraser
- Marker pens:
    - Use fine tip pens if you are working with a small puzzle
    - Use larger marker pens if you are working with large puzzle pieces
- Scissors
- Glue sticks
- Collage material (magazines, maps, greeting card fronts, or anything relevant)
- Bonus materials:
    - Prefabricated puzzle sheets (sold as pre-cut cardboard puzzle sheets, typically white-washed on one side, and die-cut by machine enough to stay together until pulled apart)
    - Recycled puzzle pieces: consider an old puzzle from a

thrift store or garage sale, or one that even has some missing pieces; used with glue

- Universal puzzle pieces: these are typically large (10 x 10 inches) and do not fit together in only one way; they can be constructed in multiple ways, since every piece can fit into any other puzzle piece

Preparation

This project needs very little preparation, since the preparation and the decisions made in the preparation stage have a lot to do with the outcome. For this project, clients will create a puzzle that depicts their integrated self. Puzzles are, of course, made up of many smaller pieces, and so are people. There are many ways to approach this art piece. Also, your materials may be largely impactful in driving the art in a particular direction. Small pre-made puzzles lend themselves to exploring a single image, or to exploring a single characteristic or value on each piece of the puzzle.

Before starting, ask your client to consider a few things: do they want to create an image first, and then break it up into smaller puzzle pieces? Would they like to work small on each puzzle piece, and then assemble it later? Some clients like to just start drawing and see what emerges, while others might want to plan what their puzzle will include. Knowing your client's way of working can be helpful here, but so can asking them about how they want to approach this piece.

Process

Your client may want to decide if they would like to assemble their puzzle before or after art making. They can create art, and then dismantle the image into many pieces, or conversely create on each individual puzzle piece and see how things come together into a whole. Both methods can be valuable and fulfilling. Assure your client that there is no right or wrong in art, and that any method of self-exploration is valid here. While working, sometimes a single puzzle piece (or more than one) is disappointing to the artist. This is not so dissimilar from when we are disappointed with an aspect of ourselves. As with part of ourselves, a part of our puzzle can also be reconsidered and reworked. The art process lends itself to problem solving. The client gets to decide when a piece is done, and if they are not happy with the outcome, they can continue to develop it. Encourage your client to lean into those opportunities.

Questions to spark reflection or discussion

- How did you approach your puzzle?
- What challenges arose as you created your puzzle?
- Were there moments of frustration, indecision, confusion? When were they, and what did you do about it?
- Were there any moments of insight that came up along the way? When was that?
- What pieces of the puzzle do you feel most confident about, and why?
- What pieces of the puzzle are most concerning to you, and why?

Alternate art therapy project ideas

Alternate art therapy project idea 1: Self-esteem journal
We recommend journals that are large enough for visual and written exploration (8½ x 11 inches or larger) with unlined white paper. Journals can be bought or made; fancy or expensive journals sometimes have a certain appeal to the journaler, but so, too, does the handmade journal. There are a number of tutorials online about how to bind paper with cardboard, string, and glue, but three-ring binders and hole punching sometimes make optimal journals too. Colored pencils or marker pens can be used to explore some of the following prompts that all point to aspects of the self. The client can try using these prompts, and also consider coming up with some new ideas themselves:

I felt fantastic when...
I felt lousy when...

One of the things I like best about me is…
Something I would like to do better is…
There is someone who I deeply admire, and here is why…
Something that really matters to me is…
Something that I am scared to tell anyone is…
One thing that I really want more than anything else is…
Something that I am not afraid of is…
It is easy for me to be myself when…
One thing I would like to be better at by next year is…
Something unique about me is…
I feel proud of myself when…
Something I have shown progress on is…
Here is a time when I showed great compassion to myself…
If I were going to adopt a mantra, it would be…

Alternate art therapy project idea 2: Flower power

The flower power concept was developed by advocates for social change who encouraged people to examine power differentials in society (Arnold *et al.* 1991). We use it with developing clinicians to encourage them to look at the impact (on themselves and others) of their own aspects of self, including gender identity, sexual orientation, race, religion, socioeconomic status, employment status, education, ability level, body type, geography, and more. Flower power can aid in the exploration of intersectional identities. Some categories resonate more with people than others, and there can be some enlightening moments when someone realizes that an aspect of their identity or experience has been more impactful than they had previously understood.

Here is how the exercise works: the client draws a flower center, and then a series of petals with an inner and an outer layer. This could also be made with collage, or printed off of the computer—there are a number of examples of flower power exercise templates and examples online.[1] On the inner most part of each petal, the client identifies a different area of identity, such as

---

[1] See, for example, www.oise.utoronto.ca/edactivism/Activist_Resources/The_Power_Flower.html

religion, education, or body appearance. On the middle layer of the corresponding flower petal (or the center point of a long petal), they write in the social norm or ideal for that item. For example, in the USA, the social norm or ideal for religion is Christianity. While there are a number of other religions present in the USA, and it could be argued that there is equal opportunity and treatment for people of all religions, the social structure in the USA favors people who identify as Christian. We see this in the way that people of other religions cannot always assume to get a day off from school or work on their religious holidays. The social norm or ideal in the USA in regard to education is a college degree. Certainly, plenty of people don't have one, but as a culture people with degrees are regarded more highly. In the USA the ideal body appearance is tall and thin, even if that does not describe the majority of people.

At the farthest point of the flower petals, on the outer edge, the client indicates their experience with whatever identity marker their petal is naming and exploring. There is an opportunity here to consider as many identity markers as they can think of. For example, were they raised in a two-parent home? Were they raised by heterosexual parents who were married? Were they raised by your biological parents? Or maybe they were adopted, or raised in foster care? The flower power exercise is designed to study the client's experiences of power, privilege, and oppression, but it is also an opportunity to learn more about their integrated self.

PROJECT EXAMPLE

In *Solving Me* (Figure 13), the artist created a puzzle based on her drawn self-portrait. Initially, she carefully hand drew the puzzle pieces on one side of the paper in pencil, before creating a likeness of herself on the other side. She used white oil pastel on black construction paper; she discussed wanting her image to be in black and white, and acknowledged these colors as a metaphor for clarity. She then chose not to use black ink (or marker pen) on white paper, as it would have been too conventional; she was working to convey the complex process that integrating herself was proving to be.

Figure 13: *Solving Me*, by an anonymous artist (2018)

REFERENCES

Abbott, K.A., Shanahan, M.J., and Neufeld, R.W.J. (2013) "Artistic tasks outperform nonartistic tasks for stress reduction." *Art Therapy 30*, 2, 71–78. https://doi.org/10.1080/07421656.2013.787214

Anonymous artist (2018) *Solving Me* [Drawing]. Private collection.

APA (American Psychiatric Association) (2022) *Diagnostic and Statistical Manual of Mental Disorders* (5th edn, Text Revision). https://doi.org/10.1176/appi.books.9780890425787

Arnold, R., Burke, B., James, C., Martin, D., and Thomas, B. (1991) *Educating for a Change*. Toronto: Between the Lines and the Doris Martin Institute for Education and Action.

Beaumont, S.L. (2012) "Art therapy approaches for identity problems during adolescence." *Canadian Art Therapy Association Journal 25*, 1, 7–14. https://doi.org/10.1080/08322473.2012.11415557

Breen, D.T. and Daigneault, S.D. (1998) "The use of play therapy with adolescents in high school." *International Journal of Play Therapy 7*, 1, 25–47. https://doi.org/10.1037/h0089417

Chilton, G. and Scotti, V. (2014) "Snipping, gluing, writing: The properties of collage as an arts-based research practice in art therapy." *Art Therapy 31*, 4, 163–171. https://doi.org/10.1080/07421656.2015.963484

Coid, J., Petruckevitch, A., Feder, G., Chung, W.S., Richardson, J., and Moorey, S. (2001) "Relation between childhood sexual and physical abuse and risk of revictimization in women: A cross-sectional survey." *The Lancet 358*, 9280, 450–454. https://doi.org/10.1016/S0140-6736(01)05622-7

Csikszentmihalyi, M. (1996) *Flow and the Psychology of Discovery and Invention*. New York: HarperCollins.

Czerny, A.B., Lassiter, P.S., and Lim, J.H. (2018) "Post-abuse boundary renegotiation: Healing and reclaiming self after intimate partner violence." *Journal of Mental Health Counseling 40*, 3, 211–225. https://doi.org/10.17744/mehc.40.3.03

Dube, S.R., Anda, R.F., Whitfield, C.L., Brown, D.W., *et al.* (2005) "Long-term consequences of childhood sexual abuse by gender of victim." *American Journal of Preventive Medicine 28*, 5, 430–438. https://doi.org/10.1016/j.amepre.2005.01.015

Fisher, J. (2017) *Healing the Fragmented Selves of Trauma Survivors: Overcoming Internal Self-Alienation*. Abingdon: Routledge.
Fleming, J., Mullen, P.E., Sibthorpe, B., and Bammer, G. (1999) "The long-term impact of childhood sexual abuse in Australian women." *Child Abuse & Neglect 23*, 2, 145–159. https://doi.org/10.1016/S0145-2134(98)00118-5
Foo, S. (2022) *What My Bones Know: A Memoir of Healing from Complex Trauma*. New York: Ballantine Books.
Franklin, M. and Siemon, T. (2008) "Toward an understanding of the fundamental healing and therapeutic qualities of art." *Journal of Thai Traditional & Alternative Medicine 6*, 3.
Gold, J. and Ciorciari, J. (2020) "A review on the role of the neuroscience of flow states in the modern world." *Behavioral Sciences 10*, 9, 137. https://doi.org/10.3390/bs10090137
Herman, J.L. (1992) *Trauma and Recovery*. New York: Basic Books.
Hill, J.L. (2013) "Using participatory and visual methods to address power and identity in research with young people." Loughborough University. https://hdl.handle.net/2134/12750
Hill, K.E. and Lineweaver, T.T. (2016) "Improving the short-term affect of grieving children through art." *Art Therapy 33*, 2, 91–98. https://doi.org/10.1080/07421656.2016.1166414
Islaeli, I., Yati, M., and Fadmi, F.R. (2020) "The effect of play puzzle therapy on anxiety of children on preschooler in Kota Kendari hospital." *Enfermería Clínica 30*, 103–105. https://doi.org/10.1016/j.enfcli.2019.11.032
Jackson, S.A., Ford, S.K., Kimiecik, J.C., and Marsh, H.W. (1998) "Psychological correlates of flow in sport." *Journal of Sport and Exercise Psychology 20*, 4, 358–378.
Kim, S. (2008) "What Is a Puzzle?" In T. Fullerton (ed.) *Game Design Workshop: A Playcentric Approach to Creating Innovative Games* (pp.35–39). Abingdon: Routledge.
Linesch, D. (2016) "Art Therapy with Adolescents." In D.E. Gussak and M.L. Rosal (eds) *The Wiley Handbook of Art Therapy* (pp.252–261). Oxford: Wiley-Blackwell.
Michalewicz, Z. and Michalewicz, M. (2008) *Puzzle-Based Learning*. Ormond, Australia: Hybrid Publishers.
Milah, A.S., Rohman, A.A., Firmansyah, A., and Roslianti, E. (2022) "Play therapy with puzzle media to improve fine motor skills for pre-school children at Madrasah Cempaka." *ABDIMAS: Jurnal Pengabdian Masyarakat 5*, 2, 2405–2409. https://journal.umtas.ac.id/index.php/ABDIMAS/article/view/2403
Nakamura, J. and Csikszentmihalyi, M. (2002) "The Concept of Flow." In C.R. Snyder and S.J. Lopez (eds) *The Handbook of Positive Psychology* (pp.89–105). Oxford: Oxford University Press.
Oaklander, V. (1978) *Windows to Our Children: A Gestalt Approach to Children and Adolescents*. Gouldsboro, ME: The Gestalt Journal Press.
Ørke, E.C., Bjørkly, S., and Vatnar, S.K.B. (2022) "IPV characteristics, childhood violence, and adversities as risk factors for being victimized in multiple IPV relationships." *Journal of Interpersonal Violence 37*, 3–4, 1988–2011. https://doi.org/10.1177/0886260520933037
Pribadi, T., Elsanti, D., and Yulianto, A. (2018) "Reduction of anxiety in children facing hospitalization by play therapy: Origami and puzzle in Lampung-Indonesia." *Malahayati International Journal of Nursing and Health Science 1*, 1, 29–35. doi: 10.33024/minh.v1i1.850
Rappaport, L. (2008) *Focusing-Oriented Art Therapy: Accessing the Body's Wisdom and Creative Intelligence*. London and Philadelphia, PA: Jessica Kingsley Publishers.
Schutte, N.S. and Malouff, J.M. (2020) "Connections between curiosity, flow and creativity." *Journal of Interpersonal Violence 37*, 3–4, NP1988–NP2011. https://doi.org/10.1177/0886260520933037

Settineri, S., Sicari, F., Pagano Dritto, I., Frisone, F., Strangis Mobilia, F., and Merlo, E.M. (2019) "Application of art therapy in adolescence: Photo-novel analysis as an expressive technique." *Mediterranean Journal of Clinical Psychology (MJCP) 7*, 2. https://doi.org/10.6092/2282-1619/2019.7.2247

Smith, L.J., Gradisar, M., King, D.L., and Short, M. (2017) "Intrinsic and extrinsic predictors of video-gaming behaviour and adolescent bedtimes: The relationship between flow states, self-perceived risk-taking, device accessibility, parental regulation of media and bedtime." *Sleep Medicine 30*, 64–70. https://doi.org/10.1016/j.sleep.2016.01.009

Snyder, K. (2021) "The digital art therapy frame: Creating a 'magic circle' in teletherapy." *International Journal of Art Therapy 26*, 3, 104–110. https://doi.org/10.1080/17454832.2020.1871389

Thomson, P. and Jaque, V. (2012) "Dancing with the muses: Dissociation and flow." *Journal of Trauma & Dissociation 13*, 4, 478–489. https://doi.org/10.1080/15299732.2011.652345

van der Hart, O., Nijenhuis, E.R.S., and Steele, K. (2006) *The Haunted Self: Structural Dissociation and the Treatment of Chronic Traumatization*. New York: W.W. Norton & Co., Inc.

Wanner, B., Ladouceur, R., Auclair, A.V., and Vitaro, F. (2006) "Flow and dissociation: Examination of mean levels, cross-links, and links to emotional well-being across sports and recreational and pathological gambling." *Journal of Gambling Studies 22*, 3, 289–304. https://doi.org/10.1007/s10899-006-9017-5

Part Three

ADDITIONAL CONSIDERATIONS

Chapter 12

IMPLICATIONS FOR CLINICAL USE

Clinically appropriate care is the cornerstone of ethical, trauma-responsive work in all therapeutic realms, and should also be applied to the incorporation of the Empowerment Wheel model with the use of art. As in all clinical work, the trained therapist functions best with good supervision and professional consultation. Additionally, we have made some recommendations for the use of this model in working with survivors of relationship abuse.

It is essential to acknowledge the risk that victims of abuse face in leaving. This is not a book about leaving an abusive relationship, but rather, a book about healing after abuse, which, for many people, happens after they leave. It is important to understand that survivors who decide to leave the relationship are often at increased risk. Additionally, the decision to leave a relationship is a deeply personal one, and the consequences for that must be carefully weighed up by the individual and their trusted therapist. Establishing a plan for safety can benefit victims of relationship abuse regardless of what outcome they pursue; this can be a valuable and necessary activity to pursue in therapy.

Breakout box: Safety planning

Safety planning is an essential exercise, regardless of whether you are planning to leave, planning to stay, or planning to return to an abusive relationship. Although creating a safety plan cannot actually guarantee your safety, the following key elements will aid you in being prepared as much as possible for a worst-case scenario:

- Identify individuals who are able and willing to support you. This might include your therapist, general or family practitioner, family, friends, co-workers, etc.

- Have a code word that can be used in a phone call, text, or instant message with one of these individuals who agrees to call emergency services on your behalf when they receive the code word, should you need it.

- Identify a safe place for you to stay should you need it. This can be a domestic violence shelter, a hotel room, or a friend's couch. Have a back-up place identified as well, in case your first choice is not an option.

- Have access to transportation, or at a minimum be familiar with public transportation options.

- Keep your purse and/or essentials in the same place along with your car keys or public transportation access card/tickets in the same place in your home, so that you know exactly where they are and can access them quickly.

- Make copies of important government documents, such as your driver's license, passport, birth certificate, marriage certificate, insurance documents, residential leases, medical records, etc., and keep them in a safe place where you can easily access them. This may mean keeping them with a trusted family member or friend rather than in your home.

- Have an overnight bag prepared with anything you might need, including medication, should you need to leave suddenly. This might also need to be stored with a trusted family member or friend rather than in your home.

- Plan to bring your cell phone or have a cell phone available to you along with a charging cord; plan to change your number as soon as you can.

- If you would normally see your partner on your way to work or class, plan out an alternate route that will minimize the risk of an encounter.

- If you are afraid to be alone, find individuals in advance who are willing to stay with you, and call on them when you need to.

- If you have shared passwords to social media or other online accounts (including email or online banking), consider changing those passwords as soon as you can.

- If you have children who are impacted by the abuse, plan to take them with you if you can. You may also need to prepare for back-up childcare options.

- Teach your children how to call 911 (in the USA) or similar appropriate emergency services.

- Have the address and contact information for your local police department.

- If you are using a written or printed safety plan, keep it in a place where your partner cannot find it. This may mean keeping it with a trusted family member or friend rather than in your home.

While this is not an exhaustive list, it is a start, and can save valuable time in an emergency. While there are many safety planning resources on the internet, be careful about searching for the term "safety planning domestic violence" or any similar phrasing in households where computers are shared. Leaving a "search" trail can escalate the tension or violence in a home. If you have safe access to the internet, the National Domestic Violence Hotline[1] has an interactive safety planning tool.[2]

Safety should always be addressed first, prior to starting any work with a relationship abuse survivor. A lot of time is given in therapy to the discussion of emotional safety (Rankin and Taucher 2003). It is also imperative to make sure that your client is physically safe. A client who is actively in a toxic relationship, living with any degree of uncertainty for their wellbeing, or going home to any form of violence or aggression may not be a candidate for the use of this therapy model. This model is designed for people who are physically safe and living violence free, regardless of whether they have terminated the relationship or not.

Be careful about using diagnosis with victims of relationship abuse. Assigning a diagnosis to a victim of relationship abuse should always include thoughtful consideration of the client's history and presentation. Adding a label to someone who is in crisis may result in additional and perhaps even unnecessary stress and confusion for a person who is doing their best to survive. An individual in crisis might appear distressed, anxious, confused, distracted, angry, scared, or depressed. They may also struggle with planning, decision making, or being able to verbalize the extent of their abuse. Many domestic violence agencies have a policy of not diagnosing their clients because of this.

The importance of person-first language. In writing this book, we have attempted to be as respectful as possible of the individual, and have avoided using stigmatizing or labeling language to describe victims of relationship abuse. Our goal has been to protect and preserve the dignity of post-abuse victims and survivors by honoring

---

[1] www.thehotline.org
[2] www.thehotline.org/plan-for-safety/create-a-safety-plan

their journey as one of healing and empowerment. In the book *What My Bones Know*, Foo (2022) speaks about the stigmatizing way that authors often write about individuals with CPTSD, and how devastating it was for her to see herself in descriptions that were harshly clinical and which failed to see her humanity. We hope that we have succeeded in honoring the individual while still illuminating the struggles and challenges that abuse can create in someone's life. We encourage the use of person-first language and caution around the tendency in mental health settings to label, categorize, or stigmatize individuals who are doing the best they can to survive and move forward.

THE THREE PHASES OF TRAUMA TREATMENT

Use of the Empowerment Wheel may be contraindicated if the abuse is so recent that the client has not been able to achieve stability. When safety and stability are not yet ensured for an individual, addressing the emotional repercussions of abuse through the Empowerment Wheel model or any therapeutic tool may be too difficult for the client. We recommend adhering to Herman's (1998) three stages of trauma treatment: safety and stabilization, remembrance and mourning, and reconnection and integration. Creating safety and ensuring client stability should always be the first phase of any trauma treatment or intervention.

Start anywhere. While we think that a good starting point to begin working with the Empowerment Wheel is *red flags*, there is no one right or best place to start. Often in a therapeutic situation, reflecting on missed opportunities or moments when someone should have known better seems to come somewhat naturally to clients. The client can determine the starting point in the model, and it may be an opportunity to feel empowered in doing so. The therapist might have recommendations for where to start as well. There is no identified "right" starting point, and the Empowerment Wheel is intentionally not linear. Sectors of it can be explored in any order, and revisiting sections repeatedly and often can be helpful to a client.

While it is true that you can start anywhere, we also recommend *not starting* with the *integrated self* sector, unless you have already completed significant therapeutic work. The *integrated self* sector explores and strives to assist in repairing the disintegrated self, and often results in exploring deep wounds that may go back further than the identified abusive relationship.

Feeling uncomfortable vs. feeling unsafe. When engaging with the six sectors of the Empowerment Wheel, it is likely that your client will experience strong emotions. At times, feeling strong emotions can be confused with feeling unsafe. We always advocate for safety in the therapeutic realm, but feeling uncomfortable is sometimes unavoidable, even valuable, in the therapeutic space. Feeling uncomfortable when processing difficult memories or experiences does not equal being unsafe. Facing the past is the only way to move into the present; it is an important part of the healing journey. It may be necessary to help your client develop increased affect tolerance by exploring the difference between comfort and safety. Providing psychoeducation about emotion and affect tolerance will help support the processing of difficult feelings when engaging with the Empowerment Wheel.

Prioritize the use of the Empowerment Wheel's sectors by considering a goal. While the Empowerment Wheel is not designed to start or end at any one spot, this does not mean that there isn't benefit to considering specifically where your client might enter their journey. Four sectors of the wheel constitute a part of what we consider the immediate healing work. These are: *red flags, boundaries, relationship authenticity,* and *locus of control.* Each of these areas is directly related to an individual's ability to establish trust and connection with themselves, permit authentic expression, draw limits, or exercise flexibility in relationships and stretch beyond their own limitations. The remaining two sectors of the Empowerment Wheel build on (and beyond) the work established in the immediate healing: *self-talk* and *integrated self.* Clients who start with self-talk or integrated self often end up returning to these sections later, after working in areas of more immediate healing.

The Empowerment Wheel model is a multidirectional and non-linear process. It is expected that some sectors will take longer than others. Most clinicians understand that it may be hard to predict the necessary amount of processing on a given topic; this type of inconsistency is amplified with trauma. It is also expected that some sectors may need to be revisited. For example, in some types of therapy, story components that trigger memories may give rise to new red flags. Messages that a person has sent or needs to learn may continue to emerge as the healing unfurls. And arriving at an integrated sense of self is indeed a process. Establishing early that this is not a journey with one set path may be helpful to clients.

Sector overlap. The different sectors of the Empowerment Wheel have connections to each other that can make talking about them as isolated conceptual strands difficult. For example, it may be difficult to discuss *self-talk* without also mentioning *locus of control*. Negative self-talk is a phenomenon that is directly related to our sense of worth. Similarly, it might be difficult to talk about *boundaries* without also discussing recognizing *red flags*. While the overlap between the sectors can be helpful in that one sector can seamlessly lead into another, some clients might find the clear distinction between them more beneficial. We leave it to the therapist's clinical intuition and understanding of the client to decide whether the client can absorb complex concepts that are inherently connected, or whether they might be better served by addressing each one as an individual concept.

IMPLICATIONS FOR THE USE OF ART WITH THE EMPOWERMENT WHEEL

Use what you have. Materials can be simplistic or elaborate. This depends on a variety of factors, including budget, session space, storage capacity, time limit, client interest, and safety precautions. More expensive art materials sometimes bring about more sophisticated artworks, but not always. Materials used for projects may vary depending on what you have or can source easily. Art therapists are often expert at learning to source materials at very little cost, and there are resources that support doing this (Brand-off and Thompson 2019). Additionally, all project materials are adaptable. Caution tape that is expensive or difficult to source could be recreated through paint, using marker pens on white tape, or by printing out images online. Beads can be kiln-fired or torch-worked glass, but can also be sourced at many dollar stores. Additionally beads can be created with aluminum foil or air dry clay. Consider what you need, and also what you already have.

Everyone is an artist. Some people identify themselves as artists; others may be novices and have much less familiarity with art making. Comfort level with art often affects the creative process in the beginning, but typically people evolve into a certain comfort creativity. This is especially true when they are invested in the subject matter at hand. Art therapists commonly hear refrains such as "I'm not an artist" or "I don't even know how to draw." They have a variety of ways of addressing these. Creativity is an inherent part of being human, even if someone might be inexperienced at allowing themselves to create. Creativity can be expressed in so many ways, and really requires some willingness to play and take healthy risks. Learning to take healthy risks is itself a process. Those who demonstrate ease, comfort, and confidence in making art are likely just more practiced at taking risks associated with visual expression. We always encourage our clients to try new things, to attempt to silence their inner critics, and to find a way forward, as when problem solving.

Value the process and the product. When making artwork an individual might sometimes take away a creation that is very special, or even precious. Meaning that comes from therapeutic exploration can be inherently tied into the now sacred object that may have emerged from that exploration. Sometimes the artwork made in a therapeutic process is ancillary. While it may be useful in facilitating a reflective process, the artwork itself may be incidental, or even unimportant. This is okay. Sometimes it's what you make that counts. Sometimes it's what you take away from the process, even if the tangible artwork does not last forever. Both process and product can be valuable when employing art in a therapeutic realm. Allow for the utility of both.

Artwork can be a way of telling without talking. Clinicians who often work with trauma will be familiar with the fact that verbally expressing trauma histories can be a huge obstacle to processing them. Research suggests that part of the difficulty with verbal expression pertain to neurophysiological changes that impact speech, as well as memory storage and recall (van der Kolk 2005). Additionally, feelings of shame, guilt, and embarrassment can further complicate a client's ability to speak of their relationship abuse. Clients will benefit from the freedom to share verbally when they are ready to do so, and also the freedom to not have to share verbally. In this way, art therapy is a powerful form of expression since it allows for expression that does not have to be articulated. The artwork itself can say what needs to be said.

The Empowerment Wheel can be an exceptional tool to help clients to unravel the impact of their own relationship abuse. We also believe that the concepts put forth in the wheel in this text, including the suggested art interventions, may be useful in examining relationship abuse that extends beyond that of intimate partners.

REFERENCES

Brandoff, R. and Thompson, A. (2019) *Quick & Creative Art Projects for (Very) Limited Budgets*. London and Philadelphia, PA: Jessica Kingsley Publishers.

Foo, S. (2022). *What my bones know: A memoir of healing from complex trauma*. NY: Ballantine Books.

Rankin, A.B. and Taucher, L.C. (2003) "A task-oriented approach to art therapy in trauma treatment." *Art Therapy 20*, 3, 138–147. https://doi.org/10.1080/07421656.2003.10129570

van der Kolk, B.A. (2005) "Developmental Trauma Disorder: Toward a rational diagnosis for children with complex trauma histories." *Psychiatric Annals 35*, 5, 401–408. https://doi.org/10.3928/00485713-20050501-06

Appendix

DEFINITIONS

Abuse: Abuse is the misuse of power against another person or thing (such as authority) in order to gain leverage or control. It is a broad term that can include a wide array of behaviors, including physical, emotional, and psychological aggression, as well as assault, rape, and injury. Abuse, as it relates to the Empowerment Wheel, is considered to be any behavior that serves to diminish the power or autonomy of another individual within the context of an intimate partnership.[1]

Angel Shot: A drink that you can order to signal that you need help. Ordering an Angel Shot drink will signal to the bartender or waiter that you need help. If you order an Angel Shot *neat*, the bartender or waiter will escort you to your car; if you order an Angel Shot *with ice*, the bartender or waiter will call for a ride such as Uber or Lyft; and if you order an Angel Shot *with lime*, the bartender or waiter will call the police.[2]

Art therapy: The engagement of the creative process and use of artistic expression facilitated by a trained art therapist toward health and wellness goals such as coping with symptoms, increasing self-awareness, raising self-esteem, developing communication skills, building trust, and integrating trauma.

Attachment: The concept of attachment, written about extensively by Bowlby (1982), describes a profound connection between two people. Attachment is believed to be developed in early life based on a child's relationship with their primary caregiver; this creates a psychological roadmap that informs how a child establishes and maintains future relationships.

Authenticity: The congruence between someone's thoughts, feelings, and actions; the act of being true to yourself, personality, and spirit, in spite of what others might want. Authenticity occurs through self-knowledge and is evidenced by an ability to express your emotions and needs.

Batterer intervention program (BIP): These are treatment interventions that seek to remediate violent behavior within intimate relationships. BIPs are often either psychoeducational or cognitive-behavioral, or some combination of both. The Duluth Model (Pence and Paymar 1993) is a BIP intervention that has been operating since the early 1980s. It is often categorized as psychoeducational, and includes a coordinated community response that is meant to challenge patriarchal tendencies

---

[1] For a thorough list of the many forms that abuse can take, see Wikipedia's page on abuse: https://en.wikipedia.org/wiki/Abuse
[2] In the UK, "Ask for Angela" (i.e., asking venue staff for "Angela") works in a similar way to ordering an Angel Shot in the USA.

in society at large, and to transfer blame or accountability for the violence from the victim to the perpetrator.

Beit Noam: A batterer intervention project (BIP) in Israel that provides temporary housing and support to perpetrators of domestic violence, intimate partner violence, and relationship abuse.

Benching: The feeling that your partner is playing you and holding out for someone better by staying active on an online dating app, or that your partner isn't committing to you in case someone better comes along.

Boundaries: A boundary is a point of demarcation between self and others. Boundaries can be physical or emotional, mental or spiritual. They can also be largely unconscious until they become uncomfortable and we are forced to pay attention to them. Boundaries define who we are and how we engage with others in the world. Boundaries can be established and manipulated with variables such as time, touch, physical space, and self-disclosure. *This is also a sector in the Empowerment Wheel model.*

Coercion (and threats): Making or carrying out threats to harm or hurt the victim in some way. This may include threats to abandon the victim or attempt suicide. Abusers may threaten to report the victim to the authorities (welfare, child services, etc.), even when aggressive acts are committed by victims in their own defense. Abusers may exert their control by making the victim do things that the victim does not want to do, including taking or using drugs or alcohol or other illegal activities.

Complex posttraumatic stress disorder (CPTSD): A psychiatric disorder that is often the result of long-lasting abuse or trauma that repeats for months or years and which frequently occurs in childhood. CPTSD can result in distortions to a person's core identity, as well as significant emotional dysregulation and disturbance. CPTSD is not a diagnosis in the *Diagnostic and Statistical Manual of Mental Disorders* (DSM-5-TR) (APA 2022).

DARVO: Freyd's (2023) acronym DARVO, meaning "Deny, Attack, and Reverse Victim and Offender." This happens when perpetrators minimize, deny, or blame the victim and refuse to take responsibility for their actions. They often reverse-blame the victim, telling them they are overreacting or that the abuse simply didn't happen. These types of behaviors weaken a victim's sense of self and self-worth, leaving that person confused and unable to seek help.

Dialectical behavior therapy (DBT): A very comprehensive therapeutic intervention that is used to treat emotion dysregulation among individuals with self-harming behaviors, borderline personality disorder, or inter-personal relationship problems.

Distress hand signal: Tucking your thumb into the palm of your hand and closing all four fingers over the thumb is a universal distress signal that indicates there is violence at home.

Domestic violence: Abuse, aggression, or violence that occurs in a home, most typically between intimate partners, but can also include family members, other household members, or friends who are cohabitating.

Domestic violence shelter: A homeless shelter that exclusively provides temporary housing and support to victims of domestic violence, intimate partner violence, or relationship abuse.

Economic abuse (also financial abuse): Economic abuse includes having limited or no access to finances, restrictions on being allowed to work or participate in work affairs, or demanding that the victim forfeit earned income (or sequestering such income) if they are allowed to work. It can also include making the victim ask for money or keeping the victim on an allowance, or denying financial access for necessary items.

Emotional abuse: Any behavior that minimizes or attacks a person's self-esteem or confuses them enough to cause them to doubt themselves more than the perpetrator.

Name-calling, mind games, humiliation, bullying, and gaslighting are variations of emotional abuse with the end goal of making the victim easier to control.

Empowerment: A process by which a person deprived of autonomy reasserts power and choice in their own life. Empowerment can include goal-setting, developing skills, accessing resources, and moving towards self-sufficiency. It can also include intra-personal constructs, such as described in the Empowerment Wheel model.

Exteroception: A neural process that helps us make sense of and assess our external environment through the use of our five senses (sight, taste, smell, touch, and hearing). Exteroception is useful in determining if a situation feels safe based on what we sense in our immediate surroundings.

Eye movement desensitization and reprocessing (EMDR) therapy: An eight-phased process that focuses on the processing of traumatic memory and helps to transform thought patterns or blocking beliefs that emerge from traumatic experiences.

Fawn response: A trauma response that uses people-pleasing behavior as a way to avoid, mitigate, or appease abusive behavior.

Fight or flight response: An automatic, physiological trauma response in which the sympathetic nervous system is activated, resulting in fight or flight responses to cues of danger.

Focusing-oriented art therapy: A therapeutic technique based on the philosophical work and approach of Eugene Gendlin (1981) which encouraged clients to find meaning and understanding through intense focus on felt senses, words, and images. Gendlin espoused the value of clearing space in the mind, moving beyond judgment and reaching for acceptance. Art therapists who use focusing techniques incorporate art making into this multistep therapeutic process.

Gaslighting: Psychological abuse that is specifically meant to make the victim feel as if they are losing their mind or slowly going mad, by creating doubt as to what they know is factual or true.

Ghosting: The act of ceasing all contact without explanation, including blocking avenues that might open contact (phone, social media, etc.), and possibly even relocating to a different location.

Grey rocking: Being as unresponsive and neutral as possible when engaging with an abusive or toxic person; not responding, showing emotion, or making minimal eye contact as a way to reinforce boundaries and stop the negative behavior.

Integrated self: A term that refers to someone's ability to connect to the breadth of their experience and to bring all dimensions of their personality into a cohesive, balanced, and integrated whole. *Also a sector in the Empowerment Wheel model.*

Interoception: One of the additional three senses, which include proprioception (movement) and vestibular (balance). Interoception is sometimes experienced on a more conscious level; it is the recognition and interpretation of body signals that can indicate emotions and "gut" wisdom that are connected or experienced within the polyvagal system.

Intervention: A specific action (usually one that aligns with a psychological theory) meant to improve a person's situation or illness.

Intimate partner violence: Abuse, aggression, or violence that occurs between individuals who either have been or currently are in an intimate partnership. This refers to individuals who are married or dating.

Intimate terrorism: Coercive and violent, the type of abuse that produces terror and fear in the victim and makes help-seeking a challenge. Intimate terrorism does not necessarily indicate the level of violence (although these relationships can be extremely violent), but rather the pattern of tactics used to gain control over the partner across time (Johnson 2008).

Intimidation: Using facial expressions, intense eye contact, non-violent physical actions, or gestures that are meant to convey intentions, expectations, and messages of grave consequences. These motions can covertly or overtly threaten and intimidate, and may include aggressive behaviors like destruction of property, throwing or smashing household items, or displaying weapons.

Isolation: This occurs when an individual has limited access to support networks, including family and friends, as well as any outside of the home involvement. Controlling who a victim has contact with, what a victim reads, watches, or has exposure to, results in a form of destructive dependency that makes accessing support for leaving a relationship almost impossible.

Kinetic Family Drawing: An art therapy projective assessment developed in 1970 by Burnes and Kaufman (1987), intended to elicit information about family dynamics, and the child's attitude towards their family. This assessment is sometimes used as a tool in case evaluations where child abuse is suspected.

Locus of control: The place (either internal or external) where reinforcement for behavior is found. *Also a sector in the Empowerment Wheel model.* **Internal locus of control:** Having a belief that outcomes in your life are related to personal efforts (personal responsibility). **External locus of control:** Having a belief that outcomes in your life are largely due to factors outside of your personal control (faith in external resources).

Love-bombing: Being showered with gifts, attention, affection, and compliments that often result in the relationship moving forward extremely rapidly.

Male privilege: Using your male gender to assert power and control over a victim. Some forms of intimate partner violence tend to be more common in households with traditional gendered partner roles. This occurs in situations where the male partner is the "head of the house" and makes all the decisions, including those related to responsibilities and activities that family members are expected or allowed to have and experience.

Medium/media: Art materials; the collection of items, objects, or tools used in the art-making process.

#MeToo movement: A global, survivor-led movement against sexual violence, dedicated to creating pathways for healing, justice, action, and leadership.

Minimizing, denying, or blaming: Minimizing, denying, or blaming the victim; refusing to take responsibility for actions; telling the victim they are overreacting, or that the abuse simply didn't happen. An abuser can make a victim believe that they are the cause of the abuse. These types of behaviors weaken a victim's sense of self and self-worth, leaving that person confused and unable to seek help.

Mutual violent control: Occurs when both partners exert violence against each other in attempts to gain control over the relationship (Johnson 2008).

Narrative exposure therapy (NET): A therapeutic intervention for survivors of multiple traumas such as war, cultural displacement, organized crime, and violence. NET was specifically designed to address posttraumatic stress disorder symptoms and to be delivered in low-income countries and in a relatively short-term manner.

Neuroception: A neural process that allows for recognition of environmental and/or visceral cues of safety, danger, or threat that often occurs outside of our conscious awareness.

Phototherapy: An art therapy application using photography, photographs, or any number of analog or digital art techniques utilizing photo technology in the context of therapy.

Posttraumatic growth: Positive psychological change that occurs in the aftermath of a traumatic event. A metaphor for posttraumatic growth might be seeing the silver lining of a dark cloud. Difficult or challenging experiences can result in positive outcomes; the two are not mutually exclusive. Someone can experience a traumatic or stressful event and wish that the event had never happened, and simultaneously be grateful for growth and positive outcomes that might not have happened without the event. For example, they might regret a divorce and wish that it had never happened, but at the same time feel gratitude for lessons that resulted in their ability to live independently and without the financial support of others.

Posttraumatic stress disorder (PTSD): A psychiatric disorder that can result from being in or witnessing a traumatic event or series of events. People with PTSD experience such events as emotionally or physically harmful or life-threatening. PTSD can affect mental, physical, social, and/or spiritual wellbeing. Examples of traumatic events can include natural disasters, serious accidents, terrorist acts, war/combat, rape/sexual assault, historical trauma, intimate partner violence, or bullying. PTSD is a diagnosis in the *Diagnostic and Statistical Manual of Mental Disorders* (DSM-5-TR) (APA 2022).

Red flags: The experience of a boundary violation; a physical reaction to a behavior that feels invasive, inappropriate, dismissive, invalidating, oppressive, or violent. *Also a sector in the Empowerment Wheel model.*

Relationship abuse: Significant negative impact on one or more persons within a significant relationship that is caused by another person within the relationship; its impact can be experienced as physical, psychological, emotional, financial, spiritual, sexual, or social. Abuse of one person towards another may be premeditated or spontaneous, intentional or unintended. Results are often pervasive and long-lasting in victims.

Relationship authenticity: A person's ability to remain true to their self (thoughts, feelings, actions) while in relationship with a partner or potential "other." *Also a sector in the Empowerment Wheel model.*

Relationship inauthenticity: Occurs when the desire for a relationship is so strong that a person is willing or forced to compromise parts of self (thoughts, feelings, actions) in order to stay in the relationship.

Safety plan: An essential exercise that is applicable to victims who are planning to leave, planning to stay, or planning to return to an abusive relationship. Although a safety plan cannot guarantee safety, creating one will help victims be prepared, as much as possible, for the escalation of aggression or violence, or a worst-case scenario.

Self-talk: Internalized messages that often become deeply embedded in the psyche and tend to run automatically or exist outside of an individual's conscious awareness. Negative self-talk can erode self-esteem and damage someone's sense of self and individuality, whereas positive self-talk can lead to feelings of confidence or competence and an enhanced feeling of self-worth. *Also a sector in the Empowerment Wheel model.*

Situational couple violence: A type of abuse in which arguments escalate to violence and where the violence is perpetrated by either or both partners. Situational couple violence can include a number of variables including chronic conflict, substance use and abuse, anger issues, and communication issues. Perpetrators of situational couple violence may have struggles in multiple areas of their lives including issues around poverty and substance abuse, especially alcohol (Johnson 2008).

Trauma: A reaction to an event or series of events that are extremely distressing, unsettling, or frightening. The lasting impact affects emotional and psychological health and can impact functioning in multiple domains, including mental, physical, emotional, behavioral, and spiritual wellbeing.

Treatment: Medical, psychiatric, or behavioral care given by a trained professional to a person who is suffering or struggling and which is meant to improve that person's condition.

Typology of domestic violence: Johnson (2008) delineated four different types of relationship violence to promote understanding of the mechanisms and characteristics that contribute to violent behaviors: (a) intimate terrorism; (b) violent resistance;

(c) mutual violent control; and (d) situational couple violence. (See definitions of each in this Appendix.)

Using children: A type of abuse where the perpetrator threatens to take children away or denies visitation. The objective is to make the victim feel guilty and afraid, as a means to control the victim and keep them trapped in the relationship. Some victims may stay to protect their children, feeling that their children are more at risk from the abuser if they leave. This category can also include pets.

Vagus nerve: The tenth cranial nerve that is a communication superhighway between the brain and key organs and systems within the body, such as the heart, lungs, and immune and digestive systems. The communication highway runs in both directions, from the brain to the organs and from the organs back to the brain.

Violence Against Women Act (VAWA): Legislation in the USA that creates comprehensive and cost-effective responses to sexual assault, domestic violence and intimate partner violence, dating violence, and stalking. It was enacted in 1994.[3]

Violent resistance: A type of abuse that can look like self-defense against a perpetrator of intimate terrorism, but can also be acts of retaliation against an abusive partner (Johnson 2008).

REFERENCES

APA (American Psychiatric Association) (2022) *Diagnostic and Statistical Manual of Mental Disorders* (5th edn, Text Revision). https://doi.org/10.1176/appi.books.9780890425787

Bowlby, J. (1982) "Attachment and loss: Retrospect and prospect." *American Journal of Orthopsychiatry 52*, 4, 664–678. doi: 10.1111/j.1939-0025.1982.tb01456.x.

Burnes, R.C. and Kaufman, S.H. (1987) *Kinetic Family Drawings (K-F-D): An Introduction to Understanding Children Through Kinetic Drawings*. New York: Brunner/Mazel.

Freyd, J.J. (2023) "What is DARVO?" http://pages.uoregon.edu/dynamic/jjf/defineDARVO.html

Gendlin, E.T. (1981) *Focusing*. New York: Bantam Book.

Johnson, M.P. (2008) *A Typology of Domestic Violence: Intimate Terrorism, Violent Resistance, and Situational Couples Violence*. Lebanon, NH: Northeastern University Press.

Pence, E. and Paymar, M. (1993) *Education Groups for Men Who Batter: The Duluth Model*. New York: Springer Publishing Company, Inc.

---

3   www.congress.gov/bill/117th-congress/senate-bill/3623

Index

Sub-headings in *italics* refer to figures.

Aaron, S.M. 53
AATA (American Art Therapy Association) 104
Abbott, K.A. 191
Abdullah, N.N. 26
Abu-Ras, W.M. 59
abuse 212
  see relationship abuse
abusers *see* perpetrators
Adams, P.E. 135
adaptive information processing (AIP) model 56
adolescent dating violence 25
Adult Nowicki-Strickland Locus of Control Scale 140
adventure and wilderness therapy 57–8
Affirmation cards 146
African American clients 57, 60
agency 141–2
Akinsulure-Smith, A.M. 59
Al-Anon 45
Al'Uqdah, S.N. 58
alcohol consumption 19, 25, 27–8, 36, 44
  alcohol abuse 30, 38, 140, 187–9
Alexander, J.H. 85
Alkhateeb, S. 59
Allen, A.B. 170
Allen, K.N. 47
Altenburger, L.E. 36
Alter-Muri, S. 80
Álvarez Lezama, M. 125

American Psychiatric Association (APA) 57
Angel Shot/Ask for Angela 21, 212
anger management 35
Anonymous artist 118, 146, 166, 197
APA (American Psychiatric Association) 185, 213, 216
April, K.A. 134, 135, 136
Ard, K.L. 17
Argentina 26
Armour, C. 30
Arnold, A. 37
Arnold, R. 195
art therapy 52, 78–9, 212
  art directives 81–2
  art therapy trauma protocol (ATTP) 57
  art therapy with the Empowerment Wheel model 85–6, 100–6
  artwork as a way of telling without talking 211
  everyone is an artist 210
  group treatment 84–5
  homework 82–4
  impact of relationship abuse on children 85
  media 80–1, 215
  reclamation of self and voice 83–4
  talk vs. art 79
  use what you have 209–10
  value the process and the product 210–11
art therapy projects 105–6

boundaries 124–31
  integrated self 190–7
  locus of control 139–48
  red flags 112–18
  relationship authenticity 158–66
  self-talk 173–80
art.b 141
Ashley, W. 57
ATCB (Art Therapy Credentials Board) 104
attachment 94–7, 212
  assessing first impressions 98–9
  attachment and authenticity 121–2
  attachment isn't always love 97–8
Austin, B.D. 80
Australia 45
authenticity 8, 99–100, 212
  attachment and authenticity 121–2
Azmat, A. 59

Babins-Wagner, R. 84
Bagwell-Gray, M.E. 61
Bagwell, R. 27
Baker, E 25
Banksy 125
Barnes, M. 9
barrier tape 125–6
barriers to leaving 22–3
Barst, J. 162
Basile, K.C. 25
Basyiroh, A.N. 85
Bates, E. 17
battered women's movement 44–5

218

INDEX

shelter movement 45–6
shelters 46–51
batterer intervention programs (BIPs) 53–4, 212–13
BBC News 125
Beaulaurier, R.L. 53
Beaumont, S.L. 109
Bechtel, A. 130
Beck, A.T. 168–9
Beit Noam 49, 213
Belenky, M.F. 169
benching 20, 213
Biden, Jo 32
Big Little Lies 36–7
bilocal expectancy 134, 136
Binkley, E. 79
Bird, J. 84
Bjørkly, S. 183
Black, M.C. 17, 24
blind contour drawing 178
Boley, M. 146
Bonomi, A. 36
Boserup, B. 26
Bosgraaf, L. 80, 81
Bouchard, C. 145
boundaries 8, 95, 102, 120, 208, 209, 213
  attachment and authenticity 121–2
  boundaries and healing 123–4
  boundary flexibility 122
  boundary line project alternate art therapy project ideas 130
  Bound 131
  Holes in My Boundaries 131
  materials suggested 127
  overview of boundary lines in art 124–6
  preparation 128
  process 128–9
  project goals 126
  purpose 124
  questions to spark reflection or discussion 129–30
  warm-ups 126–7
Boutilier, S. 27
Bowlby, J. 212
Bows, H. 26–7
Boyd Webb, N. 85
Brackley, M. 36
Bradley, L. 141
Brady-Amoon, P. 93
brain function 79, 96
Brancheau, D. 128
Brandoff, R. 78, 105, 112, 210
Bray, R.S. 125

breadcrumbing 20
breakout boxes 11, 36–7, 51, 72, 78–9, 80–1, 97–9, 101, 136, 185–6, 204–6
Breen, D.T. 191
Breiding, M.J. 109
Brooke, S.L. 83
Brown, G.K. 168–9
Brown, J. 35
Buchalter, S.I. 113
Burlae, K.K. 94
Burnes, R.C. 215
Busch, N.B. 68
Buschel, B.S. 9, 84, 85
BWSS (Battered Women's Support Services) 22

Calhoun, L.G. 69, 70
Callaghan, J.E.M. 85
Camilleri, V. 85
Campbell, J.C. 23
Canada 27, 45, 46, 84
Carlton, N.R. 80
Carr, S.M.D. 173
Cattaneo, L.B. 67, 68
caution tape 125–6
CDC (Centers for Disease Control and Prevention) 24–5
Cepeda, I. 32
Chapman, A.R. 67, 68
Charlot, N. 24
Cheng, S.-Y. 53
Chevalier, J. 146
children 85
  attachment theory 94, 95–6, 99, 121–2
  childhood abuse 153, 183
  using children as a means to exert control 18, 217
Chilton, G. 109
Cho, H. 58
Ciorciari, J. 185
clear tape human figures 130
clinical considerations 203
  diagnosis 206
  importance of person-first language 206–7
  safety planning 204–6
  three phases of trauma treatment 207–9
Clinton, Bill 32
Cobb, A.R. 69
coercion 19, 213
Cogan, R. 56
cognitive behavioral therapy (CBT) 53, 59–60, 85
Cohen, B. 9
Cohn, L. 57
Coid, J. 183
collage 80, 81, 126, 128, 176, 190, 192
Collier, A. 80
compartmentalization 183–4
compromise vs. control 151–2
confirmation bias 98
consequences of abuse 29–32
control 37–8
Cottone, R.R. 52
couples counseling 51–2
Courtois, C.A. 94
COVID-19 pandemic 23, 25–6
Craig, W. 25
Cramer, H. 53
creativity 78–9
  art directives 81–2
  non-traditional art materials 80–1
Cresci, M.B. 153
criticism vs. feedback 136
Crowe, A. 153
Csikszentmihalyi, M. 185, 186
Cukor, G. 37
culturally appropriate interventions and treatment 58–62
  empowerment 70–6
  locus of control 135–6
Czerny, A.B. 8, 9, 74, 93, 123, 134, 184

Daigneault, S.D. 191
DARVO (Deny, Attack, and Reverse Victim and Offender) 18, 213
Davis, E. 57
de Jongh, A. 57
developmental trauma 94
Dharani, B. 134, 135, 136
dialectical behavior therapy (DBT) 55, 213
did you know? boxes 32–3, 101, 151, 155, 169–70
dissociation 184–5
  flow vs. dissociation 185–6
  structural dissociation of the personality 56
domestic abuse 15–16

219

Domestic Abuse
    Intervention
    Programs 17
domestic violence
    15–16, 213
    COVID-19 pandemic
        25–6
    domestic violence
        typology 37–8, 216–17
    elder abuse 26
    shelters 45–51, 213
    solution-focused
        domestic violence
        treatment 52
    sporting events 27–8
Dube, S.R. 85, 99, 153, 183
Duke, M.P. 140
Duluth Model 17, 53–4
dysregulated states 38–9,
    55
Dziewa, A. 29

easing into reflection 101
    boundaries 123–4
    integrated self 189
    locus of control 138–9
    red flags 112
    relationship
        authenticity 157
    self-talk 172
Echeverry, B. 174
economic abuse 19, 213
ego state therapy 56
Ehinger, J. 80
Ehsan, M.K. 59
Elbert, T. 56
elder abuse and domestic
    violence 26–7
Elkbuli, A. 26
Ellis, A. 169
Ellis, S. 59
Elsanti, D. 191
EMDR 56–7, 185, 188, 214
Emotion Focused
    Therapy 121
emotional abuse 18, 213–14
empowerment 67–9, 214
    cultural context 70–6
    posttraumatic
        growth 69–70
    reclamation of self
        and voice 83–4
    Empowerment Wheel
        8–12, 85, 93–4
    art therapy with the
        Empowerment
        Wheel model 85–6
    attachment 94–9
    authenticity 99–100

bringing art therapy to
    the empowerment
    wheel 104–6
clinical use 51, 72, 203–7
*The Empowerment
    Wheel* 92
three phases of trauma
    treatment 207–9
use of art within the
    Empowerment
    Wheel 209–11
using the Empowerment
    Wheel with
    groups 100–4
Estes, T.H. 101
Exner-Cortens, D. 25
expectancy 141
exteroception 110, 214

Fadmi, F.R. 191
Falk-Rafael, A.R. 68
fawn response 38, 214
feedback vs. criticism 136
Fellin, L.C. 85
femicide 23–4
Fenner, L.B. 124
Ferraro, K.J. 53
Fifty Shades of Grey 36–7
fight or flight response
    38, 214
Finneran, C. 17
Firdaus, M.A.M. 26
Fisher, J. 153, 183, 184
Fitzgerald, J. 57
flags 112–13
    general history of
        flags 113–14
    personal emblems 117
    prayer flags 117
Flammer, A. 133
Flasch, P. 153
Fleming, J. 99, 153, 183
Fleming, M.F. 36
Flicker, S.M. 58
Flores, A.R. 15
flow 185–6
flower power identity
    exercise 195–6
focusing-oriented art
    therapy 190, 214
Foley, J. 37
Foo, S. 184, 207
Fortune, M.M. 59
Fox, C.F. 125
fragmentation of
    self 153, 183–6
Frame Blog, The 125
France 26
Francis, B. 27

Frank, P. 37
Frankland, A. 35
Franklin, M. 186
freeze response 38, 214
Freyd, J.J. 18, 213
Frost, S.B. 146
Fruzzetti, A. 55

Galvin, B.M. 137
Garg, S. 51
Gaslight 36–7
gaslighting 20, 214
Gavron, T. 80
Gendlin, E.T. 214
Gerber, N.E. 141
Germany 45
Gheerbrant, A. 146
ghosting 21, 214
Gibson, C.J. 30
Gil-Or, O. 153
Gillum, T.L. 58, 60
Giordano, P.C. 35
Glass, N.E. 61
glossary 212–17
Glowacz, F. 29
GNWS (Global Network of
    Women's Shelters) 46
Gold, J. 185
Goldsmith, S. 125
Goldsmith, Shelly 125
Goodman, H. 46
Goodman, L.A. 67, 68
Gracia, E. 17, 53
Graham, L.M. 28
graphic storytelling 139–142
Green, J. 58
Gregory, K. 47, 70
grey rocking 20, 214
group therapy 52
    art therapy 84–5
    using the Empowerment
        Wheel 100–4
Guarnaccia, C. 56
Gunter, M.A. 101
Gussak, D.E. 124, 140

Haaken, J. 45
Haen, C. 85
Haeyen, S. 174
Halpern, M.K. 125
Hansen, J.T. 93
Harbishettar, V. 51
Harshaw, C. 111
Harvey, E. 56
Hass-Cohen, N. 79
haunting 20
Heijman, J. 174
Herman, J.L. 183, 207

INDEX

Hester, M. 26
Hill, E. 178
Hill, J.L. 109
Hill, K.E. 191
Hill, N. 58
Hinz, L.D. 105
Holt, E.S. 140
Holtzworth-Munroe, A. 37
Houpt, K. 173
human tape sculptures 130
Hurless, N. 52
Hurvitz Madsen, L. 9, 84, 85
Hyer, S. 44, 45

identity 83
    true self 152–4
Ikonomopoulos, J. 83
India 73
Indigenous clients 61
integrated self 8, 100, 103–4, 182–9, 208, 214
integrated self puzzle project
    alternate art therapy project ideas 194–6
    materials suggested 192–3
    preparation 193
    process 193–4
    project goals 191
    purpose 190–1
    questions to spark reflection or discussion 194
    Solving Me 196–7
    warm-ups 191–2
interoception 110–11, 214
Interval House 46
intimate partner violence 15, 24–5, 57–8, 61, 153–4, 214
    consequences of relationship abuse 29–32
intimate terrorism 37, 214
intimidation 19, 214–15
Islaeli, I. 191
isolation 18, 215
Ivandi , R. 28
Iverson, K.M. 55
Iyengar, K. 73

Jackson, S.A. 186
James, E.L. 36
Jaque, V. 185
Jategaonkar, N. 80
Jiménez, G. 57
Joel, S. 24

Johns, J. 113
Johns, Jasper *Flag* 113
Johnson, L. 17
Johnson, M.P. 37, 38, 53, 215, 217
Johnson, S.M. 121
Jung, C.G. 146
Junge, M.B. 78

Kaimal, G. 78, 80
Kaiser, D.H. 140
Källberg-Shroff, M. 135
Karakurt, G. 30
Kasturirangan, A. 70
Kaufman, S.H. 215
Kaur, R. 51
Keane, B. 142
Keithley, Z. 146
Kellington, S. 85
Kennedy, A.C. 47
Keynan, O. 49
Kim, S. 191
Kinetic Family Drawing 140, 215
Kintsugi 81–2
Kippert, A. 45
Kirby, S. 27
Kirchmaier, T. 28
Knight, L. 26
Knowledge Networks, Inc. 109
Korell, G. 58
Kury, H. 35

Lacalle-Calderon, M. 32
Lagdon, S. 30
Landgarten, H.B. 128
Lark, C.V. 173
Laskey, P. 17
Lassiter, P.S. 8, 9, 74, 93, 123, 134, 184
Latif, M. 59
Latinjak, A.T. 169
Layton, E. 178
leaving an abusive relationship 22–4, 203
    safety planning 204–6
Leijssen, M. 174
Lemberger, M.E. 93
Levi-Belz, Y. 153
Levine, D. 58
LGBTQ girls 25
Lietaer, G. 174
Lila, M. 53
Lim, J.H. 74, 123, 184
Lindsay, R. 142
Linesch, D. 191
Lineweaver, T.T. 191

Lipscomb, A. 57
locus of control 8, 102, 133–5, 208, 209, 215
    differences by culture and gender 135–6
    feedback vs. criticism 136
    internal vs. external locus of control 137–9
locus of control graphic stories project
    alternate art therapy project idea 145–6
    materials suggested 143–4
    preparation 144
    process 144–5
    project goals 142–3
    purpose 139–42
    questions to spark reflection or discussion 145
    The Unloved 147–8
    warm-ups 143
    Where We're Headed 146–7
love-bombing 20, 215
Ludlam, J. 131
Luzzatto, P. 62
Lyman, F. 101
Lynton, N. 135

Maclaren, C. 169
Macy, R.J. 28
Magsamen, S. 78
Majaj, L. 173
Makadon, H.J. 17
Malchiodi, C.A. 110
male privilege 19, 215
male victims 28–9
Malka, M. 85
Malouff, J.M. 186
maps, personal 130, 143
Martinez Barrio, B. 174
Marx, B.P. 111
Maté, G. 99
Math, S.B. 51
Maxfield, L. 57
Maxwell, C. 58
McBride, D.L. 58
McCollum, E.E. 52
McCormick, R. 141
McKenney, M. 26
McKeown, A. 56
McNally, R.J. 69
media 80–1, 215
Meichenbaum, D. 169
#MeToo 8, 35, 215
Meyer, S. 58
Michalewicz, M. 191
Michalewicz, Z. 191
Milah, A.S. 191

221

Milbourne, M. 179
Miller, G. 9
Miller, J.G. 135
Mills, E. 85
Milner, M. 141
minimizing, denying, or blaming 18, 215
Mission Services 45
MMIW (Murdered & Missing Indigenous Women) 23–4
MoMA Learning 125
Mommie Dearest 36–7
Moon, B.L. 82
Moon, C.H. 80
Morgan, A. 85
Morgan, R.E. 24
Morgan, W. 29
Morrison, P.K. 53
movies 36–7
Murphey-Graham, E. 68
Murray, C.E. 84, 153
Museum of Modern Art (MoMA), New York 124–5
mutual violent control 37, 215
myPlan 61

Nakamura, J. 185
narrative exposure therapy (NET) 55–6, 215
National Commission on COVID-19 and Criminal Justice 26
National Domestic Violence Hotline 206
National Violence Against Women Survey 30–1
NCADV (National Coalition Against Domestic Violence) 22, 23, 26 36
Neff, K.D. 153
Netherlands 45, 46
Neufeld, R.W.J. 191
Neuner, F. 56
neuroception 110, 215
Newmeyer, M. 141
Nijenhuis, E. 56, 185
Nnawulezi, N. 47, 70
NOW (National Organization of Women) 44, 45
Nowicki, S. 140

O'Flaherty, R. 27
O'Leary, K.D. 52

Oaklander, V. 191
Obergfell-Fuchs, J. 35
Office of Family Violence and Prevention Services 25
online dating 21–2
Oracle cards 146, 147–8
Orang, T. 56
orbiting 20
Oriel, K.A. 36
Ørke, E.C. 183
Osorio, Pépon 125
ourCircle 61
Oyewuwo-Gassikia, O.B. 59

Paciorek, A. 111
Pakistan 59–60
Paolercio, M. 165
Patin, G.A. 170
Paymar, M. 17, 53, 54, 212
PBS 117
Pence, E. 17, 53, 54, 212
Penone, G. 56
perpetrators 33–5
   characteristics of the perpetrator 35–6
   minimizing, denying, or blaming 18, 215
   treatment interventions 52–4
Perry, B.D. 83, 85, 96
Peters, K. 134, 135, 136
pets 18, 23
phototherapy 190, 215
Piquero, A.R. 26
Pizzey, Erin 45, 46
Place, R.M. 145
play therapy 85
Pliske, M.M. 85
Ponic, P. 80
Porcerelli, J.H. 56
Porges, S.W. 38, 110, 111
Porter, J. 59
posttraumatic growth 69–70, 215–16
   appreciation of life 70
   new possibilities 69
   personal strength 70
   relating to others 69
   spiritual change 70
posttraumatic stress disorder (PTSD) 29, 36, 55–6, 59, 109–10, 187, 216
   complex PTSD (CPTSD) 57, 94–5, 185, 187, 207, 213
Potash, J.S. 128

Power and Control Wheel 17
prevalence of relationship abuse 24–5
   victims, groups, and trends 25–9
Pribadi, T. 191
Princer, M.K. 82
protective behaviors 20–1
psychodynamic therapy 56

Ragavan, M. 73
Rakovec-Felser, Z. 36
Ramos Collado, L. 125
Rangel, A. 140
Rankin, A.B. 9, 81, 141, 206
Rappaport, L. 109
red flags 8, 51, 95, 97, 99, 100, 102, 108–10, 207, 208, 209, 216
   authenticity and red flags 155
   neuroception, exteroception, and interoception 110–12
red flags project
   alternate art therapy project ideas 117
   Broken Frame Flag 118
   He Barks & I Bite My Tongue 118
   materials suggested 115–16
   preparation 116
   project goals 114
   purpose 112–14
   questions to spark reflection or discussion 116–17
   warm-up 114–15
relationship abuse 8–12, 216
   barriers to leaving 22–4
   books and movies 36–7
   characteristics of the perpetrator 35–6
   defining terms 15–16
   elements of relationship abuse 17
   impact of relationship abuse on children 85
   misconception of anger as the source 35
   other forms of abuse 20–2
   prevalence 24–9
   responses to abuse 38–9
   root of the problem 33–5
   short- and long-term consequences 29–33

types of relationship abuse 17–19
typology of control and violence in relationships 37–8
see treatment protocols
relationship authenticity 8, 103, 150–1, 208, 216
authenticity and red flags 155
compromise vs. control 151–2
relationship inauthenticity 151, 152–4, 216
the true self 152–4
various outcomes 154–7
relationship authenticity self sculpture project 158–9
alternate art therapy project ideas 163–4
Authentically Me 165–6
Hidden 164–5
materials suggested 161, 163–4
preparation 161–2
process 162–3
project gaols 159
Pull and Flow 165
questions to spark reflection or discussion 163
warm-ups 159–60
REPROVIDE 54
Resick, P.A. 30
retablos 139–40
Ricks, C.F. 174
Riley, S. 84
Rivera, T. 45
Robertson, E. 170
Robey, K.L. 140
Rosal, M.L. 139
Rosen, K.H. 52
Rosen, K.H. 52
Rosenblad, S.R. 141
Ross, C.J. 141
Ross, I. 78
Rothery, M.A. 84
Rotter, J.B. 133
Rowe, C. 85
Rowland, D.L. 59
Roy Lichtenstein Foundation 178
Rubin, J.A. 86
Ruby's Place 45

Sáez, G. 57
Safeopedia 125

safety planning 204–6, 216
Salis, K.L. 52
Salmon, P.R. 141
sandtray therapy 141
Santirso, F.A. 53
Satyen, L. 58
Savannah 131
Schauer, M. 56
Schnicke, M.K. 30
Schouten, K.A. 9
Schulz, K. 45
Schutte, N.S. 186
Schwab, J.H. 101
Schwartz, R.C. 56
Scott, A.L. 120, 122
Scott, E.H. 141
Scotti, V. 109
self-esteem journal 194–5
self-talk 8, 103, 168–72, 208, 209, 216
learning self-talk 169–70
self-talk finding own voice project
alternate art therapy project ideas 178–9
Finding Your Voice 179–80
materials suggested 176
preparation 176
process 177
project goals 175
purpose 173–4
questions to spark reflection or discussion 177
Untitled 179
warm-ups 175
Settineri, S. 109
sex trafficking 28
Shanahan, M.J. 191
Shapiro, F. 56, 79
shelters 45–6
living in shelters 46–51
Shenk, C. 55
Sholt, M. 80
Siemon, T. 186
signals 21
Singapore 26
Singh, A. 85
Singh, V. 36
situational couple violence 38, 216
Skill Share 178
Skop, M. 84, 85
Skora, L. 111
Smith, D.B. 30
Smith, L.J. 186
Snyder, K. 191
social learning theory 133
Soler-Baillo, J.M. 111

solution-focused domestic violence treatment 52
SoulCollage® cards 146
Speciale, M. 93
speech and thought bubbles 178–9
Spirit cards 146
sporting events and violence 27–8
Spring, D. 79
Stauffer, S.D. 85
Steele, K. 56, 185
Steer, R.A. 168–9
Stephenson, R. 17
Stinckens, N. 174
Stith, S.M. 52
Stocks, A. 135
Strailey, L. 118
Stringer, M. 30
Stronach-Buschel, B. 84
Stuart, G.L. 37
Stubbs, A. 30
Suizzo, M.-A. 153
Sullivan, C.M. 47, 70
survivors 16, 203
boundaries and healing 123–4
posttraumatic growth 69–70
reclamation of self and voice 83–4
safety planning 204–6
treatment interventions 54–8
Szoeke, C. 30

talk therapy 79
Talwar, S. 57, 79
Tanzania 62
Tarot cards 145–6, 147–8
Tate Museum, London 125
Taucher, L.C. 81, 141, 206
Taylor, J. 17
Taylor-Johnson, S. 37
Tedeschi, R.G. 69, 70
Teen Dating Violence Awareness Month (February) 25
Teoli, L. 130
Thoennes, N. 17, 22, 24, 30
Thomas, B. 146
Thompson, A. 78, 105, 112, 210
Thomson, P. 185
Thomson, S. 80
threats 19, 213
Tilley, D.S. 36
Tjaden, P. 17, 22, 24, 30
Tombourou, J.W. 58

Torralba, M. 32
Torres-Blas, N. 28
Trabold, N. 54, 55
trauma treatment with the Empowerment Wheel 207
  consider goals 208
  feeling uncomfortable vs. feeling unsafe 208
  multidirectional and non-linear process 209
  sector overlap 209
  start anywhere 207–8
treatment protocols 44–5
  couples counseling 51–2
  culturally appropriate interventions and treatment 58–62
  shelter movement 45–6
  shelters 46–51
  treatment interventions 52–8
Treviño, A.L. 52, 83
Tripp, T. 79, 128
true self 152–4
Truman, J.L. 24 24
Tucker, N. 52, 83
Turel, O. 153
Tutty, L.M. 84

Ulloa, E.C. 69
UN (United Nations) 23
United Kingdom (UK) 15, 26–8, 37, 45
United States (USA) 15, 25, 26, 27, 32–3, 44–5, 196, 205
  shelter movement 45–6

US Department of Veteran Affairs 57
USDOJ (United States Department of Justice) 28

Vaddiparti, K. 59, 80
vagus nerve 110–11, 217
Valentine, D. 68
Vallée, J.-M. 37
van der Hart, O. 56, 185
van der Kolk, B.A. 79, 94, 211
Varma, D.S. 80
Vatnar, S.K.B. 183
VAWA (Violence Against Women Act) 32–3
Verhoeven, M. 28
victims 16
  cultural context 70–6
  empowerment 67–9
  male victims 28–9
  protective behaviors 20–1
  responses to abuse 38–9
  types of relationship abuse 17–19
  victims, groups, and trends 25–9
Violence Against Women Act (VAWA) USA 32–3, 217
violent resistance 37–8, 217
voice 84, 173–4
  see self-talk
Voith, L.A. 53
Vygotsky, L.S. 169

Walker, A. 28, 29
Wallston, K.A. 134
Walsh, S.D. 28
Walton, N.L. 36
Wang, Y.N. 152
Wanner, B. 185
Wardi-Zonna, K. 80, 82
Weber, A.M. 85
websites 23, 61, 206
Weiss, E. 165
Weldon, G. 142
Wells, M. 29
Werner-Lin, A. 85
Wheat, M. 158
White, M. 85
Whiting, J. 30
WHO (World Health Organization) 26, 31–2
Wilcox, Dawn 23
Williams, L.M. 59
Winfrey, O. 83, 85, 96
Winnicott, D.W. 152
Woerner, R. 147, 180
Woessner, G. 35
Wood, L.L. 130
World Bank Group 32
Wozniak, D.F. 47
Wulkan, R. 125
Wurtz, R. 73

Yakeley, J. 56
Yalom, I. 84
Yates, C. 173
Yati, M. 191
youth.gov 25
Yragui, N. 45
Yulianto, A. 191
Yuniarti, W.Y. 85
Yunus, R.M. 26